9/03

20.⁹⁵

SPINAL CORD INJURIES

Other titles in Diseases and People

—Diseases and People—

SPINAL CORD INJURIES

Elaine Landau

Enslow Publishers, Inc.

40 Industrial Road   PO Box 38
Box 398   Aldershot
Berkeley Heights, NJ 07922 Hants GU12 6BP
USA   UK

http://www.enslow.com

For Sarah Sutin

Copyright © 2001 by Elaine Landau

Library of Congress Cataloging-in-Publication Data

Landau, Elaine.
    Spinal cord injuries / Elaine Landau.
       p. ; cm. — (Diseases and people)
    Includes bibliographical references and index.
    ISBN 0-7660-1474-6
    1. Spinal cord—Wounds and injuries—Juvenile literature. [1. Spinal cord
—Wounds and injuries. 2. Physically handicapped.]
    [DNLM: 1. Spinal Cord Injuries—Juvenile Literature. WL 400 L253s
2001] I. Title. II. Series.
    RD594.3 .L36 2001
    617.4'82044—dc21   2001001045

Printed in the United States of America

10 9 8 7 6 5 4 3 2 1

To Our Readers:
We have done our best to make sure all Internet addresses in this book were active and appropriate when we went to press. However, the author and the publisher have no control over and assume no liability for the material available on those Internet sites or on other Web sites they may link to. Any comments or suggestions can be sent by e-mail to comments@enslow.com or to the address on the back cover.

Illustration Credits: © Corel Corporation, pp. 27, 34; Courtesy of Charlene Curtiss, Seattle, Washington, p.69; Courtesy of The Cleveland FES Center, Cleveland, Ohio, p.57, 59; Courtesy of Craig Hospital, Englewood, Colorado, pp.17, 19, 51, 71, 78, 92; Courtesy of PN/Paraplegia News/Paralyzed Veterans of America, pp. 14, 54, 64, 67, 75, 98; J. Hirschman, p. 11; John Russo, p. 88; Ron Hughes, p. 30; TIRR (The Institute for Rehabilitation and Research), Houston, Texas, pp. 24, 39, 43, 48; TopGuns Corp. Photography-photo provided by the Paralysis Society of America, 83.

Cover Illustration: Skjold Photographs

Contents

SPINAL CORD INJURIES

What is it? A spinal cord injury (SCI) is damage to the spinal cord, the bundle of nerves and fibers that extends down the spine from the base of the brain to the lower back. This damage usually results in some serious consequences. These consequences can include either a partial or complete loss of movement (paralysis) and/or feeling in the affected parts of the body.

Who gets it? Anyone can injure his or her spinal cord. However, spinal cord injuries are most common among young males. Over half of all spinal cord injuries occur in people between sixteen and thirty years of age. Males are four times more likely than females to injure their spinal cords.

How does it happen? Motor vehicle accidents account for the greatest number of spinal cord injuries. The next largest category is violence, followed by falls and sports accidents.

What are the symptoms? The most obvious symptom of spinal cord injury is paralysis and a loss of sensation (feeling). Bladder, bowel, circulatory, respiratory, and sexual functions may be affected as well.

How is it treated? Presently, there is no cure for spinal cord injury. However, many researchers are working toward that end, and some significant strides have been made. Often, people with SCI benefit from working with rehabilitation therapists during their recovery.

How can it be prevented? It would be difficult to prevent spinal cord injuries entirely. Sometimes they occur as the result of accidents that are out of a person's control. Nevertheless, in some cases spinal cord injuries can be avoided by not taking needless risks. That means driving safely; wearing seat belts; never diving into shallow water; wearing safety gear for sports and following the rules; and refusing to accept sports challenges that seem risky and dangerous. In addition, injuries among young people can be reduced if they do not have access to guns and do not use drugs or alcohol.

1

It Happens
This Way . . .

It should have been the best time of his life. Willem van
Tuij, a thirteen-year-old Dutch youth, was on a five-year
trip with his parents to see the world. The family was
traveling on a 44-foot vessel they built themselves, and by
March 2000 they had already logged 40,000 nautical miles.
After visiting the Azores Islands, Fiji, and Alaska, they were on
their way home to Holland. But first the family decided to
stop near the coast of Honduras for some fishing and
relaxation.

What was to be a restful time turned into a nightmare that
would change young Willem's life forever. One day, the family's boat, the *Hyatt*, was attacked by pirates at sea. Willem and
his father had been fishing nearby on a dinghy when they saw
the men boarding the boat. In no time, the pirates had tied
Willem's mother up and had begun to ransack the vessel.

When the men saw Willem and his father approaching, they drew their guns and began firing. A bullet struck Willem just above the hip and passed through his body, severing the boy's spinal cord. Gunfire also hit the dinghy, throwing Willem and his father into the water.

Willem screamed to his father, "I have no feeling in my legs."[1] Yet miraculously, the boy was able to hold on to his father and not go under. "I thought I was going to be eaten by sharks because I was bleeding so much," Willem would later say in describing the terror he experienced.[2] After the intruders left, his father was finally able to get Willem back to the boat and radio for help.

Amateur radio operators in the area of the van Tuijs' boat picked up their signal and alerted the Honduran naval authorities, who, in turn, directed the family to the coastal town of Puerto Lempira. Among the ham operators answering the call was Miami cardiologist Jim Hirschman. Hirschman did what he could to help Willem's parents stop their son's bleeding until they could reach help.

The boy was eventually airlifted to a clinic in La Ceiba, Honduras, where doctors patched up Willem's kidney and intestine, both of which had been ripped by the gunshot round. Unfortunately, there was nothing they could do to repair his spinal cord. The physicians informed Willem's parents that their son would never walk again.

Jena's Story

Jena was a freshman at the University of Idaho when her life was dramatically spun around. It was the weekend, and she

10

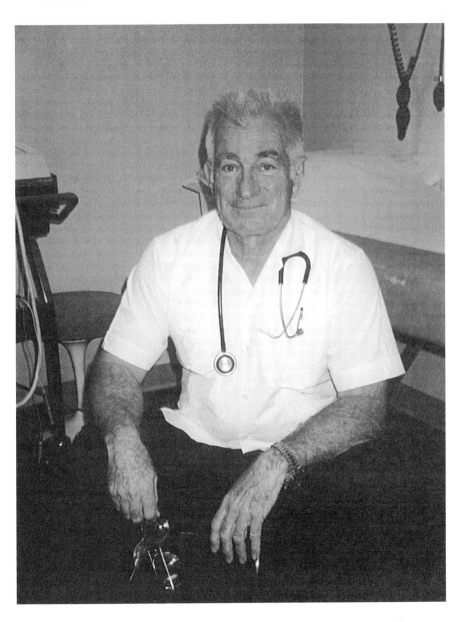

Jim Hirschman, a Miami doctor, helped Willem Tuij by ham radio after
the attack.

had been busily making the rounds of the campus parties. Yet Jena was back at her sorority house and should have been safe when the accident happened. She described what occurred as follows:

> Somehow, after walking home from the parties, I fell thirty feet from my sorority house's fire escape. I can't remember how it happened—I had been drinking pretty heavily at the parties. I woke up in the local hospital with complete numbness. . . . Then a paramedic said to me, 'You've been in a terrible accident and broken your back.'[3]

Jena's spinal cord had also been injured. Now she had a new reality to cope with. Her doctors told her that she would be permanently paralyzed. "I didn't want to believe that at eighteen years old I'd be in a wheelchair for the rest of my life."[4]

Other Stories

Matt, now nineteen, suffered a spinal cord injury when he was just eight years old. That spring, he and others in his daycare group were on their way to visit the Easter Bunny at the local mall when the driver of their van blacked out behind the wheel. The van crashed, and the vehicle's back seat flew forward. Both Matt and his good friend Josh sustained disabling injuries.[5]

Samantha was in her room dressing for school when she was injured. The six-year-old had heard her next-door neighbor mowing his lawn when a rod suddenly dislodged from the mower. Unaccountably, the machine part flew into her window, hitting Samantha in the neck. The young girl was taken by surprise. She claims to recall only the "sound of the lawnmower" and thinking about what she was going to wear. "The next thing I remember was waking up in a hospital," she later reported.[6]

In another instance, a young woman attempting to rescue a cat from the edge of a balcony fell three floors to the ground, landing on her back. She sustained a spinal cord injury that left her paralyzed from the waist down.[7] In a similar case, a young husband and father of four fell while doing repairs on the roof of his home. A spinal cord injury resulted in his paralysis as well.[8]

The Reality of Spinal Cord Injury

The people described here were injured under different circumstances, but in each case the result was the same—the person was paralyzed and lost sensation in part of his or her body. This result is typical of many spinal cord injuries. What happened to these people is not uncommon. Today there are an estimated 250,000–400,000 Americans living with spinal cord injuries. An average of 11,000 new injuries occur in the United States each year.[9]

According to the National Spinal Cord Injury Statistical Center at the University of Alabama at Birmingham, 82 percent of those who suffer spinal cord injuries are male, and 55 percent of people with SCI are between sixteen and thirty years of age. The average age at time of injury is 31.8 years.[10] Spinal cord injuries are most commonly caused by:[11]

- Vehicular accidents . . . . 44 percent
- Violence . . . . 26 percent
- Falls . . . . 22 percent
- Sports accidents . . . . 7 percent
- Other . . . . 1 percent

The fastest growing of these categories is violence. In such cases, the spinal cord injury is usually caused by a gunshot wound. In the urban areas of Miami, Houston, Philadelphia,

Doyle Harbaugh does carpentry work from his wheelchair. Eight in ten of those with spinal cord injuries are male.

Washington, D.C., Chicago, and Los Angeles, gunshot wounds have already become the leading cause of SCI.

But you do not have to live in a big city to be at risk. On April 20, 1999, two high school students named Dylan Klebold and Eric Harris walked into Columbine High School in Littleton, Colorado, and opened fire in a senseless shooting spree. Twelve students and one teacher were killed, and three students suffered spinal cord injuries that left them paralyzed. It was an affluent suburban town, yet this tragedy happened there—and could have happened anywhere.

Spinal cord injuries pose a tremendous financial and emotional burden on the injured individuals and their families. The cost of initial hospitalization, adaptive equipment, and home modification averages $140,000. The additional costs of caring for a person with such an injury over a lifetime average $400,000 and can run as high as $2 million.[12] The annual cost to the nation to care for people with spinal cord injuries averages $9.7 billion, which includes health care and other needs.[13] This is a book about spinal cord injuries—a condition that, in one way or another, affects us all.

2

What Is Spinal Cord Injury?

You cannot see your spinal cord and, unless you or someone you know has had an accident affecting it, you probably have not thought very much about this part of your body. Yet your spinal cord is actually far more important to your well-being than you might have realized.

It is called a cord, but the spinal cord is really a nearly two-foot-long bundle of nerves and fibers that is part of a vital communication network within the body. The spinal cord is part of the nervous system, which is made up of more than 10 billion neurons (nerve cells) that operate constantly all over our bodies. The electrochemical impulses of our nervous system makes it possible for us to move, feel, breathe, urinate, sweat, and do all the other things that we do to function and stay alive.

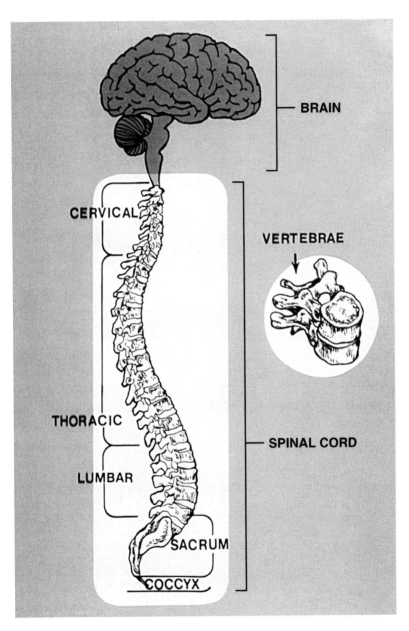

The brain and spinal cord make up the central nervous system. The different regions of the spinal cord control different parts of the body.

Think about what would happen if you touched a hot stove. You would pull your hand back right away so it would not be burned. But how does your body know that you need to pull your hand away from that hot surface?

When your hand touches the stove, the nerve cells in your hand sense the heat. They immediately send a message to your brain: "This surface is hot!" As soon as the brain gets the message, it sends another message back to the hand: "Stop touching the hot surface!" The messages move back and forth very quickly so you can pull your hand away before it gets badly burned.

Those messages to and from the brain travel through the spinal cord. The spinal cord and the brain are the primary parts of the central nervous system. The brain is like a supercomputer that controls our bodies. The spinal cord is like a cable that carries information and commands to and from the brain.

Some of the messages the spinal cord carries give the brain information about your sensations. They tell you that you are touching something hot or cold, something hard or soft, or something wet or dry. Some messages control your body's movement by telling your muscles to lift your arm or wiggle your toes. Other messages give your brain information about the position of your body so you know without looking that you are sitting down or bending over. Some messages control the muscles in your bladder so you can urinate, and other messages control the movement of your lungs so you can breathe.

Structure of the Spinal Cord

The spinal cord consists of millions of neurons in a column that extends down the spine from the base of the brain to the lower back. This column is about seventeen inches long and as wide as a little finger. Because the spinal cord can be easily injured, it is protected by the spine, which is a strong structure made up of vertebrae. The vertebrae are small bones that are stacked on top of one another like a pile of pebbles. Each vertebra has a small hole, like the hole in a donut, through which the column of neurons passes. Between the vertebrae are discs made of spongy material that protect the bones from movement. This material absorbs the jolts when you move, the

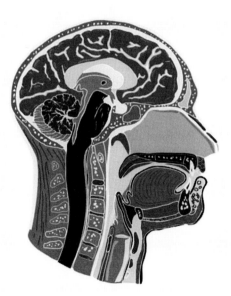

The brain sends signals along the nerves to the muscles.

way shock absorbers on a car absorb the jolts when the car hits a bump. The vertebrae and disks are held in place by the ligaments, which are thick flexible cords that allow the neck and back to twist and bend without everything falling apart.

Each neuron in the spinal cord has several important parts that allow it to send and receive messages. These parts include the cell body, the axons, the myelin sheath, and the dendrites.

The cell body is shaped like a tiny, round ball. It is the center for receiving and sending messages (nerve signals).

Axons are long nerve cell fibers that extend out from the cell body. Axons transmit (send) nerve signals from neuron to neuron. Some axons are covered by a fatty substance called the myelin sheath. The myelin sheath protects the axon and helps messages travel more rapidly and reliably.

Dendrites look a little like the branches of a tree. They are receptors that receive messages from the nerve cells in the body so they can be transmitted to the brain.

The messages the neurons send are called nerve impulses. The point at which a nerve impulse travels from the axon of one neuron to the dendrite of another is called a synapse. When the neuron sends a message, the nerve impulse travels from the cell body out through the axon. Then an electrochemical reaction causes the nerve impulse to jump across the synapse, where it is received by the dendrites of the next neuron in the pathway. The axon of that neuron sends the message across the synapse to the next neuron, and so on, until the message arrives at its destination.

The spinal cord is so important that nature has protected it well. It lies deep within the body and is enclosed within tough membranes. Yet despite these safeguards, the spinal cord is still frequently injured. When that occurs, the communication system it is part of is interrupted. Exactly which parts of the body are affected depends on where the injury occurs along the spinal cord. It also depends on the severity of the injury and which nerve fibers are damaged.

The spinal cord is divided into four different segments or areas. Nerves from each area connect to separate parts of the body. Those in the cervical or neck region relay signals to the neck, arms, and hands. Nerves in the thoracic or upper back region control signals to the torso and parts of the arms. Nerves in the lumbar or mid-back region just below the ribs send signals to the hips and legs. Lastly, the sacral area controls signals to the groin, toes, and parts of the legs.

What Happens When the Spinal Cord Is Injured?

When there is an injury, the person's body usually remains largely unaffected above the level at which the injury occurred. Things will go on working as they always have. But the spinal cord nerves below this point can no longer transport messages to and from the brain.

Therefore, the higher in the body the injury occurs, the more body parts will be affected and the worse the outcome will be. The closer the spinal cord injury is to the brain, the fewer body parts will function normally. People hurt in the neck or

Other Problems with SCI

People with SCI often lose the ability to control the muscles that allow us to move our arms and legs. They may also lose the ability to feel sensations like touch, pressure, and temperature.

Depending on the type of injury, some people with SCI also lose other functions. The messages that control bladder and sphincter muscles (the muscles that control bowel movements) might not get through the damaged spinal cord. When that happens, people cannot control when they urinate or have bowel movements.

Damage to the spinal cord does not affect how well the heart pumps. But in people with SCI, the brain cannot always send the right signals to the blood vessels. Sometimes the blood pressure gets too low, which slows down the heart.

Some people with SCI also have difficulty breathing and clearing their lungs. That is because their brain cannot send signals to the muscles that control breathing and coughing. When the nerve impulses to and from these muscles cannot get through, people may need special equipment so they can breathe.

cervical region of the spinal cord may be paralyzed in both their arms and legs. These patients have a condition known as quadriplegia (from the Latin meaning "four"), also known as tetraplegia (from the Greek meaning "four"). A chest-level injury may result in paralysis of the person's lower limbs or legs. This condition is called paraplegia, and these individuals are known as paraplegics.

Spinal cord injuries are also described by the location of the vertebrae around them. For example, an injury to the spinal cord near the fourth or fifth cervical vertebrae would be called a C-4/C-5 vertebral injury (C stands for "cervical"). An injury lower down in the thoracic region might be a T-6 (T stands for "thoracic"). A spinal cord injury is further categorized as being either complete or incomplete. The National Spinal Cord Injury Association describes the difference this way:

> A complete injury means that there is no function below the level of injury; no sensation and no voluntary movement. Both sides of the body are equally affected. An incomplete injury means that there is some functioning below the primary level of the injury [where on the spinal cord the injury occurred]. A person with an incomplete injury may be able to move one limb more than another, may be able to feel parts of the body that cannot be moved, or may have more functioning on one side of the body than the other.[1]

The nerve cells of the central nervous system are extremely sensitive, and unlike most cells in the body, they do not repair themselves when injured. Instead, when the spinal cord is damaged, the neurons (nerve cells) die or never sufficiently recover to allow the person to function as he or she formerly did.

For many years, that was the way most spinal cord injury stories ended. A success was a patient who survived the injury and went on to adjust to a fulfilling but more physically limited lifestyle. However, in recent times, that view of spinal cord injury has been challenged. Researchers have been exploring new ways to heal spinal cords that were formerly thought to be beyond repair. While they don't want to give

People whose lower limbs are paralyzed have paraplegia. This woman with paraplegia prepared this meal, which she is now enjoying with her husband.

patients false hope, many feel that there are now grounds for optimism.

New information regarding the central nervous system has been generated through a host of studies and experiments. This knowledge, coupled with advanced techniques and tools, is bringing about an important difference in the way spinal cord injuries are treated. The really exciting news is that some important changes in the treatment of spinal cord injuries are already beginning to happen.

3

A History of Spinal Cord Injury

Today, people with SCI often look forward to long and fulfilling lives. It was not always that way, however. Prior to World War II, spinal cord injuries were usually fatal. Individuals fortunate enough to survive a spinal cord injury generally did not live very long afterwards because of such complications as lung and kidney infections, respiratory problems, and badly infected bedsores.

The ancient Egyptians did not understand the functions of the brain, nerves, and spinal cord. In addition, they did not have methods to treat injuries to these parts of the body. In what is believed to be the oldest medical document in history, written over 2,500 years ago, an Egyptian doctor described 48 injuries and their treatments. He wrote of a spinal cord injury that it was "an ailment not to be treated"—that is, he could not help the patient. [1]

In Greece two thousand years later, a doctor named Alcmaeon of Croton dissected animals and noticed that the brain and eyes were connected. From this, he deduced that the brain controlled other parts of the body.[2] Another Greek doctor, Galen of Pergamum, discovered that the spinal cord carried messages between the muscles and the brain. He studied monkeys whose spinal cords had been severed. In a lecture he gave in A.D. 177, he said that the monkeys lost both "the capacity of sensation and the capacity of movement" below the point where the cord was damaged.[3]

The ancient Egyptians did not understand how the central nervous system functioned and could not treat spinal cord injuries.

Wheeling Around

The first wheeled chair we know about was called an "invalid's chair." It was made in the sixteenth century for King Philip II of Spain. It had a quilted back, hinged arms, and a mechanism for adjusting the angle of its back and legs.[4]

During the next century, several other types of wheeled chairs were invented. Some of these chairs could be operated by the person in the chair, who would use a crank to turn the wheels. Others were designed to be pushed by an attendant. Some had leg supports and other features. These chairs rode on small casters like those used today on television stands.

The first chair with large wheels was introduced in the early nineteenth century by John Joseph Merlin, the man who invented the roller skate.[5] The Merlin chair, with its large wheels and slightly smaller outer wheel (which allowed riders to control the chair without getting dirt from the wheels on their hands) was much easier to use.

The Merlin chair was made of wood, so it was heavy and awkward to use. Some inventors tried to make chairs out of lighter materials such as wicker, but the chairs were not strong enough for everyday use.

By the end of the nineteenth century, wheels with rubber tires and wire spokes like those used on bicycles were being used on wheeled chairs. These chairs were called by many names, including invalid chairs, invalid lounges, and bath chairs. The current term became popular when catalogues that sold these chairs began to advertise them as "wheel chairs."[6]

Even though they had been improved in many ways, wheel-chairs were still heavy and difficult to use. That changed in 1919. A man named Herbert A. Everest, who broke his back in a mining accident, wanted a chair he could put into a car. He worked with a friend, Harry C. Jennings, Sr., to invent a chair that was light and could be folded up. By 1973, the Everest & Jennings Company had produced one million wheelchairs.[7]

Automated, or electric, wheelchairs became widely used after the Vietnam War, when many soldiers returned with injuries that made them unable to walk. The electric wheelchair has made it much easier for people with SCI to get around by themselves.

Today, a new type of wheelchair allows people with SCI to climb stairs, move on rough ground, and even to "stand up." The chair has sensors that evaluate the steepness of a flight of stairs so the chair can adjust its position and speed. Using its sensors, the chair can travel on bumpy or uneven surfaces, such as a path in the woods.[8] Sandy Tagliareni, who says she missed walking in the woods near her home after her injury, was one of the first people to test the new wheelchair. "What I like most," she says, "is that it would give me back about 90 percent of what I used to do. . . . Could you climb over a fallen log with an ordinary chair?"[9] John Hockenberry, a radio and television reporter, likes the fact that his new chair lets him "stand up."[10] Seated in the chair, Hockenberry can raise himself so he can talk to people face to face instead of looking up at them.

Wheelchairs have improved a great deal since the nineteenth century and are now much more comfortable and functional. Here, a bride dances with her uncle, who is wheelchair-bound.

It was many centuries before new information about the nervous system came to light, partly because the Christian doctrine of the time forbade dissection of the human body after death. But in 1543, Andreas Vesalius, a Flemish doctor, wrote a medical book, *On the Workings of the Human Body*. He was the first to suggest that different regions of the brain controlled different parts of the body. In addition, his was one of the first books to have accurate illustrations of the body's interior, showing nerves running from the brain to all parts of the body.[11]

Later scientific inventions and discoveries added to knowledge about the nervous system. In 1717, using the microscope he had just invented, Dutch scientist Antoni van Leeuwenhoek observed nerve cells. He noticed that each nerve cell had a long projection sticking out like a root. Italian scientist Luigi Galvani noticed that the frog legs in his laboratory, stored on metal plates, twitched during a thunderstorm. In 1791, he published a paper that described how tiny amounts of electricity make muscles move.[12]

During the nineteenth century, scientists were able to learn how nerve cells worked to carry messages between the muscles and the brain. A German anatomy professor, Wilhelm von Waldeyer, gathered information from many sources and published a series of journal articles about the workings of the nervous system. He added a number of words to the scientific vocabulary, including the word "neuron" for the nerve cell body and the fiber extending from it.[13]

While this knowledge was crucial to understanding the nervous system, it did not immediately affect the treatment of people with spinal cord injuries. However, the medical community began to develop better techniques of caring for people with spinal cord injuries. These allowed many more patients to survive an injury and the initial period following it. For example, in the early years of the twentieth century, the technique of intermittent catheterization (a method of emptying the bladder) was developed, which led to a 15 percent decline in mortality.[14] In addition, the development and widespread use of antibiotics such as penicillin in the mid-1940s helped people with SCI fight infection, significantly improving their life expectancy.[15] In the 1950s, spinal cord injury treatment centers were developed, which further reduced mortality.[16]

During the last years of the twentieth century, enormously important discoveries were made about the nervous system and about how to treat spinal cord injuries. In fact, clinical neurologist Ira Black of the Robert Wood Johnson Medical School in Piscataway, New Jersey, noted, "There's been a revolution in our view of the spinal cord and its potential for recovery . . . . The astounding progress over the past decade dwarfs the progress of the past 5,000 years."[17]

4

Diagnosis and Treatment

In some ways, spinal cord injuries are not like other wounds. Damage to the spinal cord continues even after the accident. That is why time is often a crucial factor, and the hours immediately following the injury are known as the *acute stage.*

During this period, the spinal cord swells, and the injury's effects worsen. Blood pressure in the affected area sharply drops, cutting off the vital blood supply to the damaged cells. Hemorrhaging, or internal bleeding, starting at the spinal cord's center, spreads outward. As inflammation, or swelling, sets in, chemicals known as oxidants or "free radicals" are released. These chemicals attack the body's defenses and vital cell structures.

Nerve cells die, leaving a vacant space or opening in the spinal cord where scar tissue can later form in the region. Even if the spinal cord was initially crushed or bruised rather than broken, the effect is the same once this process has taken place. The connections within the spinal cord are severed.

Because so much occurs in the hours immediately following a spinal cord injury, it is important that the injured person receive prompt medical attention by qualified health care professionals, including immediate immobilization of the spine. This treatment can be crucial in minimizing any permanent damage to the body. Of course, that is the ideal situation. Sadly, it does not always happen that way.

An Accident in Mexico

One case in which the lack of prompt treatment caused terrible consequences involved Don Kraft, a husband and father from San Diego, California. Kraft often enjoyed driving to Mexico with his family to take fishing trips. One evening, when the Krafts were on their way home from such a trip, Don made a U-turn across a Mexican highway. As he did so, a car coming from the opposite direction hit his truck.

Don's wife Melody and their three sons were not hurt. Neither was the couple in the other car. But it was immediately apparent that Kraft was badly injured. Realizing that he would need help, Kraft asked for the sophisticated medical care available in the States. Instinctively, he called out to his wife, "Get me back across the border."[1]

But that proved to be easier said than done. An ambulance from nearby Ensenada, a town in Mexico, arrived on the scene, and Kraft was taken to a local hospital. There, X-rays showed that Kraft's neck was broken and his spinal cord

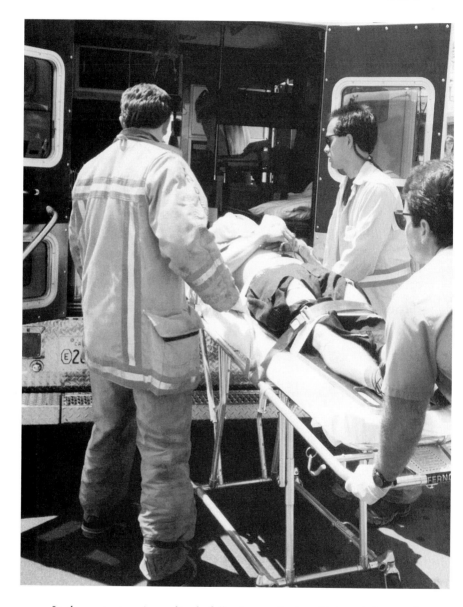

In the acute stage immediately following a spinal cord injury, it is crucial that the spine be immobilized and that the patient receive prompt medical attention.

injured. Dr. Manuel Velez, the doctor who ran the medical service, knew that paralysis would occur quickly if his patient were not attended to at once. Velez also knew that his hospital lacked the facilities to treat Kraft.

To help Kraft get the emergency care he needed, Velez arranged for an ambulance to remain just outside the hospital. He hoped to have Kraft immediately transferred to a facility in San Diego, which was only about an hour away across the border. At the time the ambulance pulled up to the hospital's door, Don Kraft could still move his arms and legs. However, Dr. Velez knew this condition would change if Kraft did not get medical help soon. Kraft was in the acute stage of spinal cord injury, and the clock had begun ticking.

Garcia Sanchez, the man driving the car that hit Kraft's truck, was also at the hospital. He was not hurt, but because Kraft had made an illegal U-turn, causing the accident, Sanchez filed charges against him. It was clear that he was going to try to prevent Kraft from leaving the country.

Three hours had now passed, and Don Kraft was still being kept on a hospital gurney in terrible pain, until the legal technicalities could be worked out. His wife was shocked when she saw an armed police officer placed outside her husband's room. Years later, she explained,

> He was under arrest. Here he has a broken neck, he's on a gurney. He's not going anywhere. He's screaming out in pain. I mean, he's in total agony. My kids [are] sitting on the floor, they're young boys, and here's their dad, they see their dad with a guy with a gun.[2]

35

However, holding Kraft in the Mexican hospital was legal under Mexican law.

Apparently, Sanchez was willing to release Kraft for $2,000 (the cost of damages), but by the time they agreed, it was late at night and all the banks were closed. Dr. Velez offered to put up the money for the Krafts, but Sanchez refused, saying he would only accept payment from the family. By 10:00 P.M., four and half hours after the accident, Don Kraft was no closer to securing medical care in the States. There was little anyone could do. Dr. Velez let the authorities at Ensenada know what was happening, but it did not help. As it turned out, Sanchez was an attorney general for the town where the accident had taken place.

Calls were made to various government offices, and the American consulate became involved. Meanwhile, time was passing and a solution still had not presented itself. It was now after midnight, more than eight hours since Don Kraft's neck had been broken. Incredibly, the price of his release bond had gone up twice during the evening. By then, it was up to $7,000.

At 3:30 that morning, Mrs. Kraft's parents were on their way to Mexico with the required cash. By then, their son-in-law's neck was badly swollen and his movements seemed stiffer. Paralysis was setting in. Finally, at 7:00 A.M., two car-loads of Kraft family members arrived at the Mexican hospital. They had the money, but had to wait until 9:00 A.M. when the courts opened.

36

The court determined that the bond was excessive and lowered it to $2,700. The family went through a great deal of red tape before Don Kraft could be released. By then, it was lunchtime (12:00 P.M.), and eighteen hours had passed since the accident. Finally, Kraft was airlifted to a hospital in San Diego—but it was too late. Don Kraft was now paralyzed.

The incident sparked a huge controversy, and the Mexican consulate agreed to investigate. It was hoped that others might be spared Don Kraft's fate, but this father of three paid a tremendous price for the delay in medical assistance. Less than two weeks later, Kraft died of pneumonia while in a hospital facility for long-term care. The swelling in his neck had affected his breathing ability. The county medical examiner noted that this complication might not have existed if Kraft had received prompt medical attention at the time of his accident.

What Should Have Happened

The preceding was the course of a spinal cord injury under the worst possible circumstances. Here is what ideally should have happened to Don Kraft or others in a similar position:

Trained emergency medical personnel arrive at the accident site as soon as possible. They bring the patient with a possible spinal cord injury to a trauma center, taking extreme care in transporting that individual. Often, the accident victim is strapped to a stiff board with padding to keep the person's body from moving. Even minimal movement during this acute stage can increase the possibility of permanent paralysis.

At this point, the medical team promptly arrives at an accurate diagnosis. In doing so, the patient's lung function, particularly in cases where the injury occurred in the neck and chest area, is evaluated. If the injury is just below the skull, the patient may not be able to breathe without assistance and could die without emergency respiratory aid.

The physicians must also find the best method to relieve pressure on the patient's spinal cord as well as stabilize the spinal column so that it is correctly aligned around the cord and does not move. To keep the patient as still as possible, the medical team may rely on traction and weights as well as special bed frames designed to limit movement.

In determining just how badly the spinal cord and nerves are damaged, a battery of tests will be administered. The physicians need to know whether the injured person's spinal cord has been partly or completely severed, rather than merely bruised or compressed.

New Drugs for SCI

To help minimize the body's reaction to injury, thus reducing damage to the spinal cord, doctors administer a steroid drug, methylprednisolone. Methylprednisolone became part of the standard treatment for acute spinal cord injuries after extensive clinical studies revealed that patients who received this drug during the first eight hours following an injury did significantly better than those who did not. Completely paralyzed patients given methylprednisolone recovered about 20 percent of their lost motor functions (ability to move), whereas patients not receiving it only regained 8 percent of these functions. Partially paralyzed patients receiving methylprednisolone got back about 75 percent of their motor functions as compared to 59 percent of patients not given the drug.[3]

Doctors are learning more about other drugs that might be useful during the acute stage of spinal cord injury. Among these is a medication called GM-1 ganglioside. This substance occurs naturally in the body's cells. Laboratory studies have revealed that neurons that are soaked in GM-1 ganglioside

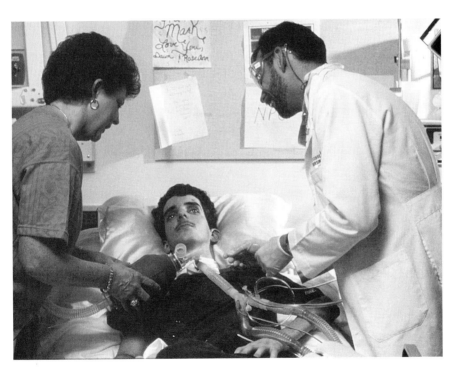

Some people with SCI need help to breathe. Here, a nurse is showing a patient's mother how to suction his ventilator.

grow vine-like fibers like the ones damaged in spinal cord injuries. In a 1991 study, patients with spinal cord injuries who were given the drug through a series of injections within 72 hours of being hurt experienced some reversal of the nerve damage.[4]

GM-1 ganglioside was used in 1992 when New York Jets football player Dennis Byrd broke his neck after colliding with a teammate on the field. Although he initially retained some feeling in his arms, Byrd was otherwise paralyzed. However, after prompt treatment with methylprednisolone, surgery, and a series of shots of GM-1 ganglioside, he regained feeling and movement in his lower body. He is now able to walk without assistance.[5]

The drug was also tried on the Chinese gymnast Sang Lan, who injured her spinal cord during practice for the 1998 Goodwill Games in New York. As had been the case with Dennis Byrd, the doctors needed to obtain special permission to use GM-1 ganglioside, since it is still considered experimental and has not yet been approved by the United States Food and Drug Administration (FDA). But in Sang Lan's case, an unexpected complication arose. When the gymnast's doctors contacted the drug manufacturer, they were told that the only person who could authorize the use of the restricted drug was the company president, and he was away on vacation and could not be reached.

Since acting in time is vital with spinal cord injuries, the hospital called New York Senator Al D'Amato to personally intervene. He did, and within an hour the doctors had permission to try GM-1 ganglioside on Sang Lan. For the next six weeks, the seventy-seven pound gymnast was given the drug in the hope that it would be as successful for her as it had been for Byrd. However, this time the results were less dramatic. Although she regained some feeling in her chest, Sang Lan felt nothing below that level.[6] Further clinical trials using the drug are presently under way.

Surgery

In some instances, surgery may be necessary during the acute stage of spinal cord injury. This may be done to stabilize the spine, to relieve pressure on the cord, or to reduce swelling. Surgery also often permits physical therapy to begin earlier. In addition, new magnetic resonance imaging (MRI) has helped doctors to precisely pinpoint damaged areas to more effectively aid their patients. Once the patient's condition is stable, attention is focused on rehabilitative therapies.

Recovery from SCI

When dealing with spinal cord injuries, the level of recovery varies from one person to another. As Dr. Daniel Lammertse, medical director at Craig Hospital in Englewood, Colorado, explains:

> Why is it that some people with SCI get better and others do not? That is a very difficult question. Actually, almost all patients get better. It is a matter of how much

they get better. Some get very much better and some get very little return. The difference has to do with the nature and extent of the injury. Patients who receive excellent care during the acute stage often have better odds for a fuller recovery. In some cases, after pressure on the spinal cord is reduced surgically, nerves in the area may begin working again. . . . Many patients show some evidence of incompleteness [having some feeling and movement below the injury level] within the first week of injury. Because of the way the spinal cord is wired, the first sign of this evolving incompleteness is usually some sensation—sensation almost always precedes recovery of some movement. A hopeful prognosis starts to drop off fairly rapidly after the first three, four, or five days if there is no sign of at least sensory recovery. By the time a week has elapsed, it drops further, and every day that goes by without some function coming back makes the prognosis of recovery less likely. It is rare for someone to have major functional recovery who was truly complete: that is, with no sensation, no movement for more than a week. [7]

Cuban-born singer and songwriter Gloria Estefan might be considered among the most fortunate people to have experienced SCI. While on tour in 1990, she was nearly killed in a bus accident. The Grammy Award–winning artist broke her back, injuring her spinal cord, and was temporarily paralyzed. Today, two metal rods still stabilize vertebrae broken in the accident. However, after months of intensive physical therapy, she was able to resume her active stage career.

With physical therapy and adaptive devices, many people with SCI can regain some motor function. This woman has braces that enable her to perform such everyday activities as putting on makeup and using a computer.

Rehabilitation and any degree of recovery is often a lengthy process requiring a good deal of effort on the part of both the patient and those assisting him or her. During this period, patients must learn to live with the effects of spinal cord injury—the physical as well as the emotional ones. Success at this level is essential to the patient's future and quality of life.

5

Recovery and Rehabilitation

I t is clear that people with spinal cord injuries lose their ability to use their limbs, but it is not so well known that spinal cord injuries involve a number of other health concerns, as well. Learning to cope with these and avoid possible problems is part of the person's recovery.

SCI Complications

One complication of spinal cord injury involves both bladder and bowel function. Due to the loss of sensation following a spinal cord injury, the affected individual may not feel when his or her bladder is full and may also not be able to control the release of urine. Therefore, many people with SCI have tubes known as catheters inserted into their bladders through which urine can drain into a bag strapped to their leg. Other types of catheters are not worn continuously but are inserted at scheduled intervals throughout the day and removed after the bladder is emptied.

Bowel functions are also frequently affected in individuals with SCI. In such cases, laxatives, suppositories, or manually removing the stool may be necessary to initiate a bowel movement.

Spinal cord injuries also make skin care an extremely important health concern. Skin protects the body from injury and infection, as well as from excessive fluid loss. But following a spinal cord injury, there will be a decrease or, in some cases, a total loss of sensation in the skin covering certain areas of the body. People with SCI will not be as aware of pain, pressure, heat, or cold as they were previously. Therefore, they need to be especially alert to the possibility of being burned by bath water that is too hot, hair dryers, hot beverages, or heating pads. When outdoors, the person has to be careful not to get a sunburn.

The Spain Rehabilitation Center at the University of Alabama described how quickly heat can cause a burn:

> A girl with SCI was riding with her family in a pickup truck. Her feet were on the floorboard of the truck. Although she had on tennis shoes, her feet were in one position for too long. The hot floorboard caused the bottom of her feet to blister. The blisters developed into sores.[1]

The skin of a person with SCI can easily be injured by insect bites, chemicals, or friction as well. There is also the possibility of not realizing that one's skin has become scratched or irritated.

Pressure sores, sometimes known as pressure ulcers or bedsores, are still another concern for people with spinal cord injuries. These sores tend to develop when an individual lies or sits in the same position for too long, causing the skin and tissue in a particular spot to break down. Such sores can also easily occur as the result of skin rubbing against a wheelchair, brace, or other appliance. Ill-fitting shoes or garments—especially clothes that are wet or too tight—often contribute to the problem as well. Pressure sores and the complications that arise from them are among the most common reasons that people with spinal cord injuries are hospitalized.

Another complication that can result from spinal cord injury is spasticity. This condition occurs when, due to the breakdown in the body's communication network, the brain is not able to tell the spinal cord to turn muscles off. According to Dr. Richard Bruno of Englewood Hospital in New Jersey, spasticity results from damage to the spinal cord or the brain:

> When this happens, the motor nerves will go off on their own, like unsupervised children. If there isn't a parent around to tell them to stop running around the room that's exactly what they're going to do. Your brain is the parent of your muscles and motor nerves. Why aren't you dancing around the room right now? Your brain is telling you not to do that, but to just sit there and be quiet. When you cut the spinal cord or damage the brain, the brain is no longer able to tell the motor nerves to stop firing, therefore the muscles contract. A paraplegic's muscles might contract and relax and his/her leg might dance up and down."[2]

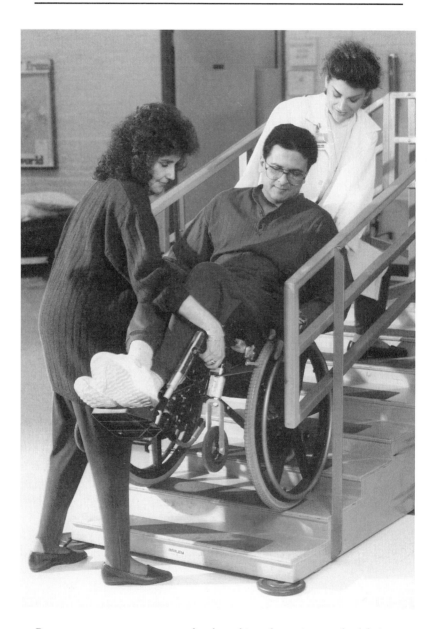

Because pressure sores can result when skin rubs against a wheelchair or other appliance, people with SCI must take special care of their skin.

Autonomic dysreflexia (AD), also known as hyperreflexia, is a serious complication of spinal cord injury. Sometimes, it can be life-threatening. When this condition occurs, the person's blood pressure rises to the point at which he or she is at risk of a stroke or death if not treated. AD can happen when an irritation located below the point of injury causes blood vessels in the abdomen and legs to tighten, raising the person's blood pressure. People experiencing AD usually have a sudden pounding headache and their skin may become flushed. There may also be increased perspiration, a slowed heart rate, nausea, nasal stuffiness, and goosebumps.

It is crucial not to ignore these symptoms. The irritation or stimulus causing the problem needs to be promptly identified and remedied. Often, AD is due to a full bladder that needs to be emptied, a bladder infection, or a plugged catheter. Another common cause is constipation or an impacted bowel. Pressure sores have also been known to cause AD. AD is a risk during pregnancy, so an obstetrician needs to know about this potentially lethal complication.

People with spinal cord injuries must be taught to avoid these complications. This special education is part of a long-term treatment program. The plan includes rehabilitation designed to give each person the best possible quality of life.

A Team Approach

The medical specialty dealing specifically with the diagnosis and treatment of physical disabilities is known as physical medicine and rehabilitation, often referred to as "physiatry." A physiatrist is a doctor who helps patients with the physical and psychological disabilities that remain once the initial medical or surgical treatment has been completed.

According to the National Spinal Cord Injury Association:

> The physiatrist often coordinates a team of doctors and health professionals in developing and carrying out a comprehensive rehabilitation plan, which extends beyond hospital walls into the patient's family, community, occupation, friends, and ultimate life style. This rehabilitation team may include physical, occupational, and/or speech therapists, nurses and doctors from various specialties, including neurology [the branch of medicine concerned with the nervous system] and orthopedics [the branch concerned with skeletal deformities], psychologists, counselors or social workers, rehabilitation engineers, and others. The physiatrist's success comes through a team effort where the patient is an integral part of the team process. Each improvement in function, however subtle, can significantly improve the life of a patient.[3]

Through various rehabilitation techniques, patients learn to make the most of their remaining abilities. Drugs to combat spasticity and other conditions resulting from spinal cord injury may be prescribed. In addition, intensive physical therapy has proven crucial for people with SCI. According to the National Rehabilitation Information Center, "Almost all patients with spinal cord injuries can now achieve a partial return of function with proper physical therapy that maintains flexibility and function of the muscles and joints."[4] A physical therapy program can include exercises with weights, pulleys, and special exercise machines; a tilt table, which helps the patient's cardiovascular system adjust to being upright; exercises performed on a mat that help the person learn to change position in bed, get dressed, and move from place to place; and classes in using a wheelchair. [5]

The mother of a teenage boy who injured his spinal cord while playing ice hockey described the rehabilitation phase of her son's recovery. As she noted, it is not a quick cure-all: "For

Rehabilitation techniques enable people with SCI to make the most of their abilities and, as much as possible, to return to everyday activities, such as walking the dog.

51

spinal-cord-injury patients, there is no defining moment at which everything 'goes back to normal,'" she recalled. "Recovery is a long, slow series of little miracles, and even then, there may be setbacks; a movement today may become impossible tomorrow. So we learned to mark our triumphs one at a time and be grateful for the smallest sign of progress."[6]

Chinese gymnast Sang Lan's post-injury therapy is a good example of the slow but steady gains that can be made. Sang Lan's rehabilitation began just ten days after her accident. Through an intensive physical therapy regime she built up strength in her arms, shoulders, and neck, and is now largely able to feed, bathe, and dress herself and to use a manual wheelchair.

Over the months, Sang Lan worked with several therapists. An occupational therapist worked with Sang Lan to teach her how to accomplish such basic tasks as getting dressed and brushing her hair. Another therapist taught the young gymnast to roll herself over to prevent bedsores from developing. Commenting on Sang Lan's dogged determination, the physical therapist Deborah Lewis noted, "If she doesn't get it, she'll try and try again. She doesn't seem to give up."[7]

One of Sang Lan's proudest moments came when she was finally able to eat on her own. She had been fitted with a metal splint device for her right hand that permits her to attach a fork or spoon, enabling her to bring food to her mouth. Lan uses the same appliance to brush her teeth and hold a pen.

How Technology Helps People With SCI

Sang Lan's hand splint is one example of an adaptive device that enables a person to perform everyday activities. In addition to using adaptive devices, people with SCI often need to have changes made in their environment that allow them to be more self-sufficient. These changes can include wider doorways (to accommodate wheelchairs), nonskid floors, specially adapted bathtubs or showers, and controls for lighting, faucets, and appliances that can be reached and operated easily.[8] In addition, many people with SCI drive cars that have been fitted with hand controls, extra-wide doors, a wheelchair or scooter lift, and other modifications.[9] Unfortunately, such modifications to homes and cars cost thousands of dollars.

In some cases, functional electrical stimulation (FES) can also be an effective tool in rehabilitative work involving spinal cord injury patients. With FES, an electrical current is applied to paralyzed muscles to produce movement. In most FES systems, a control unit determines the strength of the current to be applied, while a stimulator unit generates the current. Electrodes transmit the electrical stimulus to the muscles. Through this process, neurons that previously could not be stimulated, due to the breakdown in the communication system between the brain and the spinal cord, are now stimulated electrically. The FES technology first captured the public's attention in 1983 when it was used to enable Nan Davis, a young paraplegic at Wright State University in Ohio, to get out of her wheelchair and walk to the podium to receive her

53

diploma. While that was a dramatic moment, FES is not a cure for paralysis. However, it has been used in exercise training for people with SCI and to assist them in standing and moving.

The FES leg cycle ergometer, a sophisticated exercise bike of sorts, is a good example of how FES can be effectively administered. The cycle uses low-level electrical impulses to stimulate a person's muscles through electrodes placed over the motor nerves of the legs. The electrical stimulation causes the paralyzed person's legs to move against the cycle's pedals, enabling him or her to have physical exercise. Susan Steele became a quadriplegic in August 1979, when she was still in

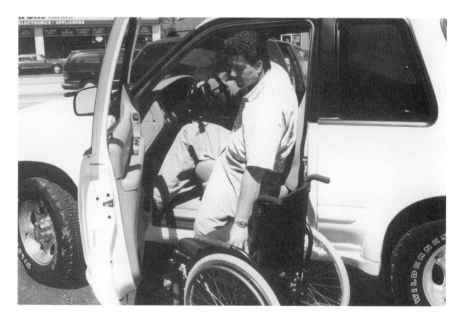

Modifications such as hand controls enable people with spinal cord injuries to drive cars.

Doing Ordinary Things

People with SCI often need help doing things that people without spinal cord injuries do without thinking. Here are some of the creative ideas that people have come up with:[10]

- Button hook/zipper cuff: Kevin Robinson says that the person who invented this gadget "should get the Nobel Prize. Not only does it do what it's supposed to, the zipper end is great for cleaning fingernails, ripping open CD packages, and letting the air out of the tires of ABs [able-bodied, or nondisabled people] who take my parking spaces."

- Sliding solution: Hugh Gallagher uses a thick piece of cowhide that is smooth on one side and rough on the other to slide from his chair into a car seat. "It rolls up and fits in my briefcase," he says.

- Door locks: Roxy Meck's dad replaced the buttons on her deadbolt locks with four-inch wooden dowels that are easier for Roxy to slide shut. Now Roxy can lock her doors without help.

- Page turners: Don Deal says that one of his favorite tools is "a piece of Tupperware used to peel oranges . . . and they're given away as favors at Tupperware parties. They make great page turners."

- Document grabber: June Price glued two Popsicle sticks across one end of a yardstick. She uses her new gadget to lift documents from her computer printer.

- Speakerphone switch: A rubber eraser glued to her speakerphone button lets Laura Hershey turn on the phone by pressing it with the tray on her wheelchair.

high school. She has taken part in research studies and has always wanted to reap the benefits of physical exercise. In describing her experience with this special exercise bike, she noted that it "definitely gives you a workout and the exercise leaves you with the same glow and feeling that motivates the able-bodied."[11]

Other potential benefits from using various FES technologies include better control of spasticity, increased muscle strength, decreased risk of developing bedsores, and improved bladder and bowel function. FES can also improve respiratory function (breathing ability) and, in some cases, restore sexual function in affected males.[12] In addition, some people think that FES may prove to be an invaluable training tool in re-teaching people to walk if there is eventually a cure for SCI. They believe that patients who have kept their leg muscles in good shape will be further along on the road to recovery.

It is likely that increasing numbers of people with SCI will also benefit from FES through sophisticated electronic devices known as neural prostheses. (A prosthesis, plural "prostheses," is an artificial device to replace a missing part of the body.) While other FES aids are worn externally, neural prostheses are surgically implanted, similar to the way a cardiac pacemaker is. In some cases, these devices have replaced respirators for paralyzed individuals who needed them to breathe.

A number of other neural prostheses for patients with spinal cord injuries are now being used. Among these is the Freehand System, which restores some degree of hand movement. Ideally, patients would use their shoulder muscles to control the device, enabling them to perform a number of valuable daily activities such as using silverware to feed themselves, writing a note, and answering the phone. The FDA predicts that it may help as many as 54,000 patients whose spinal cord injuries allow some use of the body.[13]

During test studies, sixty-one quadriplegic patients in whom the device was implanted regained the ability to grasp and release objects such as forks and pens. Many of those

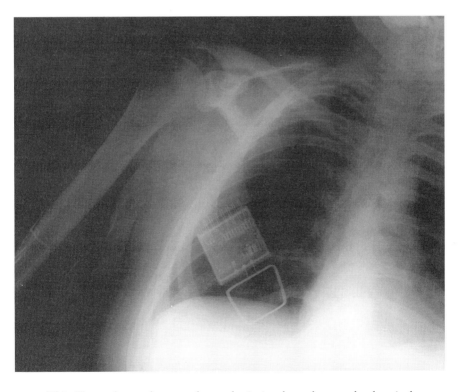

This X-ray shows the neural prosthesis implant that sends electrical impulses to paralyzed muscles to cause movement.

involved in the study reported a general improvement in their daily activities, as well as increased independence. Kathie Bates of Salineville, Ohio, found that the Freehand System made a world of difference for her. Bates's quadriplegia resulted from an automobile accident in which her spinal cord was damaged. She retained some shoulder movement and could flex her elbows, but might have ended up in a nursing home without the Freehand System. With it, however, she was able to move into her own apartment as well as retain custody of her four children. "Now I cook with my kids," Bates stated. "It's done wonders for my self-esteem, my motivation."[14]

Nevertheless, a great deal of work still needs to be done on neural prostheses. These devices are extremely complex, and numerous technical considerations come into play. For example, it is essential that all the electronic components be as small as possible. The electrodes must also be compatible with human body tissue. Researchers also need to develop better ways of safely sending electrical currents into the body. Currently, a variety of neural prostheses are being evaluated by research teams for their effectiveness and long-term safety.

While the devices currently being tested took years to develop, it has been argued that in the future, neural prostheses will be greatly enhanced. There will be improvements in both the materials used and the technology employed. Among the most recent technical advances are tiny probes that fit sixteen electrodes on a shaft slimmer than a strand of human hair. Such a device would allow patients both more refined muscle control and a greater range of movement. Those using

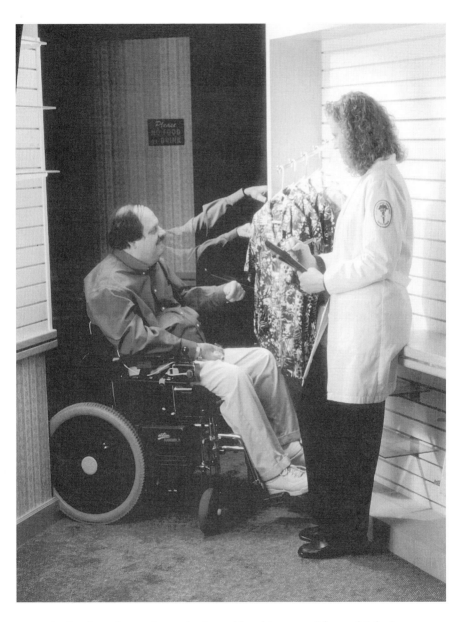

An implanted neural prosthesis enables this man with quadriplegia to reach out and grasp a hanger.

these neural prostheses would enjoy faster and more natural motion. In the future, researchers expect to perfect devices that do not need external cabling systems or externally mounted sensors.

In addition, scientists hope to one day develop neural prostheses that deliver sensory information to a person's brain. These would be designed to enable people with spinal cord injuries to stand on their own. By using such devices, the person's movements would be controlled by signals from the brain rather than from muscles.

6

Coping With a Spinal Cord Injury

On February 3, 1995, my life changed forever. Shortly after
noon, I was driving on California's Interstate 15 when my
car veered off the road. I hit a 4.5-foot dirt embankment
and in about one second, my car's speed went from about
sixty miles an hour to zero. When that happened, the
inertia threw me forward, and I became a C-4 quadriplegic.
No one can ever be prepared for such a change in life.[1]

These are the words of Ken Hall. In high school, he had
been a football fullback and wrestler. Later, Hall enlisted in the
Navy, spending four years as a submarine quartermaster and
diver. As he put it, "Most of my energies for thirty-five years
had been channeled into physical activity."[2]

We may illustrate Hall's personal story here, but the consequences of spinal cord injury are similar for most people.
Health care professionals and rehabilitation therapists may be

extremely helpful with the physical aspects of SCI. But there is also an enormous emotional adjustment to be made, and the vast majority of people with SCI will experience a broad range of feelings, including intense sadness, frustration, and rage. As a young college student with a spinal cord injury recalled:

> At first, the psychological effects were as devastating as the physical ones. For months, I was in absolute denial. Adding to my misery was a sense that life was going by without me. My friends were at college, while I was paralyzed in the hospital. Many people came to visit and sent cards and encouragement, but none of that could change what had happened.[3]

Some people focus on trying to figure out why this tragedy happened to them. Although this may not seem like a constructive use of their time, it is important to remember that people with spinal cord injuries are dealing with a complex combination of major health, emotional, and financial concerns. At first, many feel completely overwhelmed.

One doctor gave his new patients this advice:

> In one sense, you'll never get over it. In another sense, you'll gradually feel a bit better each week. . . . There is a period of grief and a sense of loss that is, I guess, like having someone close to you die, whether it be family or a very close friend. You have to say goodbye to a part of yourself, the way your body used to be. But certainly that doesn't mean your life is over. You're going to have a period of pain; but you have to slug it through like anybody would.[4]

Peter Addesso, director of the Eastern Paralyzed Veterans Association, explained what those feelings may be like:

> Having a disability such as a spinal cord injury produces a lot of questions about who you are, who you want to be, how others, including your family, will interact with you, and how you will live your life as a person with a disability. Unlike questions about your physical needs, personal and social issues do not have exact answers or procedures to follow. What you decide to do with your personal and social life is up to you. Some of these issues are difficult, and sometimes very complex.[5]

Getting Help

In trying to get their lives back on track, many people with spinal cord injuries profit from sessions with a psychologist or counselor. Professional advice can help the injured deal with their reactions and the challenges ahead.

Many people with SCI have also found it especially helpful to speak to others who have already gone through what they are going through. It is important for the person to know that he or she is not alone and to learn what emotional reactions to expect.

A loved one's injury can also have a tremendous emotional impact on his or her family. At first, family members may be shocked at the effect of the injury, as well as concerned about the extent of the care and financial resources that may be necessary. Family members will have a lot of questions, and often

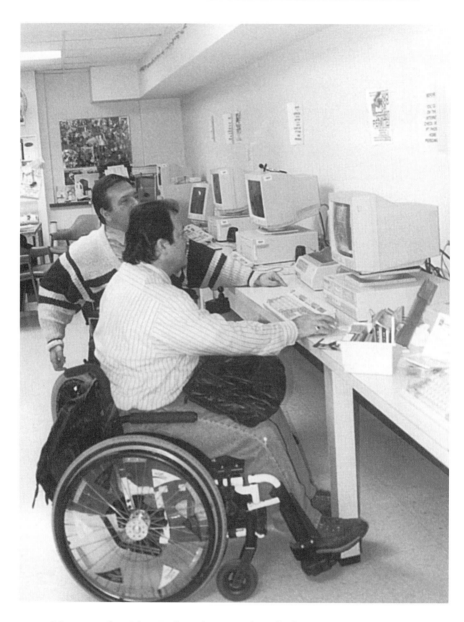

Many people with spinal cord injuries benefit from talking with others who have been through similar experiences.

the answers may not be simple or immediately forthcoming. The mother of a quadriplegic described her frustration after hearing about her daughter's injury:

> At first, you experience disbelief, shock, anger and terror. You just don't know what will happen. I went to the library and took out every book about quadriplegia I could find. Most of the information, I later found, wasn't true. I wish I had known more about what was happening. Sometimes things aren't going to be all right, and it would've been real helpful to talk to someone who had been there. So much is happening; it's rough to deal with it all alone.[6]

As time passes, people with spinal cord injuries usually find that they are able to do things that they first thought they could no longer do. Now, however, they are doing most of these things in a wheelchair. Numerous people with SCI earn advanced degrees, hold meaningful jobs, and lead active social lives. It is especially important to remember that a person with a spinal cord injury is essentially the same person he or she was before the accident. An individual's personality is not going to change as the result of an injury. As Peter Addesso neatly summed it up, "If you were smart, friendly, obnoxious, hard to get along with, finicky, argumentative, bossy, or goal-oriented before your injury, the chances are very good that you'll be the same person after your injury."[7]

Nevertheless, those with spinal cord injuries must still confront the stereotypes many people have about people with disabilities. Sometimes, a person with SCI must confront even his or her own misconceptions. As Addesso noted:

> It is often said that one of the hardest things about coping with the abrupt onset of a disability is that you're suddenly thrust into it, with all your able-bodied beliefs, attitudes and misconceptions. If you know anyone with a disability, say a friend or family member or fellow employee, you probably would discover that the disability would seem less important as the relationship grew. First impressions or initial attitudes are not always accurate and may change over time.[8]

In dealing with SCI, it is important to concentrate on what people can do rather than what they cannot do. Recapturing old skills is an ongoing process as the injured person learns new ways of doing things and begins increasingly to do more for himself or herself. According to experts at the Jackson Memorial Medical Center at the University of Miami, people with SCI will be more successful if they can

- ask for and accept realistic help from others;
- use positive thinking;
- set realistic goals for themselves;
- be willing to try new things; and
- involve themselves with positively oriented peers with SCI.[9]

Even with efforts to maintain a positive attitude, many people with SCI experience depression, an emotional illness that goes beyond feeling sad or being "down in the dumps."

Walt Royca is a championship bowler. Many people who experience spinal cord injuries are able to do things they first thought they could no longer do.

When this happens, it is important for them to get help. A primary care physician can refer people to a mental health professional such as a psychologist, social worker, psychiatrist, psychiatric nurse practitioner, or family therapist. Treatment can involve psychotherapy (also known as counseling or "talk therapy"), medication, or both.[10]

Assistive Devices

Another adjustment to be made by people with spinal cord injuries and those around them is acceptance of such assistive devices as wheelchairs and scooters. In time, they may learn to view these devices differently than they may have in the past. An Internet site known as "A Celebration of Wheels" perhaps best addresses the issue as it states:

> "Confined to a wheelchair" is a commonly used term. But for many men and women wounded by accident, illness, or birth defect, the wheelchair is not a prison. Quite the contrary: They are confined *without* a wheelchair. With one, they are enabled to experience life more fully.[11]

Ron Miner is a consultant who advises California architects and developers on how to make their buildings wheelchair-accessible in conformity with state access codes. Miner is also a quadriplegic who has used a wheelchair for more than thirty years. He described the importance of activity in his everyday life:

> I had to take the philosophy, the more I can do for myself today the more I can do for myself tomorrow. Even after I

was first injured, I would brush my own teeth and shave myself, even though it was kind of difficult. A lot of the guys would have nurses do it, but I just kept working at it until it got easier. . . . The more you accomplish, the more you can feel good about yourself. The more you depend on other people, the more you don't feel positive about yourself. You just mentally have to psych yourself into it, the feeling that as long as I work to take care of myself, I'm going to feel better, get around better and enjoy life.[12]

Given the right attitude, families can provide a good deal of support and encouragement as people with SCI carve out

Charlene Curtiss (top) and Joanne Petroff (bottom), of the performance group Light Motion, perform the dance "Laughing Games," showing how beautiful movement in a wheelchair can be.

active roles for themselves. "How your family and friends respond to your new disability is a big influence on how you will respond to it," cited physical therapist Sharon Grady of Orange County, California. "They need to allow the person to participate in normal, everyday activities, even if it means that they also have to learn to do things a little differently than they used to."[13]

As the months pass, people with SCI tend to develop new approaches to life. One teenage girl with a spinal cord injury recalled:

> My trauma changed my way of thinking. I don't let the pettiness of others bother me. I gained a new appreciation for life because I miss all the things I did so casually before the accident—hiking, biking, simply going up stairs. But I discovered that there are many activities I can still enjoy. There are at least fifty sports for people with disabilities.[14]

Sports

Sports can serve as a wonderful means of both recreation and exercise for people with SCI. Just a few of the sports that can be done in a wheelchair are tennis, basketball, fishing, archery, air-rifle shooting, and sailing. In the Wheelchair Sports, U.S.A., National Junior Wheelchair Championships, young participants engage in competitions in table tennis, weight lifting, track, swimming, and other sports. Such events give youthful wheelchair athletes an opportunity to spend time with one another. Frequently, lasting friendships are forged.

On an international level, top athletes with disabilities can participate in the Paralympics. These games are the equivalent of the Olympics for outstanding athletes who are physically or mentally challenged. Like the Olympics, the Paralympics are held every four years.

One exceptional athlete who is also a paraplegic is Mark Wellman. Wellman, who has been climbing mountains since he was twelve, has scaled over fifty Sierra Nevada peaks as well as climbed in the French Alps. But in 1982, he injured his spinal cord while mountaineering in the John Muir Wilderness in California.

Team sports, such as wheelchair basketball, are a good way for people with SCI to stay active and social.

Despite his injury and the physical limitations it imposed, Wellman continued to climb, using specially adapted equipment that he designed. The climbing gear consists of a belt, a chest harness, and leg supports that attach to a horizontal pull-up bar. After attaching the bar to fixed ropes along the rock face, Wellman pulls himself up, six inches at a time.

In 1989, with the help of his climbing partner, Mike Corbett, Wellman made it up the 3,000-foot face of El Capitan, the world's highest cliff, in Yosemite National Park. And ten years later, he repeated the feat, this time choosing a more difficult route to the top. Wellman and Corbett carried about 250 pounds of gear, which included 100 pounds of water along with sleeping bags, rainwear, headlamps, cameras, and other items. As if that were not enough, there were another 40 pounds of rope and protection devices to be hauled up. During the journey, the men ate and slept either on El Capitan's rocky ledges or while suspended in midair. After eleven days—and, for Wellman, six thousand chin-ups—they reached the top. Wellman made his purpose in climbing El Capitan especially meaningful when he said, "My message isn't for the disabled to come and climb El Capitan. It's to climb whatever mountain that is a barrier in their lives. And that can be anything."[15]

Wellman continued to enjoy kayaking and skiing as well. He became a member of the United States Disabled Ski Team and competed in two Paralympics. In the spring of 1993, he became the first paraplegic to sit-ski across the Sierra Nevada Mountain Range. That meant that this outstanding athlete skied fifty miles with only the use of his arms. In describing his achievements, Wellman has said, "Everyone faces the world with different abilities and disabilities. But everyone has at least one goal in common . . . to break through their own barriers."[16]

Overcoming Obstacles

There are countless other people with SCI who made the most of their recovery and went on to achieve results that many able-bodied people would envy. For example, with a sense of fierce determination, Annie Drophin opened a completely wheelchair-accessible beauty salon in her hometown in New Jersey by the time she was twenty-seven.

Drophin had been a quadriplegic since she was twelve as the result of a diving accident. Using a wheelchair made Drophin especially sensitive to the accessibility needs of others. This sensitivity went into her plans for the design and operation of her first business:

> I've visited salons where the chairs at the cutting stations are bolted to the floor, chairs are connected to the sinks at washing stations, and hair dryers are connected to chairs. All these factors prevent wheelchair access. I know firsthand the daily obstacles faced by the handicapped, so I wanted my salon to be as accessible as possible.[17]

Her salon, From Hair to Eternity, has wide doors, movable chairs, and ample space to permit clients in wheelchairs to move about the premises easily. Although now a successful businesswoman, at times Drophin had been frustrated in the work world. "I had a lot of trouble finding a job," she recalled, "Sometimes I would call about a job, tell the person I'm in a wheelchair and set up an interview, only to find when I got there that the work site was not handicapped accessible. It was annoying and a little demoralizing."[18]

Another success story is that of Dr. Ed Nieshoff, who was paralyzed from the chest down in a diving accident when he was twenty-one years old. Following the accident, Nieshoff spent fourteen months recovering in the hospital. Then, to the amazement of many, he got into medical school. The path was not always easy. Nieshoff had to meet the challenges medical school presented despite the physical limitations imposed by his injury.

When Nieshoff came up against something in medical school he was physically unable to do, he made up for it by learning to listen and observe more. These skills proved to be especially beneficial later in caring for his patients. Ed Nieshoff graduated from The Medical College of Ohio in Toledo in 1991, and completed his residency in 1995 at Detroit's Rehabilitation Institute.

Today, he treats patients at the Institute and serves as an assistant professor in the rehabilitation department of Wayne State University Medical School in Detroit. Perhaps, most importantly, Dr. Nieshoff has been a vital role model and inspiration to his patients dealing with spinal cord injuries.

Among his patients was a young man named Christian Mageli. Mageli was one of two medical technicians shot when a woman opened fire in a Detroit clinic, claiming that her husband had failed to receive proper care there. Mageli, who sustained a spinal cord injury, credits Dr. Nieshoff with convincing him that people can still have meaningful lives after such an injury. "Going through medical school healthy is enough of an achievement in a lifetime," Mageli stated. "But doing it as a quadriplegic in a wheelchair, that's an incredible achievement and powerful motivation."[19]

Mageli's sentiments were echoed by Darrell McQueen, another of Nieshoff's patients. McQueen, an auto mechanic in his early thirties, was injured while doing somersaults at a party. "He [Nieshoff] was the doctor who made me get up out

A teacher in a wheelchair leads a discussion in her math class. Numerous people with SCI earn advanced degrees and hold meaningful jobs.

of bed," McQueen recalled. "Here he was, in a wheelchair, and I could see all he could do. He told me I wasn't as bad off as I thought."[20]

To many people, recovery from a spinal cord injury means a return to the way their bodies were formerly, or at least regaining significant feeling and movement. If someone who was not expected to walk again does so through healing and physical therapy, that person may often be said to have made a good recovery. However, Ed Nieshoff believes there is a broader and better way to view recovery.

> Society defines recovery as getting up and walking. [But] what's important is doing something meaningful with your life; to have a job, a home, a wife, whatever, to pursue the American dream. . . . I'd define recovery as being happy with who you are and leading a productive life. If that's your definition, you have an excellent chance of recovering.[21]

7

Society and People With SCI

Over the last thirty years, there has been a dramatic shift in how society views and treats people with disabilities. Earlier, people with SCI often felt forced to remain on the sidelines. Too frequently, they were placed in nursing homes. The limitations these individuals faced were very real. Public transportation and buildings simply were not designed to accommodate those in wheelchairs. Many people with SCI who were well qualified for positions were barred from the workplace because businesses were usually not wheelchair-accessible.

However, by the late 1960s, large numbers of the disabled population were no longer willing to spend their lives on the outside looking in. People in wheelchairs had come to believe that the problem was not with their wheelchairs but with the basic design of most buildings. Any design that excluded whole groups of people needed to be changed.

That kind of thinking sparked the disability-rights movement—one born to ensure equality for people in wheelchairs as well as for those with other disabilities. These activists argued that the way society treated people with disabilities was more disabling than their actual medical conditions. Being denied a job because the doors and aisles of the workplace were inadequate kept people in wheelchairs in poverty. The

The disability-rights movement was born to ensure equality for people with disabilities, such as those in wheelchairs.

lack of access also prohibited their participation in community activities, which only added to their sense of isolation.

New Laws

People with SCI and other disability-rights activists petitioned legislators and politicians to enact important changes into law. On numerous occasions between the 1960s and the 1990s, they held "wheelchair marches" and sit-ins to protest the discrimination they were routinely subjected to. During one instance, demonstrators even occupied the rotunda of the Capitol Building in Washington, D.C. They fought long and hard and eventually achieved some success. The following changes are evidence of that:

- The Architectural Barriers Act of 1968 required that any building or transportation facility built or paid for by the federal government be accessible to people with disabilities.

- Section 504 of the Rehabilitation Act of 1973 prohibited businesses receiving federal funds from discriminating against people with either physical or mental disabilities.

- The 1975 Individuals with Disabilities Education Act (IDEA) ordered that young people with disabilities be guaranteed a free public education in the "least restrictive environment." This would have a tremendous impact on children with spinal cord injuries. Previously, small classrooms and narrow doorways and halls often meant that students in wheelchairs received their education in a leftover space or a converted storage room. In many cases, they had remained completely cut off from other students and the interaction that is part of a well-rounded education.

- The Fair Housing Amendments Act of 1988 affected housing practices. It prohibited discrimination against the disabled in housing sales or rentals as well as in the financing necessary to purchase a home. Now people with SCI could not be told that they could not rent a particular apartment because of their disability or be denied a mortgage on the same grounds.

- In 1990, the most far-reaching legislation protecting the rights of the disabled was signed into law by President George Bush. It was the Americans with Disabilities Act (ADA). This act extended the protection already granted to the disabled through Section 504 of the Rehabilitation Act of 1973. While that legislation prohibited discrimination against the disabled in federally funded business, the ADA now guaranteed the same protection to disabled people in the private sector. This landmark legislation required that all schools, workplaces, public offices, and transit systems be wheelchair-accessible.

Today, disability-rights advocates firmly believe that there is still more to be done. The American Coalition of Citizens with Disabilities (ACCD) is a nationwide organization dedicated to advancing the rights of the disabled. One of the group's primary goals has been to ensure that disabled people are made aware of what they are entitled to under the law and that they insist on getting it. Unfortunately, it is often up to the disabled community to monitor compliance with the new standards. So far, these laws have been enforced largely through complaints, usually after an individual or a group has waged a lawsuit.

Carol Gill, who uses a wheelchair, found out how important ADA can be to the disabled in the health care arena. "When I called one of Chicago's major teaching hospitals to make an appointment at a woman's health clinic," she related, "I was told that I couldn't be seen unless I could get myself onto and off the examining table." Gill argued that this requirement was inherently unfair but was simply given the runaround while being transferred to different people and departments.

Finally Gill thought of the Americans with Disabilities Act and everything fell into place. "I asked to talk to their ADA compliance person and when I did that, it was just incredible. 'Of course we'll have someone there to assist you,' I was told. 'That's your right.' After that, I had no further problems getting access to the examination services. I hung up the phone and felt like wiping off my sword. The ADA! The ADA did this."[1]

To attain genuine equality, activists for the disabled believe that lawsuits, protests, and political persuasion will all be necessary tools for the future. Many leaders and role models have emerged within the disabled community. Among them is Marca Bristo, who, as a young woman, was paralyzed in a diving accident in Lake Michigan. The accident irrevocably changed her life, bringing her "face to face" with her "own finiteness and powerlessness."[2]

Marca Bristo became chairperson of the National Council on Disabilities, an independent federal agency that makes recommendations to the president and Congress on issues affecting the nation's disabled. She had graduated from Beloit College in Beloit, Wisconsin, in 1974, and over twenty years later, in May 1999, she addressed Beloit's graduating class. In describing her own path to empowerment, Bristo said:

> I found personal power through others who had crossed that bridge before me, other people with disabilities who taught me the power of accepting who I was and using my newly changed self to change the world around me. . . . People taught me that the world looked at us wrong, and that we had a responsibility to help the world see through our eyes. . . . It is that paradigm shift, that change in the world view, that gave the disability-rights community its power. . . . When we are challenged with a major policy issue, and people tell us that it cannot be done, such as passing the Americans with Disabilities Act, we know something they don't know and that is we will not go away![3]

The Disability-Rights Movement in Japan

While significant strides have been made in the United States, the disability-rights movement is international. Until fairly recently in Japan, it was extremely rare to see a person with a spinal cord injury or other disability out in public in a

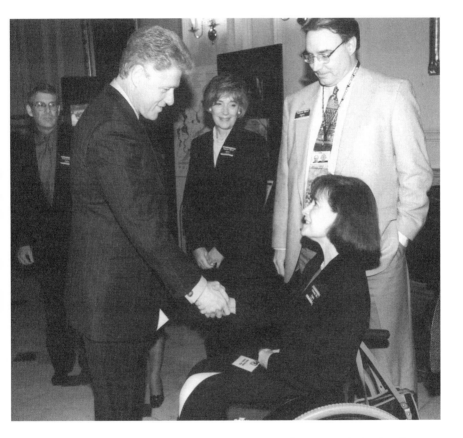

Nancy Starnes, Director of the Paralysis Society of America, shakes hands with former President Bill Clinton. The efforts of activists and political supporters are necessary for continued improvement in the rights of the disabled.

wheelchair. A combination of embarrassment, prejudice, and the inaccessibility of buildings and transportation made them virtual shut-ins.

However, by organizing and actively lobbying, this formerly invisible group has made some important strides. Laws have been enacted there to improve both transportation facilities and employment opportunities for the disabled. Other legislation to create a barrier-free society in Japan includes incentives to private corporations to improve wheelchair access. Public education campaigns have also begun to alert people to the obstacles—both physical and psychological—that those in wheelchairs deal with daily.

A number of disability-rights activists have been crucial in the attitudinal and legislative gains in Japan. These include Yasiro Eita, the first person with SCI to be a member of the Japanese cabinet. Prior to becoming the posts and telecommunications minister, Eita was a professional entertainer. However, his show business career ended in the 1960s after a fall from a stage left him paralyzed. Following his spinal cord injury, he was told that there was no longer a place for him on television. It was thought that his physical condition would upset the viewers.

Nevertheless, in 1978, Eita managed to be elected to Parliament, the Japanese legislative branch of government, where he pushed through numerous reforms enhancing the rights of the disabled. He even helped convince politicians that creating a barrier-free society would spur the economy by providing a boost to the construction industry. Yashiro Eita summed up the goal: "We have to create an environment in which disabled people don't just sleep indoors all day, but are given the opportunity to go out and have fun."[4]

Other Voices for the Disabled

In Canada, Rick Hansen, a person with SCI, took up the cause. Hansen inspired people everywhere in 1987 when he launched his wheelchair journey across Canada known as the Man in Motion World Tour. A decade later Hansen would say of the experience:

> When I look back ten years to the world tour, I always try to remind myself of the original goals and objectives. We wanted to raise awareness about the potential of people with disabilities and to get people thinking about barriers—both physical and social—that make life a challenge when you have a disability. We wanted to raise money, plain and simple, so more research into spinal cord injury could take place and new initiatives in prevention and rehabilitation could go forward.[5]

Hansen's efforts paid off. By the tour's end, he had raised over $24 million. His work also helped to bring about a change in how people in wheelchairs are viewed in Canada. Since Hansen's tour, more attention has been focused on the rightful place of disabled people in society. As in the United States, accessibility has come to mean more than being able to get to the restroom—it now means having access to jobs and social outlets.

In the United States, the most visible activist for SCI research is actor Christopher Reeve. Reeve became a quadriplegic in 1995 in a riding accident when he was thrown from his horse during a competition in Virginia. Prior to the accident, Reeve had sailed, skied, played piano, and flown his own plane. Between 1978 and 1987, he starred in four *Superman* movies, portraying the man of steel who traveled "faster than a speeding bullet" and was able to "leap tall buildings in a single bound."

Shortly after his accident, Reeve became involved in raising funds to change the face of spinal cord injury in America. It was a fitting role for the actor, who had long been passionately involved in social and environmental causes. Now Reeve was determined that his physical limitations not stop him from bringing the cause of SCI to the public's attention. As Reeve described the path he pursued, "Either you vegetate and look out the window, or activate and try to effect change."[6]

Reeve has argued that humanitarian concerns aside, investing in research to find a cure for SCI would save the nation a tremendous amount in health care costs. "I'm sitting listening to the budget debate," he noted. "A lot of it is over Medicare. And I'm thinking that the way to save the Medicare-Medicaid issue, the way to turn it around, instead of talking about cuts, is to talk about research and the efficacy of research."[7] In addition to advancing the case for SCI research, Reeve has fought to prevent insurance companies from setting lifetime limits on payments to people with SCI.

To a large degree, Reeve has focused the limelight on SCI. Besides securing a pledge for $10 million in new research funding from President Bill Clinton, Reeve inspired philanthropist Joan Irvine Smith to donate $1 million to start a spinal cord injury research center at the University of California at Irvine.

Lois Pope, wife of the late publishing magnate Generoso Pope, responded to Reeve's pleas by donating a lump sum of $10 million to the Miami Project to Cure Paralysis and pledging an additional $100,000 annually. Numerous other donations have come in. Reeve also formed the Christopher Reeve Foundation, which merged with the American Paralysis Association to become the Christopher Reeve Paralysis Foundation. The foundation has raised over $18 million and successfully funded the spinal cord injury research of more than 350 investigators around the world.

Although the whole world appreciates all Reeve has done, some people with SCI feel he has placed too much emphasis on finding a cure. They feel that the money would be better spent developing resources to improve the day-to-day lives of people with SCI. They argue that a cure may still be years off and that paralyzed people need more timely assistance in many areas of their lives.

"I'm in favor of research too," stated Cyndi Jones, who publishes Mainstream, a monthly magazine focusing on the rights of the disabled. "But I'm in favor of research that makes a difference in the lives of people with disabilities as they live them," she continued. "Things like bowel and

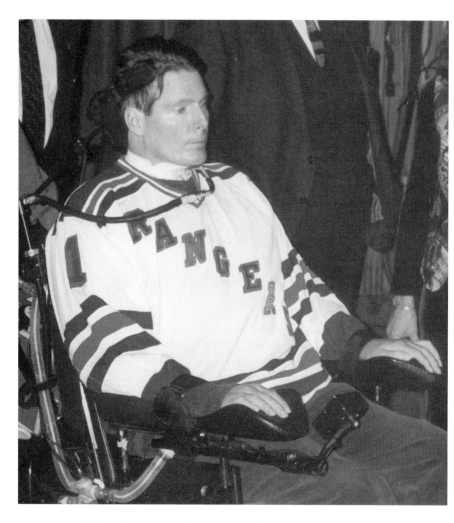

Actor Christopher Reeve, who was injured in a riding accident, has been a highly visible activist for SCI research.

bladder function—there's all kinds of stuff that they could put a little bit of money into."[8]

Other activists have argued that someone of Reeve's stature and visibility would be more valuable to the disabled community if he took on issues such as fairness in housing and fuller compliance with ADA requirements. There are also some disabled individuals who feel that emphasizing a cure for paralysis reinforces the damaging societal stereotype that someone in a wheelchair is less capable than someone who can walk and therefore needs to be "cured." One disability activist explained their viewpoint this way: "When you say you want to cure me, you're saying there's something wrong with me. I'm fine. I just get from point A to point B differently than most people."[9]

Yet Reeve feels he is on the right path and intends to continue raising funds for a cure. Believing that this is not as unrealistic a goal as some would think, he stressed:

> We should always remember that when Kennedy promised a man on the moon by the end of the 60s, many thought that was not only impossible but irresponsible. Some feel the same way about diseases of the brain and central nervous system [spinal cord injury], but the information I continually receive convinces me that the push for a cure is reasonable, appropriate and absolutely necessary.[10]

8
SCI and the Future

In the last decade or so, things have begun to change for people with SCI. While in the past most people with spinal cord injuries died within a short time, today people have a much better chance of at least a partial recovery if they receive help immediately after a spinal cord injury. In addition, exciting research prospects are currently being explored.

One such measure, which seems simple but may prove extremely beneficial, was tried experimentally with animals in a study at the Miami Project to Cure Paralysis in Florida. There, researchers found that lowering the body's temperature just one or two degrees following a spinal cord injury can reduce the inflammation that leads to cell damage and subsequent paralysis.

Scientists are working on a number of other possibilities as well. In 1988, they identified a gene that produces proteins that stop the nerve cell connections from regenerating. This protein is what prevents the spinal cord from healing following an injury. This discovery led to a vital question: If these harmful proteins could somehow be blocked, could the spinal cord repair itself?

A team led by Dr. Martin Schwab of the Brain Research Institute at the University of Zurich in Switzerland worked on that premise for a number of years. The researchers developed antibodies that block these harmful proteins.

In test-tube experiments, the antibodies were tried on nerves dissected from rats. The results were extremely encouraging: The treated nerves regrew several hundred nerve connections, or axons. In further experiments, the antibodies were given to rats whose spinal cords had been cut. After receiving the antibodies for two weeks, the paralyzed rats showed some changes: Their nerves regenerated, or regrew, and the animals regained some of their lost functions.[1]

Other laboratory work may hold even greater promise for people with SCI. In 1996, scientists from Karolinska Institute in Sweden severed the spinal cords of twenty-three rats, leaving their hind legs paralyzed. Using microsurgery, they then attempted to repair the damage. Using nerves from the rat's chest muscles, the researchers constructed nerve bridges across the spinal gap.

Nerve transplantation had been tried by a number of researchers over the years, but the Karolinska team was careful to avoid the pitfalls that had led to past failures. Encouragingly, this time the results were better. The signs of success did not appear immediately, but after about three months the animals began to flex their hind muscles. Then they started to crawl, and after a year they were able to move their hind legs and support their weight.[2]

The work was applauded by the medical community. New York University neurologist Dr. Wise Young wrote of the experiment results: "The possibility of effective regenerative therapies for human spinal cord injury is no longer a speculation but a realistic goal."[3] Because in humans spinal cord

A man plays tennis in a wheelchair. New developments in research hold out hope that spinal cord injury may one day be curable.

injuries usually involve cords that are crushed rather than severed, the implications of this advance are not yet precisely clear. Nevertheless, the work does show that damaged spinal cords are repairable, and that is an important step in the right direction.

Stem-Cell Research

Still other promising, if controversial, work involves the use of cells from early-term embryos. Known as embryonic stem cells, these cells have the potential to develop into all of the body's different types of cells. As early as 1994, Dr. David I. Gottlieb, a professor of anatomy and neurobiology at Washington University in St. Louis, found that if embryonic stem cells were exposed to a chemical known as retinoic acid, they would develop into nervous system cells.

In 1996, Gottlieb teamed up with doctors Dennis W. Choi and John W. McDonald to do further research. These scientists wanted to see if stem cells could successfully replace damaged cells in the spinal cord. If this could be done, it would be a dramatic step forward. Dr. McDonald, director of the Spinal Cord Injury Unit at Washington University School of Medicine in St. Louis, summarized the challenge. "One of the major problems in trying to restore spinal cord function is that the central nervous system is incapable of generating a sufficient number of cells to replace those that have been lost," he stated.[4]

Their work would help determine if this apparent difficulty could be overcome. McDonald and his research team

93

began transplanting embryonic stem cells that had been treated with retinoic acid into the injured spinal cords of rats. Two to five weeks later, the hind legs of the rodents receiving the transplanted cells were able to support the weight of their bodies. The rats could also move their legs somewhat. "Our work is still at a very early stage," McDonald warned, "and it needs to be repeated by other groups. But it's a tremendous feeling to have breached a barrier that has not been crossed before."[5]

The work is especially significant since the researchers waited nine days following the injury before transplanting the cells. Previously, no spinal cord injury therapy tried on rats more than twenty-four hours after the injury had ever been successful. Hopefully, this increase in the time interval between injury and treatment will bode well for future work with humans.

This new approach is very controversial. That is because stem cells come from early embryos, and the embryo is destroyed when the stem cells are taken. In 1996, people opposed to abortion succeeded in obtaining a ban that stopped government funding for research that involves human embryos. Those opposed to the ban argued that the cells did not have to come from embryos that were aborted voluntarily. They could come from embryos that were aborted spontaneously or from embryos that had been created for in vitro fertilization but were not used.

Things changed in August 2000. New rules from the National Institutes of Health allowed researchers to use stem

Help from Technology

One day, people with SCI might be able to use their own thoughts to pick up a glass of water, pet a cat, stand up from a chair, and even walk. Researchers have already taught a few paralyzed people how to use the signals from their brains to move the cursor on a computer. But even that tiny amount of movement is still very hard for people to do. It will be many years before technology makes it possible for people with SCI to use their thoughts to move their arms and legs.

But research is progressing. Thirty years ago, scientists put electrodes into the brains of monkeys.[6] They learned that certain cells in the brain plan a movement before they send out the signal that tells your arm to lift or your leg to bend.

Now, scientists have learned how to use the signals from a monkey's brain to move a robot's arm. They discovered that, before the monkey reaches out to pick up a piece of food, the monkey's brain plans the movement. Scientists recorded the patterns made in the brain during the planning process. Then they used computers to turn the patterns into instructions that could operate a robot.[7]

One of the scientists, Dr. Miguel A.L. Nicolelis, said, "As the monkey brain prepares the pattern required to make the movement, we record it and send the signal to a computer. As the monkey starts to move, our prediction is sent to the robot, and it moves at the same time."[8]

For people with SCI, this research is good news. Even though their spinal cords no longer send signals to their arms and legs, they can still plan the movement in their brains. Someday, scientists hope, devices in people's bodies will receive the signals from their brains and tell their limbs to move, just by thinking about it. When that happens, people with SCI may no longer have to use wheelchairs or need help getting dressed. Instead, they will be able to move around and do things for themselves.

cells from embryos that fertility clinics were going to destroy because their owners did not want them. Researchers would be able to use a small number of stem cells to create many more by growing and duplicating the stem cells in cultures. However, the status of research in this area remains uncertain. President Bush opposes using federal funds for research that involves destroying living human embryos. He intends to review all previous government regulation in this area.

Because there is so much controversy about using fetal cells to repair damaged spinal cord nerves, researchers are looking for alternatives. Scientists found one possibility in an area of the spinal cord that has stem cells with the ability to produce more neurons. They hope to find out how to take stem cells from a person who has SCI, get those cells to divide in the laboratory, and inject them back into the person's spinal cord.

Research in Germany

While the debate over the use of embryonic stem cells continues, another wave of research has already begun to change the lives of some people with SCI. It all began with an experimental program in Germany based on the seemingly unlikely premise that the adult human spinal cord can learn to perform some of the functions necessary for walking without the brain's help. Thorsten Sauer was a young man who had been using a wheelchair since a 1989 motorcycle accident that left him almost totally paralyzed from the ribs down. After learning about an experimental research program through which people with SCI might regain additional mobility, he wanted to be part of it. Sauer became one of the participants in the groundbreaking research program conducted by Anton Wernig, a neurophysiologist (a doctor who studies the physical functioning of the nervous system).

At Wernig's clinic, a specially trained therapist put Sauer in a harness and hoisted him into position just above a moving treadmill. While Sauer held on to the parallel bars of the treadmill, the therapist helped him to walk on the machine. To enable Sauer to perform a simple stepping motion, the therapist would extend Sauer's leg for him, put his foot down on the treadmill, and then bring it up again.

By feeding the spinal cord the sensory input involved in walking, over and over, the cord was able to develop its own memory. Over the weeks of training, the spinal cords of Sauer and the other study participants came to recognize familiar nerve signals from their leg muscles and continued the learned movement. These were the first steps Sauer had taken in six years.[9]

Sauer completed the ten-week training program at the clinic in 1995. Today, he no longer always has to use his wheelchair for mobility. He is now able to move around his apartment with a walker, and he can reach objects on shelves he once needed help to reach. With assistance, he can even walk up a few stairs. Sauer's improvement is not considered a fluke or a miracle. There are numerous other patients like him who have benefited from Wernig's program.

Alan Faulkner uses a mouthstick to operate his computer. The technology of the future will provide even more remarkable tools for people with SCI.

"There's just been this strong underlying viewpoint that the human nervous system is unique and special, and that the brain was essential for everything," one of the researchers involved in the present experiments commented.[10]

New Directions

With programs like the one at the clinic in Germany, and with other new research, viewpoints are changing. "It is now clear from a lot of areas that the whole nervous system changes continually in response to development, to learning, to trauma," explained Dr. Jonathan Wolpaw, chief of the laboratory of nervous system disorders at the Wadsworth Center of the New York State Department of Health. "There is plasticity and the capacity for change throughout the central nervous system, and that includes the spinal cord."[11] And Dr. James Grau, a professor of psychology at Texas A&M University who studies spinal cord injuries, neatly summed up the idea when he said, "The spinal cord is a lot smarter than you think."[12]

Much of the research under way holds out tremendous potential. Only a few of the most promising avenues explored have been described here, but many other paths are also being examined by researchers. While most researchers acknowledge that a cure may not be just around the corner, many believe there will be one in the foreseeable future. As Dr. Barth Green, founder of the Miami Project to Cure Paralysis, recently said:

When you talk about work on spinal cord injury you're talking about one of the most exciting things in neuroscience right now. A couple of years ago, I used to teach medical students that you could not regenerate the central nervous system. Now, we know from work in multiple laboratories around the world that we are getting the central nervous system to regrow. I think the sky is the limit in terms of what we will be able to accomplish.[13]

Millions of people around the world are rooting for their success.

Q&A

Q. How common is spinal cord injury?

A. Not counting those who die at the scene of an accident, there are about eleven thousand new spinal cord injury cases in the United States annually.

Q. Is spinal cord injury curable?

A. Presently, there is no cure for spinal cord injury. A good deal of research is being done in this area, however, and hopefully one day a cure will be found.

Q. Can people with spinal cord injuries have jobs?

A. Yes. Eight years after injury, an average of 37 percent of people with paraplegia and 27 percent of people with quadriplegia are employed.

Q. Can people with SCI have sex?

A. Spinal cord injuries often affect sexual functioning. Yet there are various therapies that can permit affected individuals to have a satisfying sex life.

Q. Can people with SCI have children?

A. Some men with spinal cord injuries find that their fertility (the ability to have children) is affected. Fertility treatments similar to those used for able-bodied men often remedy the problem. Most women with spinal cord injuries are able to conceive and carry their babies to term.

Q. If someone has fallen or has been in a car, diving, or other type of accident, should you move that person to make him or her more comfortable?

A. No. If there is a possibility of spinal cord injury, do not move the person. Call for help and let the professionals decide what to do. The only exception is if the person's life is in immediate danger, for example, if he or she is in a burning car.

Q. Is there any connection between guns and SCI?

A. Violence is presently the fastest-growing cause of SCI. In most violence-related cases, the injury is caused by a gunshot wound.

Q. If a business owner does not want to bother making his or her establishment wheelchair-accessible and is willing to lose the business generated by people in wheelchairs, does the business owner have that option?

A. No. Disabled people are guaranteed the right of accessibility by law. It is against the law for business owners to neglect their obligations to make their places of business accessible to the disabled.

Q. Do all people with SCI use wheelchairs?

A. No, but wheelchairs greatly enhance the mobility of paralyzed individuals. Depending on the extent of their injury, some people with SCI use braces and crutches, yet they may also use wheelchairs to cover longer distances. People who rely on wheelchairs are not always in them, though. They also drive, fly planes, and do many other things out of their wheelchairs.

Q. What do you say when you meet someone in a wheelchair?

A. The National Spinal Cord Injury Association suggests that you say, "Hi." A person with SCI is no different from a nondisabled individual except in a few specific ways. People with SCI have the same hopes, interests, and desires as other people. Although disabled people do some things differently from nondisabled people, the result is usually the same.

Spinal Cord Injuries Timeline

1700 B.C.—An Egyptian physician wrote that a spinal cord injury was "not to be treated."

440 B.C.—Alcmaeon of Croton, a Greek doctor, observed connections between the eyes and the brain in dissected animals.

177 B.C.—Galen of Pergamum described what happens when the spinal cords of monkeys are severed.

A.D. 1543—Andreas Vesalius wrote *On the Workings of the Human Body*, in which he showed nerves running from the brain throughout the body.

1717—Antoni van Leeuwenhoek, a Dutch scientist, observed a nerve fiber through a microscope.

1791—Luigi Galvani published information about electrical stimulation of frog nerves.

1891—Wilhelm von Waldeyer coined the term "neuron"; published articles about the workings of the nervous system.

Early 20th century—Care for people with SCI improves; technique of intermittent catheterization was developed, leading to a 15 percent decline in mortality after SCI.

Mid-1940s—The widespread development and use of antibiotics such as penicillin improved the life expectancy of people with SCI.

1950s—Spinal cord injury treatment centers built to manage the care of people with SCI.

1968—Architectural Barriers Act passed in United States, requiring buildings funded by the U.S. government to be accessible to the handicapped.

1973—Section 504 of the Rehabilitation Act prohibited businesses receiving funds from the U.S. government to discriminate against people with physical or mental disabilities.

1975—Individuals with Disabilities Education Act ordered that young people be guaranteed a free public education in the least restrictive environment.

1988—Fair Housing Amendments Act prohibited discrimination against the disabled in housing sales or rentals.

1988—Researchers at the University of Zurich in Switzerland discovered a gene that produces proteins that prevent nerve-cell connections from regenerating after a spinal cord injury. Work to develop antibodies to block these proteins began shortly thereafter.

1990—President George Bush signs the Americans with Disabilities Act, which prohibits discrimination against the disabled in the private sector as well as federally funded businesses.

1990—The use of steroid drug methylprednisolone within eight hours of a spinal cord injury becomes standard treatment.

1996—Scientists from the Karolinska Institute in Sweden use microsurgery on paralyzed rats to enable the rodents to regain some movement.

1996 (approximately)—In an experimental program in Germany, people with SCI, strapped into a harness and assisted by specially trained therapists, begin to take some steps on a treadmill.

1997—Work using cells from early embryos known as embryonic stem cells show definite promise in healing SCI.

For More Information

Christopher Reeve Paralysis Foundation
500 Morris Avenue
Springfield, New Jersey 07081
Phone: (973) 379-2690
Fax: (973) 912-9433
<http://www.paralysis.org>

Craig Hospital, Research Department
3425 South Clarkson Street
Englewood, Colorado 80110
Phone: (303) 789-8308
<http://www.craighospital.org>

National Spinal Cord Injury Statistical Center
619 19th Street South
Birmingham, Alabama 35249-7330
Phone: (205) 934-3320
Fax: (205) 934-2709
<http://www.spinalcord.uab.edu>

Chapter Notes

Chapter 1. It Happens This Way . . .

1. Thomas Fields-Meyer, "No Time to Lose," *People*, April 24, 2000, p. 70.

2. Ibid.

3. Jena Coghlan, "I May Never Walk Again," *Teen Magazine*, November 1998, p. 84.

4. Ibid.

5. Connie Panzarino, *Tell It Like It Is*, National Spinal Cord Injury Association, 1997, p. 20.

6. Ibid., p. 18.

7. Office of Science and Health Reports, National Institute of Neurological and Communicative Disorders and Stroke, NIH Publications, No. 81-160, February 1981, p. 1.

8. Ibid.

9. "The Facts About Spinal Cord Injury and Central Nervous System Disorders," *Christopher Reeve Paralysis Foundation Page*, 1999, <http://paralysis.apacure.org/progress/facts.html> (March 6, 2001).

10. "Spinal Cord Injury: Facts and Figures at a Glance—June, 2000," *National Spinal Cord Injury Statistical Center Page*, <http://www.spinalcord.uab.edu/show.asp?durki=21446> (March, 2001).

11. "The Facts About Spinal Cord Injury and Central Nervous System Disorders."

12. Ibid.

13. Ibid.

Chapter 2. What Is Spinal Cord Injury?

1. "Common Questions About Spinal Cord Injury," Factsheet 1, National Spinal Cord Injury Association, July 1996, p. 2.

Chapter 3. A History of Spinal Cord Injury

1. "The Edwin Smith Surgical Papyrus: the first use of 'neuro' words in recorded history," *Neuroscience for Kids Page*, n.d., <http://faculty.washington.edu/chudler/papy.html> (August 5, 2000); Robert H. Wilkins, "Neurosurgical Classic-XVII-Edwin Smith Surgical Papyrus," *American Association of Neurosurgeons and Congress of Neurosurgeons Page*, n.d., <http://www.neurosurgery.org/cybermuseum/pre20th/epapyrus.html> (August 5, 2000).

2. Edwin Clarke and C. D. O'Malley, *The Human Brain and Spinal Cord: a Historical Study Illustrated by Writings from Antiquity to the Twentieth Century* (Berkeley: University of California Press, 1968), p. 3; Susan A. Greenfield, *The Human Brain, A Guided Tour* (New York: Basic Books, 1997), p. 4.

3. Clarke, p. 292.

4. Pamela Tudor-Craig, "Times and Tide," *History Today*, vol. 48, January 1998, pp. 2–4; and Joyce Faust, "60 Years of Portability," *Accent on Living*, vol. 38, Winter 1993, p. 104.

5. Ibid.

6. Ibid.

7. Ibid.

8. Audrey T. Hingley, "Spinal Cord Injuries," *FDA Consumer*, Vol. 27, No. 6, July/Aug 1993, p. 14.

9. Robert Samuels, "A Wheelchair for the New Millennium?" *New Mobility Page*, November 21, 2000, <httm://newmobility.com/review_article.cfm?id=240&action =browse> (March, 2001).

10. Ibid.

11. "Milestones in Neuroscience Research," *Neuroscience for Kids Page*, n.d., <http://faculty.washington.edu/chudler/ hist.html> (August 5, 2000); Greenfield, p. 68; Walther Riese, *A History of Neurology*, New York: MD Publications, 1959, p. 191.

12. "Milestones in Neuroscience Research."

13. Clarke, p. 114.

14. Personal communication from David F. Apple, MD, July 19, 2000.

15. Ibid.

16. Ibid.

17. Jeffrey Kluger, "Will Christopher Reeve Walk Again?" *Time*, November 8, 1999, p. 85.

Chapter 4. Diagnosis and Treatment

1. "South of the Border," *Dateline*, January 10, 2000 (transcript of television show).

2. Ibid.

3. "Spinal Cord Injury: Emerging Concepts," *National Institutes of Health Page*, n.d., <www.ninds.nih.gov/health_and_medical/pubs/sci_report.htm> (March 14, 2001).

4. Audrey T. Hingley, "Spinal Cord Injuries: Science Meets Challenge." *FDA Consumer*, vol. 27, July 1993.

5. John W. McDonald and the Research Consortium of the Christopher Reeve Paralysis Foundation, "Repairing the Damaged Spinal Cord," *Scientific American*, September 1999, p. 9.

6. Lucy Grealy, "Triumph of the Spirit," *Women's Sports and Fitness*, May 1999, p. 100.

7. Daniel Lammertse, "Why Doesn't the Body Heal After SCI?" in Sam Maddox, ed., *Spinal Network*, 1988, p. 158.

Chapter 5. Recovery and Rehabilitation

1. Department of Physical Medicine and Rehabilitation, "Preventing Secondary Medical Complications: A Guide For Personal Assistants to People With Spinal Cord Injury," Spain Rehabilitation Center, University of Alabama at Birmingham, 1996, p. 4.

2. "Muscle Spasms and Spasticity," *Accent on Living*, March 22, 1996, p. 34.

3. National Spinal Cord Injury Association, Factsheet 11, July 1996, p. 1.

4. "Did You Know?" *National Rehabilitation Information Center Page*, n.d., <http://naric.com/didyouknow/> (March 13, 2001).

5. "Spinal Cord Injury Treatment & Rehabilitation," *National Institute of Neurological Disorders and Stroke Page,* n.d., <http://www.healthtouch.com/bin/Econtent_HT/hd ShowLfts.asp?lftname=NINDS082&cid=HTHLTH> (March 13, 2001).

6. Nancy Peyton, "Ben's Miracle," *Ladies' Home Journal,* December 1998, p. 28.

7. Eve Heyn and Nick Charles, "The Will To Win," *People,* September 28, 1998, p. 170.

8. "Other Rehabilitation Issues in SCI: Home Safety and Modifications," *Louis Calder Memorial Library of the University of Miami/Jackson Memorial Medical Center Page,* 1998, <http://calder/med.miami.edu/pointis/safety.html> (March 13, 2001).

9. "Special Section: Accessible Driving," *Infinitec Page,* n.d., <http://www.infinitec.org/driving_mod.html> (March 13, 1991).

10. Barry Corbet, "Disability: Grandmother of Invention," *New Mobility Page,* n.d., <newmobility.com/ review_article.cfm?id=15&action=browse> (March 13, 2001).

11. Spenser Bevan-John, "FES and Leg Cycles," *Therapeutic Alliance Page,* n.d., <http://www.MusclePower .com> (March, 2001).

12. G.H. Creasy, "Restoring Bladder, Bowel and Sexual Function," *Topics in Spinal Cord Injury Rehabilitation,* vol. 5, no. 1, 1999, pp. 21–32.

13. U.S. Department of Health and Human Services, Food and Drug Administration, "FDA Approves New Hand Implant for Quadriplegics," press release, August 18, 1997.

14. Mary Broophy Marcus and Stacey Schultz, "Grace Under Pain: Science Is Coming Closer to a Cure for Spinal Cord Injuries," *U.S. News and World Report*, May 11, 1998, p. 61.

Chapter 6. Coping With a Spinal Cord Injury

1. Kenneth Hall, "What To Do When Your Life Goes Upside Down," *SCI/Life*, Spring 1999, p. 30.

2. Ibid.

3. Jena Coghlan, "I May Never Walk Again," *Teen Magazine*, November 1998, p. 2.

4. Patricia Anstett, "Dr. Ed Nieshoff: An Inspiration To His Patients With Spinal Cord Injuries," Knight-Ridder/Tribune News Service, June 20, 1997, p. 620.

5. Peter Addesso, "Advice For The Newly Spinal Cord Injured," *EPUA Action*, December 1991, p. 17.

6. Theresa Jaworski, *Family Adjustment to Spinal Cord Injury*, Spain Rehabilitation Center, University of Alabama in Birmingham, 1988, p. 2.

7. Addesso.

8. Ibid.

9. "Feelings and Reactions in Spinal Cord Injury: The Patient," *Louis Calder Memorial Library of the University of Miami/Jackson Memorial Medical Center Page*, 1998, <http://calder.med.miami.edu/pointis/patient.html> (March 13, 2001).

10. "Depression: What You Should Know," *Consortium for Spinal Cord Medicine, Paralyzed Veterans of America Page*, 1999, <http://www.pva.org/prof/9811cpgs/Depression.pdf> (March 13, 2001).

11. "A Celebration of Wheels . . . " n.d., <http://lehmac.tripod.com> (March, 2001).

12. Kimberly La Marche, "Winners and Losers," *Accent On Living*, Winter 1998, p. 26.

13. Ibid.

14. Coghlan.

15. "Wellman Strikes Again," *PN/Paraplegia News*, October 1999, p. 26.

16. "Return to the Challenge," *No Limits Page*, n.d., <www.nolimitstahoe.com> (May 4, 2001).

17. James C. Sheil, "DOING DOs," *Accent On Living*, Winter 1997, p. 78.

18. Ibid.

19. Anstett.

20. Ibid.

21. Ibid.

Chapter 7. Society and People With SCI

1. Fred Pelka, "Bashing the Disabled: The Right-Wing Attack on the ADA," *The Humanist*, November 1, 1996, p. 26.

2. Marca Bristo, "Power To Change the World," *PN/Paraplegia News*, October 1999, p. 66.

3. Ibid.

4. Johnathan Watts, "Japan Puts the Rights of the Disabled Into the Spotlight," *The Lancet*, January 15, 2000, p. 209.

5. "Man In Motion," *Maclean's*, May 26, 1997, p. 51.

6. Kendall Hamilton, "Fighting to Fund An 'Absolute Necessity,'" *Newsweek*, July 1, 1996, p. 56.

7. Roger Rosenblatt, "New Hopes, New Dreams," *Time*, August 26, 1996, p. 41.

8. Hamilton.

9. Ibid.

10. Ibid.

Chapter 8. SCI and the Future

1. Ingrid Wickelgren, "Rat Spinal Cord Function Partially Restored," *Science*, December 3, 1999, p. 182.

2. Christine Gorman, "A Step Beyond Paralysis: Doctors Prove That Spinal Co rd Can Repair Itself," *Time*, August 5, 1996, p. 63.

3. Ibid.

4. Linda Sage, "Touching A Nerve," *Outlook*, Winter 1999, p. 19.

5. Ibid.

6. Sandra Blakeslee, "Brain Signals Shown to Move a Robot's Arm," *New York Times*, November 16, 2000, p. A20.

7. Ibid.

8. Ibid.

9. Ingrid Wickelgren, "Teaching the Spinal Cord To Walk," *Science*, January 16, 1998, p. 319.

10. Erica Goode, "No Dullard; Spinal Cord Proves It Can Learn," *New York Times*, September 21, 1999, p. 9.

11. Ibid.

12. Ibid.

13. Charles Marwick, "Spinal Cord Injury Research Shows Promise," *Journal of the American Medical Association*, December 8, 1999, p. 211.

Glossary

acute stage—The hours immediately following a spinal cord injury.

automatic dysreflexia (AD)—A life-threatening complication of spinal cord injury that occurs when a person's blood pressure rises to the point at which he or she is at risk of a stroke or death if not treated.

axon—A long nerve cell fiber that transmits electrical impulses.

catheter—A tube ins erted into the bladder through which urine can drain out.

central nervous system—The brain and spinal cord.

functional electrical stimulation (FES)—The process of electrically stimulating nerves or muscles to react as though they are receiving impulses from the brain.

methylprednisolone—A steroid drug given to patients with spinal cord injuries to reduce secondary damage (damage which occurs after the initial injury).

neuron—A nerve cell.

oxidants—Chemicals that attack the body's defenses and vital cell structures.

paralysis—A partial or complete loss of movement and feeling in a part of the body.

paraplegia—A condition caused by a spinal cord injury in which the person has lost the ability to move or have feeling in the lower part of his or her body.

physiatrist—A doctor specializing in physical medicine and rehabilitation who deals with the physical and psychological aftermath of spinal cord injury.

pressure sores—Sores that develop as a breakdown of skin and tissue that occurs when a person lies or sits in the same position for too long.

quadriplegia—A condition caused by a spinal cord injury in which the person has lost the ability to move and have feeling in his or her lower body as well as all or part of the upper body (also called **tetraplegia**).

spinal cord—The ropelike bundle of nerves and fibers that carries messages to and from the brain to various parts of the body.

spinal cord segments—Divisions of the spinal cord along its length.

tetraplegia—See **quadriplegia**.

vertebrae—The bones that make up the spine (backbone) and protect the spinal cord.

Further Reading

Kent, Deborah. *The Disability-Rights Movement.* Danbury, Conn.: Children's Press, 1996.

Philips, Jane H. *Gloria Estefan.* Broomall, Penn.: Chelsea House, 2001.

Stalcup, Brenda, editor. *The Disabled.* San Diego, Calif.: Greenhaven Press, 1997.

Walters, Gregory J. *Equal Access: Safeguarding Disability Rights.* Vero Beach, Fla.: Rourke Corporation, 1992.

Wren, Laura L. *Christopher Reeve: Hollywood's Man of Courage.* Springfield, N.J.: Enslow Publishers, Inc., 1999.

Internet Addresses

Healthlink USA (links to websites which may include treatment, cures, diagnosis, prevention, support groups, e-mail lists, message boards, personal stories, risk factors, statistics, research, and more)
<http://www.healthlinkusa.com/Spinal_Cord_Injury.htm>

National Institute of Neurological Disorders and Stroke
<www.ninds.nih.gov>

National Spinal Cord Injury Association
<http://www.spinalcord.org>

Index

I

Individuals with Disabilities Education Act (IDEA), 79–80

J

Jackson Memorial Medical Center, 66

K

Karolinska Institute, 91
Kraft, Don, 33, 35, 36, 37

L

Lan, Sang, 41, 52, 53
laws, 79–82
Leeuwenhoek, Antoni van, 28

M

magnetic resonance imaging (MRI), 41
Miami Project to Cure Paralysis, 87, 90, 99

N

National Council on Disabilities, 82
National Institutes of Health, 94
National Rehabilitation Information Center, 50

National Spinal Cord Injury Association, 23, 50
National Spinal Cord Injury Statistical Center, 13
neural prostheses, 56, 58, 60
Nieshoff, Ed, 74, 75, 76

P

Paralympics, 71, 72
paraplegia, 23
physiatry, 49–50
physical therapy, 42, 50–51, 52

Q

quadriplegia, 23, 58

R

Reeve, Christopher, 86–87, 89
Rehabilitation Act, 79

S

Spain Rehabilitation Center, 46
spinal cord,
    role of, 16, 18
    structure, 19–21
spinal cord injury,
    categories of, 23
    causes of, 6
    complications arising from, 45–47, 49

THE
TIGERS
ARE
BURNING

THE
TIGERS
ARE
BURNING

Martin Caidin

HAWTHORN BOOKS, INC.
Publishers / NEW YORK

For
Bob Button,
topkick

CONTENTS

PART III

THE RUSSIANS

PART IV

THE BATTLE

Part I

Introduction
to the Battle
of Kursk

1

THE PLAN BEHIND
OPERATION CITADEL

In his book *Die Ersten und die Letzen* (The First and the Last) General Adolf Galland, who commanded the fighter forces of the German air force in World War II, refers to the greatest land surface battle ever fought in history: "In July [1943] the German troops at Kursk lined up for the last large-scale offensive. It was repulsed."

It was repulsed.

That's all. Nothing is said about the greatest number of tanks, armored vehicles, and self-propelled guns amassed for the monumental struggle between the armies and air forces of the Russians and the Germans. Nothing is said of the stupendous concentration of firepower of both sides. Nothing is said of the hideous casualties endured by both sides. Nothing is said of the extraordinary shift in the balance of power on the Russian front following what has entered the historical volumes of World War II as the Battle of Kursk.

Galland described, albeit with startling brevity, the Battle of Kursk as the last large-scale offensive of the German army along the Russian front. This is true, but not because the German forces were "repulsed."

From the failure of the Wehrmacht to inflict crippling punishment
against its enemy there arose the grim specter that the German army
was no longer capable of dictating the terms of battle to the Russians.
In its simplest form, the Battle of Kursk, which began on July 4,
1943, ended one reign and began another.

Prior to the debacle at Kursk—and debacle it was for the Germans
—it was the Wehrmacht that called the shots for major confrontation
with the Russians. There had been defeats, of course, and notable
among them were Moscow and Stalingrad, where German strength
blunted and bled itself white against hysterically determined Soviet
defenses. Even in their defeat at Moscow and Stalingrad the Germans
had taken a terrible toll of the Russians. Even in their defeat the
Germans withdrew with the power, speed, and mobility to dictate
future struggles to the battered but stolid Russians.

Kursk changed all that. Or rather, the military clash at Kursk, at
Orel to the north, at Kharkov to the south—all of which is inclusive
in the single struggle—forged a new temper in the war.

That Kursk, and the great sweeping tide of two huge forces clawing
at one another, could become *the* military pivot of the war in Russia
was quite apparent to the two mortal enemies. If the Germans succeeded in their Operation Citadel as the attack plan was finally approved by Hitler himself, the stage would be set to apply vast new
pressures against the Russians. Far more was at stake than the city
of Kursk or the sweep of countryside to the north, south, and east.
What would never show on the charts and maps would be the savaging of the Russians, and that was the heart and soul of the German
plan: to punish, maul, disperse, kill, capture. There was no real
objective in terms of a specific geographic or political goal. No
Stalingrad or Moscow awaited as the immediate target for destruction
or occupation.

Not immediately. Later was a different matter. Later, if Citadel
went as Hitler anticipated, there would be a great new assault on
Moscow. Later he would implement his very top secret plan, Polar
Fox, and German forces in a lightning stroke would invade and
occupy Sweden.

Later he would shift his forces where he willed, moving expertly
across his chessboard of military strategy. More strength into Italy to

blunt and throw back the Allied invasion he knew was coming. Massive reinforcement of the Atlantic Wall—enough perhaps, to break the back of the invasion from England.

Operation Citadel, unlike many other moves by the leader of the Third Reich, was no sudden, impulsive stroke. No ringing declaration went forth in the dark of night to exhort the German soldier to perform the impossible. Citadel emerged slowly. It grew from defeat and from the battered ego and chagrin that such defeat inevitably evoked within Hitler. And let no mistake be made about it. The plan from its inception stemmed from Hitler. Whatever happened subsequently, events involving any number of high-ranking officials and military officers, occurred as handmaidens of Hitler's desires, of his objectives.

No one knew better than Adolf Hitler, as the supreme commander of the military forces of Germany, that the nation was in desperate need of a spectacular victory of arms against the barbarians to the east. In February 1943 the Russians were assuming new stature as the ultimate in destruction of everything for which Germany stood. The glorious victories that followed the invasion of Russia on June 22, 1941, had tarnished. Exultation had yielded to checked emotional reins, then to caution, deepening to concern, and now it bordered on paranoia. For the horrors of Stalingrad were all too real. The mauling of vast armies by the Russians was a grim portent of the future. Winter, and the Russians, had grown huge bristling teeth sunk deep into the German jugular.

Now the summer of 1943 was approaching, and Hitler demanded of his armies that they "make up in summer what had been lost in winter." A noble aspiration, but clinging blindly to the supposition that the Russian cannot fight when the land is not covered with snow and ice. Blind suppositions are poor material from which to wrest the advantage from an enemy growing steadily in strength, and Hitler's insistence that warm skies must token good tidings on the battlefield brought little comfort to members of the German general staff who counted their omens in the form of the order of battle of the German army. The Reich had lost perhaps 700,000 men in the meat grinder of the Russian front. Not all were German troops, to be sure, for the Germans were quick to hurl into the chopping blades of fighting with

the Russians whatever human fodder they could muster from their allies.

Show a Russian a battlefront with Italian or Hungarian troops—poorly equipped and beset with the urge to be elsewhere, anywhere but on the Russian front—and you had an Ivan eager to come to grips with his enemy. A whimsical appreciation of reality at the front? By no means; no whimsy here. Ask those who have been there.

Yet masses of men, despite being held in contempt by their German masters, do fill the areas of a military front. They are composed of a sufficient number of bodies, and this may further be broken down into armor and transport, aircraft and artillery, machine guns and rifles. If men must be sacrificed, then throw them into the seething center of the Russian attack, and keep the elite of the Reich for those fronts where skill, courage, strength, and reliability were essential.

Yet the Germans had to reckon their forces in totals, and no matter how they pondered the numbers, they were confronted with the inescapable fact that they had lost 700,000 men—and all the equipment and weapons that went with those men—in battle with the Russians. As defeat and catastrophe took hold on the eastern front, Hitler demanded and received a new "total mobilization" of German manpower. Yet it was not enough. Shortages in trained men were acute. Replacements for forward combat divisions lacked toughness and experience. Anything less against the sharpening steel of the Russian combat soldier spelled continuing disaster.

Another enemy was time. It poured all too quickly through the martial hourglass by which Germany reckoned its existence as a nation of military might. The nation could replace only half the men already chewed up by the Russians. While Germany's flow of replacements to the front ebbed, the Russians gained astonishingly in their new strength. They seemed to pluck soldiers from the far ends of the earth. They had suffered gaping wounds, but they still fought. Whatever the Germans and their allies had lost, the Russians had lost more. German factories spewed forth a torrent of armaments to be rushed to the eastern front. The Russians had lost great sections of their country, including entire cities, and this loss had to be reckoned also in terms of cities occupied, transportation facilities destroyed or

overrun, millions of civilians placed under German rule, factories occupied or destroyed.

Nevertheless—and it was both astonishing and frightening—Russian production of armaments grew. Men and women toiled day and night in Russian factories to grind out not simply a staggering quantity of matériel but weapons of extraordinary quality. To the Nazis, who had encountered inferior products in the air and on the ground, the concept of Soviet engineering and products being equal, let alone superior, to those of the German mind was intolerable and unacceptable.

But it was true. And the longer the war lasted, the longer the Russians continued to widen the rivers of supply to the front, the more ominous boded the future for the Reich.

Time does not wait. Therefore it must be served.

Could the war against the Soviets still be won? In the spring of 1943 this was a very real question. Most histories prepared by the Germans state or imply that almost no one in the hierarchy of German command believed that victory could be extricated from the deepening morass of the Russian war. Those who were in the know accepted the inevitability of defeat on the eastern front. The German general staff and its ranks of subordinates no longer believed in the miracle of destroying the Communist horde.

This writer finds such a widely shared conclusion to beg much of an objective look at both the war and the Germans. On the one hand, they hold high the banner of disclaimer to hope for victory against the Russians. On the other hand, they take no pains to conceal their elaborate plans to smash the structure of the Soviet Union once Operation Citadel achieved its goals. It would seem an unacceptable level of hedging on the part of those Germans to accept that they intended us to believe *both* points of view. If Citadel failed, they would nod in their wisdom of recognizing reality and predicting the future. If Citadel achieved its goals of mauling the Russian army beyond any point or hope of immediate repair, opening wide the gates to a fresh German onslaught into the very heart of the Soviet Union, their claim to utmost faith in the German army would clearly have been sustained.

If there was no hope for victory, as so many insist, what was the

origin of the plans for strengthening German defenses against the invasion of Italy? How would it be possible to add to the steel of the Atlantic Wall? From what source could they produce the men and weapons to execute Polar Fox and invade and occupy Sweden? By what legerdemain would the German army race deep into bristling Russian defenses and succeed now, where they had failed before, in smashing into Moscow?

History questions severely this stated German disbelief in the future.

Kursk was everything. What happened there would decide the future.

The geographic scale involved would be much less than the pivotal operations of the German army in the past. The front would extend no more than 150 miles north and south. But within that front there would be more tanks and armored vehicles, in this one impending battle, than could be counted throughout the *entire* western front after the invasion of Europe by the Allies.

It was not only the tide of Russian fortune that would be decided at Kursk. It was the war itself.

2

ZHUKOV: THE MIRACLE MARSHAL

The Germans had been thrown back from the gates of Moscow. They had been mauled severely at Stalingrad. They had been hurled out of Kharkov and in brutal fighting had clawed their way back.

Recapturing Kharkov, however, was not enough to serve the needs of Hitler's image or that of the power of the Third Reich. There was more than Russia. North Africa had been swept clear of German forces. The Italians grumbled to a new pitch in their anxiety to abandon the war. Bomber formations over the Reich were changing from a matter of annoyance to staggering destruction, with the future promising a continual cascade of ruin from the skies.

No matter what happened or threatened in any other sector, Hitler kept his gaze steadfastly on the Russian front. That was where the war would be decided. If the Russian back could be broken, the Reich could freewheel its military strength to attend to any other contingency that might arise. The Hitlerian dream was clear enough. Military victory in Russia was essential. From this triumph the critical economic, political, and propaganda battlements could be successfully assailed.

If personal and historical sources are sustained in what they have recorded, then Hitler in the early months of 1943 was determined to first stabilize the Russian front, then inflict a smashing defeat upon his enemy. Afterward, with this German victory as his impetus, he would spring wide the floodgates of revived military strength to slash deeply into the Soviet heartland.

Hitler studied his maps, pinpointing the precise boundaries of the front that must be held. A line that began in the north at the Gulf of Finland and extended southward to the Sea of Azov marked the area to hold. German fortunes held promise along that line save for one bulge—a salient that the Soviets had punched deep into the German line. A salient with the city of Kursk as its center—a huge boil in the German skin stretched taut from north to south.

What was there about Kursk to render it such magic?

The fortunes of war. No more and no less, for Kursk itself had precious little to offer as a prize of war other than its geographic location and the presence of massed forces of the Russian army.

The city of Kursk lay across the low plateau of central Russia at the confluence of the Tuskor and Seym rivers. Moscow was more than three hundred miles to the north. The land in all directions left much to be desired in terms of military operations. The roads were passable only in dry weather. The countryside offered a mixed bag of hills, flatland, gullies, brush, sand, and the like. Not the best for the hammering movement of armored forces.

Kursk had its beginnings nearly a thousand years before it became the fulcrum for what would be the greatest armored clash in the history of war. Its age was interesting but totally unrelated to the moment, for Kursk was much like hundreds of other Russian cities. The population at the outbreak of the war was estimated at 120,000. In the spring of 1943 no one knew the population. Every able-bodied man had been taken for military service. Many had already perished in earlier battle on the eastern front.

To leave Moscow for a journey to the coast of the Black Sea, one invariably traveled through Kursk. There was little enough to catch the eye. The countryside was like much of the vast Soviet landscape with its tilled soil producing sugar beet and wheat, and the inevitable orchards. If you were a pilot or a geologist, you knew about this city

and the surrounding countryside, for beneath the otherwise ordinary landscape were vast deposits of magnetite. This produced what has been known as the Kursk magnetic anomaly, an effect to render a compass worthless.

These were hardly the special qualifications for the intense interest of Adolf Hitler and the German high command. But the Russians stood fast in Kursk, and they had secured their position in the great bulge into the German line. Therein lay the problem that concerned Hitler's forces.

The Kursk salient thrust into an area heavily manned by the German army. Orel lay to the north and Belgorod to the south of the salient. The Russians were pouring into this position with every weapon at their disposal. If they could amass sufficient firepower and bring up a great quantity of supplies, then the salient could be transformed into a giant springboard for a devastating offensive from within the security of their entrenchments aimed at a breakthrough—not simply to the west, but also to the northwest as part of a sweep back into the Orel and Bryansk area, and, at the same time, to the southwest in an attempt to regain the Ukraine.

Kursk had thus become a great punchbowl of gathering Soviet power. Into the salient they poured tanks, artillery, all manner of armored and motorized equipment, and hundreds of thousands of troops. They repaired forward airfields and brought up great numbers of fighters and bombers. They converted the railroad system leading into Kursk to the Russian wide-gauge standard, and they stockpiled supplies sufficient for a dozen armies. More than using the salient for an enormous assembly area, the Russians turned the countryside into a hornet's nest of powerful gun emplacements and thousands of miles of crisscrossing trenches.

All this the Germans knew, and more. The Russians would not be content to sit out the summer, playing the game of defense in summer and offense in winter. This time they would strike under weather conditions heretofore considered more advantageous to the Wehrmacht.

And there they were, ripe for the kill.

To Hitler, the first order of business was to hold fast to the long front from the Gulf of Finland to the Sea of Azov. The next move would be to crush the Russians where they had gathered in their

greatest strength. It was almost as if the Russians had maneuvered themselves into exactly the trap that so delighted Hitler. For the strength of the Kursk salient could also become its fatal weakness.

If the German panzer forces struck with speed and cunning, the Russians would be caught in one huge basket. There would be no need for a long, drawn-out pursuit. There would be no room for the Russians to maneuver. The Wehrmacht could slash its way from the north and from the south, driving hard to close a massive pincers that would trap the Russians behind the spearheading armored columns.

In addition, the Nazis realized that to counter so powerful a blow, the enemy must respond with an overwhelming commitment of reserves. As a result, the destruction of the Russian forces would be that much greater. Indeed, the pouring in of operational reserves was to be sought. If the elite of the Wehrmacht were to perform as in the old days, the entire tide of the war could be reversed. Stalin would lack the strength to maneuver his vast forces to counter slashing thrusts by the panzers.

At the risk of moving ahead of our story, it must be stated here, in order to prevent any incorrect assumptions about the Soviet judgment of German plans, that whatever Hitler and his chosen generals elected to do with respect to the Kursk salient was anticipated with extraordinary accuracy by the Russian command. All through the months prior to the first crashing barrage of artillery, as well as during the actual battle, the brilliant strategic touch of the deputy supreme commander of all Soviet forces, Marshal of the Soviet Union Georgi Konstantinovich Zhukov, would be abundantly evident.

The Germans, to be sure, were more than familiar with both the name and the maddening skills of Zhukov, for here was the military genius in whom Stalin placed extraordinary trust and confidence. Extraordinary because Joseph Stalin was unique among men of national power for his compulsive and paranoiac distrust of almost all his close associates in government. Stalin, as history has recorded in gripping terms, had long employed the purge and whatever bloodletting he felt was necessary simply to alleviate his suspicions of people around him. He had gutted the ranks of Soviet military leadership before the war, an act of internal savagery that was to wreak its

havoc long after the event, when a Soviet army, pounded by German invaders, was sorely pressed to find the officer leadership it then needed so desperately. Be that as it may, it was Zhukov who again and again snatched first survival and then victory from the jaws of destruction applied by the invaders.

Zhukov was a brilliant tactician and strategist. He was also a man accustomed to succeeding where those about him failed. His utter disregard of human life—if success could be assured by expenditure of that life no matter how appalling the numbers—was well known to Stalin and his immediate staff long before the Germans smashed into Russia in June 1941. To Marshal Zhukov, a man who lost a battle, no matter *what* the reason, had no excuses.

In 1939 Zhukov served on the distant edge of the Russian frontier, in Outer Mongolia. And he was the man who commanded Soviet forces when Outer Mongolia was invaded by 75,000 men of the Japanese Sixth Army, well protected by hundreds of fighters and bombers. The Japanese were tough, seasoned veterans of fighting in China, and they expected the Russian defenses to topple under their relentless pressure. Zhukov led his men in a brilliant, vicious assault upon the stunned Japanese, who suffered losses of 41,000 dead and wounded and fled headlong from a caliber of Russian they had never expected to meet.

Then came the German invasion. Leningrad, furiously assailed by the Wehrmacht, was on the edge of collapse. Its chances of surviving destruction and occupation were considered to be nonexistent. Zhukov appeared on the scene to galvanize his battered and bloody countrymen. They held. The Germans then turned their attention to Moscow, its ramparts clearly visible to the spearheads of their armored columns. Moscow must fall, Hitler had ordered, and he was about to realize his greatest aspirations.

Zhukov took command of the defense, and the Russian army ultimately stopped the enemy almost at the gates of the city. The defenders wavered but held grimly to their positions long enough for a shrieking winter to descend upon the battlefield. The Russians rose like white ghosts from the snow-covered ground and hurled themselves upon the stunned Germans, who were thrown back as much as 150 miles from their deepest penetrations into Russia.

Stalingrad was next. It *must* fall to the tremendous pressure exerted by the invaders. But Zhukov was there. Under him the Russians not only held fast but launched a counterattack. Before the rampaging Soviet forces spent their fury, they destroyed the entire German Sixth Army and shattered a major portion of the German Fourth Army. All told, the Russians burst out of Stalingrad to reduce to only a shell of what then had been no fewer than twenty-two divisions of German and allied troops.

Then, in the early weeks of 1943, while Zhukov was on the northwest front of the line against the Germans, the situation along the Voronezh front began to shred. Stalin pulled Zhukov from the northwest and sent him hurriedly to where German forces were hammering back the Russians. It was too late, by the time Zhukov arrived, to save the city of Kharkov, which for the third time had been overwhelmed and fallen under control of the German army. Yet Kharkov was only one element of growing disaster.

"We must move everything we can from Stavka Reserve [Soviet supreme headquarters] and the reserves of the neighboring fronts at once," he radioed Stalin, "because if we do not the Germans will capture Belgorod and develop their offensive towards Kursk."

These were blunt words from a man of Zhukov's proven record, and Stalin did not fail his "miracle marshal." Before the hour was up, Zhukov had been informed by the chief of the Russian general staff that his message had galvanized the entire area involved and that the Twenty-first and Sixty-fourth armies were already moving under emergency orders to the Belgorod area.

Further evidence of the total trust placed in Zhukov came with the message that the First Tank Army was also on the way to the area, to be placed directly under Zhukov's command, so that he might utilize this powerful armored striking force when and where he felt necessary. It was a critical situation, and disaster was averted by the narrowest of margins. By March 18 the Germans had stormed into Belgorod, but against steadily stiffening resistance. Three days later, the Russians were dug in immediately east of Belgorod. North of that city, yielded to the Germans, more defensive positions were set up. Zhukov moved the First Tank Army into assault position south of Oboyan where it could be used for defense or, if the situation opened,

for thrusting into the flanks of the German push toward Kursk. Along the eastern banks of the Donets River he had the Sixty-fourth Army throw up defensive positions.

By the end of the month Zhukov had bought the breathing space the Russians needed so desperately. Ice on the Donets was breaking up, transforming the river into a defensive moat along its entire length. The spring thaw settled across the countryside, and the frozen roads, effective for transport during the winter, became quagmires. The farmlands and open fields were much the same. The Germans took stock of the situation and ended their drive.

For the moment an uneasy and precarious quiet settled along the front. The thaw had bought time. Zhukov had stiffened the backbone of the Russian defensive positions and added a strong measure of depth. Would it be enough?

The answer lay in part, of course, with German intentions. Zhukov was not sanguine about the position of the Russian army. The enemy would not wait long to mount a major offensive, and Zhukov sensed that the Germans were fully aware that time was not on their side, for with the full backing of Stalin he would use every day and every night to pour in reinforcements.

So the Germans must strike, reasoned Zhukov, and if they committed without delay, he knew he would be hard-pressed to hold even the newly prepared defensive lines. The Russian forces about Kursk were now in the position of a salient deep within the German front.

Two things could happen. If the Germans moved swiftly and in strength, they could transform the area into a charnel house of encircled Russian forces. If they did not commit to keeping the Russians off balance before they built up their strength, then there was every chance the Wehrmacht would find itself attacking an enemy of unusual power and skill. No one could ignore the presence of Zhukov. Too many times in the past he had blunted German steel and used the other edge of the sword to devastate German armies.

Time. It was all on the side of the Russians, who waited for the new onslaught.

Then they found a new, unexpected ally. Hitler.

He delayed in pressing the death blow against the Kursk salient.

Zhukov seized the incredible opportunity. In the next three months he poured in supplies, men, and weapons on rebuilt rail lines. Five hundred thousand freight cars rolled into the Kursk salient.

The greatest battle in history was in its makings.

3

THE FATAL FLAW IN
THE TIGER TANKS

During the early winter and spring of 1943 the members of the Soviet high command never lost sight of the stakes involved in the Kursk salient. The armored clash that had been accepted by both sides—with the Kursk area as the arena—could literally decide the advantageous position in the war. To the Russians, Kursk had all the promise of becoming a modern-day Battle of Kulikovo, the historic struggle of 1380 in which Prince Dimitri Donskoi routed mighty Tartar forces.

With the sound of the ticking clock growing louder and louder, and fully aware that they must take advantage of every minute, the Russians continued their frenetic efforts of reinforcing their position. Meanwhile, for reasons unknown to the Russians, the German delay continued.

It was an unexpected, extraordinary advantage to the Soviet forces. By the time the first long-range artillery guns would rip the air with shells heading for Russian positions, Zhukov would assemble the most concentrated and powerful military force ever known.

Twenty percent of the entire Russian army would mass in the

Kursk salient and reinforcement positions immediately to the east. The unparalleled concentration of armor would be composed of more than one third of all the available first-line tanks in the country. One out of every four first-line combat aircraft would be concentrated in the area.

The scale of the armaments involved, the numbers of men, the intricate and complex movement of the opposing forces, the critical moments of the struggle—all these defy the mental grasp of the observer. There is a tendency to impart to the relating of such an event favored terms. All too often the histories of such battles have been characterized by entire armies "wheeling smartly" to impose their force upon a given situation. It reads well enough and it has its flair of drama, but we are also left wondering. Can we effectively extract from the smoke and fury of an event such as the Battle of Kursk cohesive understanding, a full appreciation of what transpired? It takes more than mere numbers, yet we must start with declarations and numbers.

The very magnitude and concurrency of events of a battle that raged fifty days over a front that was 350 miles long and often reached a depth of 175 miles defy even the wildest attempts to paint the proper word canvas.

Kursk was not simply a battle. It was a series of interconnected struggles, fought by men whose daring and courage and panic and dying—all the elements that make up so epic a clash—were obscured by the savage fury and enormous scale of the conflict. When we turn back the clock to such moments, it must be with the understanding that we are confined to knowledge of those stories that survived the moment and the years between.

If we were to visit the battlefield today, it would be impossible to take in the complete area of struggle—350 by 175 miles—at a single glance. If we could stand high enough, we might see the entire terrain, but we would also be so remote from our point of interest that all would become as blurred and featureless as is the surface of the earth to a pilot flying in thick fog. Even a walk across the former battlements would offer only a scant reward. There are relics everywhere, even to this day. Rusted hulks of artillery, tanks, trucks, armored vehicles, motorcycles, spent shell casings, rifles, helmets. Their

stories would be muted forever, for it must all be pieced into a meaningful pattern.

It is not enough to study maps and the lines scrawled across their surface. No more than moving lead soldiers and tiny weapons across a model of terrain. No more than comparing reality on the battlefield with chess pieces. In any such struggle as the Battle of Kursk, it is necessary to appreciate that many battles were going on at one and the same time in an interwoven shuttle of events. Many actions immediately affected other actions, bringing on a falling-domino pattern of events. Other actions took hours or even weeks to produce a noticeable effect upon the situation. Yet we cannot, by any stretch of liberty, separate one from the other.

Through all the chaotic happenings before, during, and after the Battle of Kursk, men play their significant part. Some, like the generals and well-known combat leaders, inevitably play a role in the structure of re-creating the key segments of the conflict. Others remain unknown, unseen, playing roles critical to everything else, but without identification, let alone credit or blame—the effect of men, of a man, in the right place, at the right time. Courage, cowardice, stoicism, panic —emotions in battle are the prodding finger of fate, and much of that story we may only surmise, for the sound and fury have long ago disappeared forever into the chronicles that now constitute our means of looking back into history.

There is a strange parallel in the Battle of Kursk to an earlier, much different, but equally critical conflict of arms—the Battle of Britain, when a comparative handful of men in lithe winged craft held off the German air force until attrition wore down the ranks of the black-crossed machines and the Luftwaffe retired from daylight skies to attack at night. The German fighter aircraft of that period, when England stood alone against the Reich, was the Messerschmitt Me-109E. One may question why a particular designation of such a machine is important, why this airplane is singled out from all the others. The answer is that the Me-109E, used for bomber escort and attacking the British fighters, although it was one of the finest aircraft ever built, possessed a single flaw that, had it been remedied, might have enabled the Germans to win their air struggle over the

British Isles. The invasion that never happened might well have become reality.

It was simple enough. The Germans needed their fighters to protect the bombers all the way to target. With a screen of the fast, deadly Me-109E fighters, the bombers could penetrate to any point in England. They could go after the most distant fighter fields used by the Royal Air Force. What the Germans could not do in the air they could do against British fighters on the ground. They could destroy hangars, maintenance shops, supply depots, fuel farms—all the critical support paraphernalia so necessary to keeping aircraft where they belong: in the sky.

But the Me-109E, through an incredible oversight in design, lacked a simple, easy-to-manufacture device called an auxiliary fuel tank carried beneath the airplane, to be jettisoned when the pilot willed, which added an additional hundred- or two-hundred-miles flying range to the machine.

With this external tank the Me-109E fighters could have gone all the way in their escort of the German bombers. Without it the fighters were forced to turn back before reaching target, leaving the bombers on their own—and they were promptly and efficiently slaughtered by Spitfires and Hurricanes.

All this took place at a time when the Royal Air Force was nearly shattered. The line between continued fighting and almost complete ineffectiveness was alarmingly slender. If the German fighters had been able to go all the way to the bomber targets, there is every chance England would have been denied the ability to stay in the same sky with German aircraft. Without this protecting umbrella of firepower in the heavens, there would have been little to prevent the Germans from launching, and carrying out successfully, the planned invasion of England.

To a lesser extent, perhaps (and certainly the exact consequences will never be known), the Germans repeated this same kind of error in the Battle of Kursk. That a simple mistake with disastrous consequences happened so late in the war is astonishing. That it happened in an area in which the Germans prided themselves on absolute superiority—the quality of their armored vehicles—is to beggar credulity.

Into the Kursk struggle, delayed again and again by Hitler—listening to his generals and his advisers clamoring for more and more time to rush new tanks and tank destroyers to the front—the Germans poured their best Tigers and other weapons. For the moment let us consider only the Mark VI Tiger tank, considered by the contemporary authorities to be the finest weapon of its type in the world. A rolling fortress, a huge chunk of armor racing forward against the enemy, it was a weapon nigh unto itself in all those characteristics that breed reliability and lethality.

But there was a flaw in the Tigers produced by the Porsche company. No flaw in engine, in cannon, in treads, in operating systems. Porsche built their Tigers with efficiency, with skill, with proud reliability. The flaw was in a decision, which was all the more extraordinary when one considers that the men who *knew* the fine points of tank warfare ever permitted such a decision to be made and, second, that they compounded the error by repeating it with armored vehicles other than the Porsche Tiger.

There were no machine guns. What is called secondary armament. There was a long-snouted cannon, a deadly piece of supreme efficiency that characterized the heavy German tank. There was the thick armor plating that made the Tiger so wicked an opponent. But with all its attributes in battle, a tank is not a weapon to fight and survive unto itself. Like all other major weapons, it must be utilized as part of a system.

Soon after the battle started along the edges of the Kursk salient, with the Germans hammering against the massive Soviet defenses, a number of Russian soldiers noted a curious thing. They had run into the Porsche Tigers (and other weapons with the same defect). More to the point, they had run into the Porsche Tigers under unusual circumstances. All of them had to fit—and they did.

First, the Tigers broke through Russian lines. The great 88-mm. cannon rifled shells into Russian armor and defensive positions, and the defenders gave way. The Tigers roared ahead, clanking and snarling like compact dinosaurs.

They broke through the Russian lines without benefit of German infantry accompanying them. That in itself may beg of disaster, for flanking attacks gnaw at the more vulnerable sides of the armored

beasts. But a tank defends itself, or attacks, in different ways. One of them is to assail the infantry it attacks with its machine guns, its secondary armament.

But because there were no machine guns on the Tigers, the deadly German tanks that had shattered the Soviet armor and defensive positions were revealed to be utterly naked to attack by Russian foot soldiers. Once the Russians were fully aware of this weakness, the battlefields resounded to their curious cry in combat of *Hurrah!* as they swarmed against the Tigers, clambering onto the steel backs, hurling bottles of explosive fuel into exhausts and ventilation slits and other vulnerable points.

Where the Porsche Tigers had been feared, now they were sought out as the dumb, mechanical brutes they truly were. And whatever hopes the German combat leaders had placed in these weapons to crack the Russian line evaporated in the exultant battle cries of the Russian soldiers and the gutting boom of flames disemboweling the tanks, consuming them in the white heat of burning fuel and exploding ammunition.

A small point. Over England, no more than the lack of an auxiliary fuel tank.

Across the face of central Russia, no more than the missing machine guns, the secondary armament, of the great Tigers.

Enough, to whatever extent history may tell us or choose to keep hidden within the fury, smoke, and complications of a vast struggle, to have, perhaps, changed the course and the outcome of that struggle.

The term "battle," as we understand it, cannot be applied to the huge conflict at Kursk. What happened in and about the salient, its repercussions extending outward for hundreds, and then for thousands of miles, can in no way be embraced by this restrictive term. The word "battle" in this sense, then, as it is used in these pages, is more acceptance of the common expletive than it is to contain the events of the Kursk salient as a single, easily focused combat.

What happened at Kursk salient transcended by far the geographic-physical aspects of the event. Kursk rose from a multiplicity of factors, not the least of which was thorough, painful, risk-ridden decision-making long before plans were implemented by hot steel. Some

battles arise from circumstance, as the unexpected and sometimes unwanted bastard product of a conflict or set of conditions elsewhere. This was by no means the case with the Battle of Kursk, which involved extraordinary commitment by both sides long before the event. In addition, each side, in a war so often dramatized by the term "blitzkrieg" and all that it brings to mind, was provided with months in which to prepare.

Kursk represented a German attack, and it arose from the decision in Berlin to attack first—and from the decision in Moscow to permit the Germans to initiate hostilities.

So Kursk began with a violent thrusting of German armored forces into the Soviet defensive positions, accompanied by a wild and continuing melee in the skies, then a gradual stiffening of Russian resistance, a grinding down of German momentum, an explosive counterattack by the Russians, followed by a huge forward drive that sent the Germans (and the Russians as well) into a monstrous grinding machine that pulped the men and the armor of both combatants. Through all this frenzied large-scale action there were countless lesser struggles—lesser in number but not in bloodletting and savagery. It was all part of the greater picture.

It is apparent to the discerning analyst of warfare that despite the planning and tactics of the German general staff, no hard-cut operational goal had been formulated. True, there was the contemplated annihilation of Russian military strength. True, Hitler and his generals sought to cripple their enemy, but at what point would this be accomplished? What *was* the German plan beyond this decimation of Russian military strength? At what point would they commit to an advance against a particular city or other goal? Did they expect to chew up the Russian army and then spread out in all directions?

Studying the documents of Operation Citadel, one fails to grasp this clearly defined goal. One seeks the typical expression of specifics, and it is curiously always beyond grasp. To the Russians, the battle shaping up in the Kursk salient was not simply to wait for the German assault, but even to invite it, to draw in the Wehrmacht so that it must fight on Russian terms, in the midst of massive Russian defenses, under the guns of the elaborately prepared Soviet army.

That was the basic plan, the basic goal. Let the Germans come. And when they come, decimate their ranks. Counterattack when the moment is ripe, and then judge the situation and make plans accordingly. The Zhukov meat grinder had worked before, and the marshal had no doubt it would work again.

There was another intangible presence on the battlefield, one that had never appeared before and that had an inescapable effect on the battle. This was the Russian soldier. The Russians who fought in the Kursk salient were not the same type of men who had been encountered previously by the enemy. Ivan had long been held in contempt by the Nazi soldiers. He was little more than an animal, a beast of the lowest order. That attitude, officially, had been altered prior to the opening cannonade of Kursk. The Germans acknowledged the Russian troops were of uncommonly high morale and, in a startling judgment, officially graded Ivan as "tolerably trained"—a long way from those men the Germans had considered subhuman and incapable of any technical or soldierly proficiency.

Obviously, if the Russians had managed the events of Moscow, Leningrad, Stalingrad, and other areas of their country where the Germans had found victory beyond their grasp, and had done so with subhuman troops for whom technical competency was a hopeless task, to face the "new" Russian soldier of high morale and some degree of training (i.e., competency and discipline), Ivan would now constitute a compelling new force on the field of combat. This must, and did, affect the final outcome.

Meanwhile, it must be understood that the world of the soldier—even for the man in the front lines—is not all military, not constant vigilance, not unending confrontation with the enemy. Men who dig in for any period of time seek at once to improve their miserable lot in life, and the longer the period a force remains in one location, the more elaborate and unmilitary their daily life. The German troops, their own diaries show, at the first opportunity would use ingenious methods to transform utterly Spartan conditions into some semblance of comfort. When one does not know how long it may be before combat will be joined, there is a turning to gardens, to creature comforts, to "settling in." Much of the German front became an area where home-

making was of even greater interest than long-term preparations for the next military engagement.

The countryside of central Russia where the Battle of Kursk would be fought demands an appreciation of its nature. Here the broad mixture of terrain was subject to almost instant change. With no more than a crack of thunder and an ensuing cloudburst, land that was passable became an instant quagmire. Thick mud sucked fiercely at men and their machines. Tanks, trucks, half-tracks, self-propelled vehicles, just as quickly became immobilized. This factor, as much as the others, must be assessed for its influence upon the struggle.

Kursk is accepted as the single greatest armored clash of all history. No other single battle or campaign approached the numbers of armor that were involved at Kursk. And yet it would be a grave error to envision the struggle as one of strictly these thick-slabbed monsters. There were other fighting elements to be considered, beyond the tanks and the machines and the men.

Chief among these were the Russian horses, carrying cavalry that struck fast and hard in terrain considered almost impossible for the swift movement of large phalanxes of men. And not merely behind the lines, but in the thick of battle. Horses by the thousands, the mounted cavalry who learned how to use their sturdy animals to take advantage of their swift maneuverability and their skill at striking without warning. They, too, played a significant role at Kursk.

This is another instance of how difficult it is to look at Kursk, at that slaughterhouse of a battle, from a distance, while trying to comprehend the nature of that conflict. One tends to count numbers without following through to details, and that can lead to misconceptions. In judging the effect of horses in the Russian winter, for example, one must understand that at a temperature of $-4°$ F. a German horse will freeze to death.

Why a *German* horse? The specification is important. When protected from the wind, a Russian horse, as used by the cavalry, will survive temperatures down to $-58°$ F.

Were horses truly such a factor in Europe during World War II? And especially on the Russian front with all its armored and mechanized weaponry?

On the Russian front alone, German forces counted from *their* ranks *one and a half million horses dead* from combat and related actions.

Not by any stretch of imagination can the Battle of Kursk be judged by anything other than what it was—the elimination of the ability of the German army to dictate when, where, and how future engagements would be fought on the Russian front. It is really no more complicated than that. In describing Kursk as "one of the most decisive events of World War II," Marshal Zhukov added that what Kursk accomplished, beyond anything else, was to force the "Fascist Command . . . to go over to a strategic defense once and for all."

No one would dare suggest that the Germans had lost their ability to wage war on a massive and devastating scale. But they could no longer, after the fifty days of Kursk, choose the time and place. That privilege was now reserved by the Russians. And this would be the situation right to the end of the war until the Russians massed before Berlin, along a front that averaged out to three hundred heavy guns and thirty tanks (along with all other weapons such as aircraft, rockets, and infantry) *for every mile of front*.

There were high-ranking Germans, to be sure, who recognized Kursk for what it was—an attempt to shatter the Russian army that failed. They accepted Kursk and its ramifications with unjaundiced vision, and they called Kursk by what it was: a debacle, a disaster of unspeakable proportion because of the manner in which it dictated the conduct of the rest of the war.

Most German officials, however, chose to avert their gaze from the battlefield and all that it revealed. They will tell you that no German army was encircled by the Russians, and this is true. They will tell you there was no panic among the soldiers of the Wehrmacht. Again, for the most part, this is true. They will describe the brilliant rearguard actions of their troops, but they find it difficult to admit that this was brilliance in defeat and not in victory. They will say that the Russians, were the truth to be known, suffered even more casualties than did the Germans. Whether this calls for a readjustment of final numbers (if the German premise is true, and it is rather in doubt)

is a moot point. The important end result of Kursk is this: When the last shots had echoed off into the hills, it was the Russian army that had gathered to itself the impetus of the war, and it was the Russian army that dictated when and where that war would be fought.

4

SHERSHAVIN GETS HIS BRIDGE

There is a kind of fascination to raw, mass power, yet it has its limitations. And in the Battle of Kursk a strong counterthrust can be found in the specially organized bands of men who fought as shadows, ventured far beyond the rigid lines of trenches, operating in complete freedom from the restrictions of divisions and battalions. These individuals came from two ranks: special teams dispatched by the Russians into and behind the German lines with specific targets to be attacked and destroyed, and the partisans who fought constantly behind the German lines—from vehicles, from horses, and most often on foot. These were men—and women—who struck in the dead of night, beneath the cover of angry storms, phantoms who tied down tens of thousands of German troops, snarled the Nazi supply system, riddled their communications, and posed a constant, ever-shifting threat to German security.

There was a prelude of exactly these types of sorties to the Battle of Kursk, and one chapter from the extensive and critical activity is vital to the telling of this story, for it will assist in placing a proper

perspective on the preparations for the final fight. There is a tendency to become mired in the staggering numbers of armor and weapons and to lose sight of the vital human element.

The Russians made maximum use of special combat teams to penetrate the German lines during the Wehrmacht's long siege of preparations. To the Russians, time was everything. The longer the delay before the Germans struck, the stronger would be the Russian defenses and the greater the number of reserve forces available. One way to assist in delaying the German attack, as well as weakening German communications when they would be most needed, was to destroy as many key points of the enemy supply system as was possible.

During the last week of June 1943, ten days before the Germans fired their first salvos of the Battle of Kursk, the Russian command sent sapper teams into enemy lines to strike at bridges and rail lines. One such group went after a bridge the Germans had erected on the Severny Donets, in the Kharkov region, south of the Kursk salient.

This is the story of Sergeant Sergei Shershavin of the 480th Infantry Regiment, who spent three harrowing days behind German lines.

Shershavin's special support team penetrated the Wehrmacht lines during a nighttime sortie and came upon the bridge, unseen and unheard. The one German sentry encountered during their approach to the target area died quickly, Shershavin's hand clapping across his mouth while he plunged a knife to the hilt between the man's shoulder blades. Shershavin dragged the dead German from the bridge approach, dumping him off to the side in sand.

The men with Shershavin moved quickly and silently. The odds were against them. The last two attempts to demolish the span had ended with dead Russians and an intact bridge. Working against time, the Russians carried their packages of high explosives to bridge center, spotting them where the charges would have the greatest effect. Sergei Shershavin ran to the charges and connected his detonation wire. Immediately he started back, unreeling wire as he moved. A sudden sound penetrated the stillness, and he froze, listening intently. It was now eerily quiet. All he could hear was the normal sounds of the night. Nothing from the Germans. The Soviet luck was holding.

A man behind Shershavin gasped. He snapped his head around,

reaching for a knife. It was only one of his sappers, gasping for air from a combination of nervousness and excitement. This was the fellow's first mission behind the lines. Shershavin touched the other man lightly on the shoulder, then started up again with the cord unreeling behind them. He reached the end of the bridge and slid to the side.

"Here," he whispered. "This will do." The other man hurried to his side as Shershavin squatted on his heels and began to wind the end of the detonation cord about one finger. He worked more by feel than sight. The bridge seemed to have been swallowed up completely in darkness.

"Sergeant."

Shershavin glanced at the sapper, barely able to make out the face. "Quickly, then," Shershavin said, "what is it?"

"L-let me d-do it," the sapper stuttered. He took a deep breath and gained control. "Pull the cord, I mean."

Shershavin smiled. He felt a tinge of regret as he unwound the cord from his finger and passed it carefully to the sapper. "Go ahead," he said. He knew how the man felt. He had never jerked the detonation wire without a strange and childish feeling of power when the world erupted in a shattering roar.

The sapper was ready. "Pull," Shershavin told him. The other man waited, then tugged sharply. Shershavin felt the motion more than actually seeing the sapper move. They held their breath, muscles tensed, waiting for the great light flash and the following explosion.

Nothing! Air exploded from their lungs. Silence seemed to crash about them, stabbing violently in their ears, so great was their expectation for the thunder from the blast on the bridge. There was no roar, no crashing sound. They remained frozen where they were. What could have gone wrong? Again the silence was broken. Shershavin listened without moving. A nightingale—bursting into song.

"Comrade Senior Sergeant!" the sapper hissed to Shershavin, a note of embarrassment in his voice. No answer. "Sergeant?" Not a sound. Only the cry of the nightingale, for with no more cover than the song of the bird, Shershavin was gone, hustling crablike in the dark.

Shershavin was angry and upset. To have come so far for this! He would not leave the bridge. He *couldn't*. The Germans had been using the bridge to move reinforcements across to the left bank of the

river. They had brought in dangerous amounts of ammunition and fresh supplies. To leave the bridge intact meant the enemy could swing the weight of arms to their side. But if the bridge could be blown, the Germans would be forced to make do with what they had. Shershavin's regiment could pour on the pressure, eroding the ammunition and other supplies, setting up the enemy bridgehead for destruction. There was more to it than that. Something big was in the wind. It was essential to disrupt enemy communications, to break the German supply lines, in every place possible. There was no way, Shershavin knew, that he could voluntarily leave the scene, no matter what the danger to his own life.

He was close to the explosives cache when he heard the guttural murmur of German speech. For a moment the Russian sapper froze, for now voices were not all he heard. There was the hollow clatter of heels on the bridge planking. And it was coming closer.

Shershavin cursed beneath his breath. He went prone, crawling as fast as he could move to reach the explosives. He was almost there, but the Germans were perilously close.

The charges had been placed in the exact center of the bridge. Shershavin clambered to his feet and ran desperately to reach the precious packs. As he ran, he jerked a spare fuse from his pocket, readying it in his hand for immediate use. German voices were suddenly shouting now, and there were muffled curses. The darkness split wide in a blazing orange glare. At the same instant the Russian heard the clattering roar of submachine guns.

Shershavin threw himself forward bodily, smashing headlong onto the hard planking. He gasped for air, reaching for the explosives. He heard the machine guns firing again, bullets whistling directly above him. His hand grasped the explosive charges, the detonating system. Swiftly he pulled free the faulty fuse and tossed it aside; in almost the same motion, as boots pounded toward him, he shoved home the spare fuse. The guns roared again, but Shershavin ignored certain death and pulled free the safety pin.

The world tore apart in his face. Something huge and blinding smashed into him, plunged against his body. He tried to think, but he was a tiny mote in a crescendo of bursting energy—then everything went blank.

He came to with the startling knowledge that he was still alive. Consciousness returned in the passage of a single moment, and he had the wild notion that he had been through a deep and wholesome sleep. He must have enjoyed incredible good fortune. To be directly in the heart of that ripping blast and still be alive.

He couldn't open his eyes. Forcing himself to stay absolutely still, he concentrated on what he must do next. Slowly he tried to open his eyes, and immediately a surge of panic swept over him. No matter what he did, his eyes stayed closed. The lids refused to move. How badly could he be hurt? Make no noise, he warned himself. You do not know what—or who—may be near. His self-admonition bringing full discipline to him, he tried to raise his right arm. Nothing happened. In the next few moments Shershavin realized he was numb everywhere. He felt no sensation anywhere in his body. It was as if he had neither hands, feet, face, nor anything else. Only—but he could hear!

He cursed himself for a fool. Hear? Nothing of the sort. He was listening to a monotonous, even rumble that dinned into his brain. *The dead rumble of emptiness,* he realized. He was as deaf as a stone.

The next moment a sharp pain tore through him. Shershavin was never so wildly delighted to feel something, even the awful pain. Pain meant life. A change in his condition was occurring, and even as this realization reached him, he was aware of feeling in his body. So! Death was not yet here. He explored his body with his hand. For the most part there was no reaction or sensation. The paralysis was still there. Shershavin made certain not to hurry. He must determine his injuries. After a moment he noticed a strange thing. Where his hand touched his body feeling returned slowly. He continued his probing and discovered that his clothing was torn and shredded. Sudden weariness swept over him, and he let his hands drop.

Cold . . . the upper part of his body was on sand, his legs immersed in water. Of course—the river. He tried to move his legs, but they had stiffened with the cold. Slowly, gasping for breath, he dragged himself onto the bank. He struck his legs with his fists, began to rub them as hard as he could. Feeling came slowly, accompanied by sharp pains. Shershavin brought his hands to his face, prodding gently. He winced. His face was a mass of soft pulp. He felt about his eyes. Inwardly he

felt ill. Huge swellings covered where his eyes *should* be. Now he understood why he could not see. He couldn't open his eyes through the fierce swellings.

The dull roaring in his ears changed. Changed? He stirred his body, tried to climb to his feet, tried to understand what was happening. Sounds were coming to him, but he wasn't sure. He eased his body back to the sand. The sounds faded. He lurched up. The sounds were louder. Shershavin covered his ears with his hands. Silence. He removed his hands. The sounds—! His hearing was coming back. He knew now what had happened. The explosion. It had hammered him with terrible blows. Most of his body systems were smashed, but the loss seemed to be temporary. But what was that sound? Signals. High-pitched. In the darkness of still being blind he couldn't repress a smile. The nightingale. The blast was gone. It followed its callings and again was singing.

Then came a new sound. Voices! Shershavin felt his heart beat faster. He needed help and out there were— He forced himself to think. He had no idea what was out there, wherever. He had started to shout for help before he even knew who might be listening. He must use his head. A moment later he realized just how close had been his escape. *German voices* . . . He heard them distinctly. And he lay on the riverbank in sand, blind, still not knowing just how badly he was hurt in other parts of his body. But he would not be taken prisoner, blind or not. He reached into a pocket of his jacket, his fingers closing about a hand grenade. He was ready at any second to pull the pin.

The voices passed him in his darkness. Shershavin listened carefully. Quiet again; only the bird. The sergeant moved his lips. It was a painful process, and he realized how swollen and cracked they were. But he needed, if nothing else, his own assurance.

"I will live," he said aloud, and he was startled by the harsh sound of his own voice.

He fought his way to his knees. A moment later he swayed and groped wildly for support as faintness washed over him. Then he collapsed, again unconscious, to the sand.

When he came to once more, he forced himself to plan his actions. This time he crawled back to the water, moving downslope. He must

know *where* he was. He plunged his left hand into the river. He stayed absolutely still, trying to feel. The water flowed softly against the back of his hand. He realized then that the explosion had hurled his body onto the right bank of the river, well behind the German defense line.

On the left bank of the river the Germans had established a forward combat group. They occupied a stretch of land between the river and a long, narrow lake. With the bridge destroyed the German group was cut off from its main body. Shershavin ran it all through his mind. The outposts of the 480th Infantry Regiment were actually quite close to the Germans on the bank of the lake. Well, there it was. If he wanted to live, he must make it back to the Russian outposts.

It took Shershavin perhaps a half hour, his body stiff and painful from his wounds, to remove his torn clothes. Still blind, he tied his clothes into a bundle and slid into the river. He moved slowly, carefully, wading away from the bank. He knew he dared not slip. It was more than losing his clothes. He could lose his balance. Blinded, wounded, it could be the end. Above all, he knew he must keep his wits about him. Panic would kill him faster than any other enemy.

Soon the water reached to his chin. He held the bundle of clothing as high as he could and pushed himself to a swimming position. He fended the water with his side against the current to prevent being carried too far downstream. Several times he held his breath and let his body sink, trying to feel with his toes for the bottom. Each time he was forced to swim again. The river was wider than he thought. Finally his toes brushed sand. He moved to the riverbank, crawling carefully from the water, sitting still to catch his breath.

Now what could he do? Think, he ordered himself. He listened to the birds filling the air with their trills. If one thinks, he mused, one learns. The birds. They sang only in the morning. The night was gone. Well, he'd learned that much.

Soon he felt the warmth of the early morning sun on his face. If he could only see! He opened his right eye with his fingers. Nothing. The darkness within his eyes, even with the sun stabbing brilliantly across the land, was just as deep as it had been during the night. He brought his hands to his left eye and forced away the swollen tissue. He sat very still. It was far from seeing, but the blackness had been

replaced with a yellowish impenetrable mist, but evidence that light was reaching the optic nerve. There was hope. The eye was still sensitive to light. Shershavin sat on his heels, squatting for proper balance. Now he raised his head to the sky, holding open the lid to his left eye. He made a slow, complete turn.

When he finished, he felt keen disappointment. He had failed to see even the brilliance of the sun. He pushed aside the sudden depression. He hadn't come this far to give up now. He began to crawl forward. Something stiff and prickly stabbed his skin. A low bush, he knew. Well, then . . . low bush. There would be more than one. The bushes could have prevented his seeing the sun, especially if it was barely over the horizon. The lesson hit him at once. If that were so, then he might still be able to detect the sun, and he would have a compass direction.

He pulled himself clear of the bushes. A moment later he broke out into a smile and winced with the pain. His lips were black, sore crusts, and the smile had cost him dearly when the skin split. No matter. He had felt another pain and it was good—the sharpness of looking directly into the sun with his left eye. That way was east.

He had his bearings. So he knew where to go. He slipped on his clothes and began to crawl. For balance he gripped the bushes that stabbed his skin. He must get to the lake. When he felt his sense of direction leaving him, he sought out the sun with his smoky lens of an eye.

Shershavin knew that if he were to survive, his other senses must compensate for his blindness. The eye was improving as the facial swelling went down—he was sure of that—but he had no idea how long it would be before he could actually see. When the air became much more humid than he had experienced while crawling over the ground, he knew he must pay particular attention to what might be about him. Of course: the ground beneath. Damp. Soft. It yielded before the pressure of his knees. He had reached the lake.

He felt no exultation. He was too exhausted. Dragging himself painfully to bushes, he removed his shirt and covered his head with the garment. Something had changed. The warmth of the sun was gone, so Shershavin was not surprised when he felt the first soft touch of the light rain that began to fall. About him he heard leaves catching

the rain, releasing water. The shirt kept the rain directly from his face. He fell asleep.

When he awoke, enormously refreshed, it was dark again. The rain had stopped. Shershavin put his shirt back on and crawled from beneath the bush. He sat quietly, trying to regain his bearings. He heard voices but couldn't identify their source. He listened intently and froze. Germans! His hand shot into his pocket, reaching for the grenade. He realized this was the third time in no more than a day that he was prepared to deliberately take his life, along with as many of the enemy the grenade might include.

The voices came closer. They sounded as if they were only a few feet away. They passed overhead. His fingers on the ground felt the earth tremble slightly, then a blade of grass moved by the foot of a man. They failed to see his body in the night. The voices faded away into the distance. Shershavin breathed deeply. It had been incredibly close. He sat quietly for a long time. Then the signs came again. The birds, warmth against his face. Dawn.

He waited until he had his compass direction once more. The swift heat of the day surprised him. He removed his clothes for them to dry. He lay quietly on the grass, thinking that it had been a long time since any food had reached his stomach. He was surprised that he felt no hunger.

Time to go. He dressed and began crawling. An hour, perhaps two, went by when he froze, then pulled back almost in fear. He saw something green before him, and—he could see! Not much, but infinitely better than before. It was a strange kind of vision, for he could see colors, but not the shape of the objects before him. No matter; what was better would continue to improve. He knew he must go through more pain as the eye struggled to regain the capability of vision. His eye felt as if someone were kneading fingers against the eyeball, driving hard and twisting. The struggle to see became too much. He closed his eye and rested.

Time to push on again. No walking yet. He must crawl. But he crawled now without rest. His hands had long been calloused because of his work as a combat engineer. He had been in the front long enough for his body to toughen. His hands and his knees would be even tougher than before. He crawled all the rest of that day, coming to a

halt to rest only when he "saw" darkness descend and felt the first chill of night.

But the night felt less cold than his first full exposure in darkness. Shershavin took this as an omen of good tidings. His strength must be returning. It was easier to keep his eye open in the cool darkness, and he was stunned to realize he could even make out different forms in the night. He heard the gurgling sound of a small brook, and he worked his way to a shallow ravine. Moments later he heard voices. He held his breath and reached for the grenade. His hand froze. Russian voices! His heart pounded so loudly in his chest he failed to make out the words. He raised up on one elbow.

"Help!" he cried. "Help! Over here!"

No one heard his call. He realized his voice was weak, hardly more than a shouted whisper. Despair assailed him and he plunged forward. Abruptly the ground gave way and he tumbled. Helpless, he waited for jarring impact and the snapping sound of his own bones. He was surprised, almost amazed, when his fall ended without any injury. He groped about and felt steep earth walls. Walls? He felt from the ground up. They were no more than five feet high. He felt again with his fingertips. The walls were smooth, pitted only slightly with grooves. Suddenly he realized where he was. The pits and grooves were from shovels. He was in a trench.

Russian? German? No way to tell. It seemed to be empty. He began to probe. His fingers moved across hand grenades. Quickly he held one in both hands and moved his fingers along the metal ribs to the handle. It was a German grenade.

He understood now. He had moved at too great an angle from his intended path from the lake and stumbled into the German trenches. He looked up at the sky. He had seen a few brighter stars before, but now they were gone. The sky must be overcast. Good! He worked his way laboriously across the lip of the trench, aimed himself in what he believed was the direction of the Russian lines, and once more began to crawl. Raindrops spattered about him and turned quickly into a heavy shower. He felt desolate, cut off forever from his comrades. Weariness assailed him. The urge to collapse and die was overwhelming. He struggled as much against his own perverse emotion as he did the physical world.

He froze, one knee ahead of the other. Something sharp had stabbed him directly in the forehead. Just that sharp stab. Nothing else. He knew then what it was. Barbed wire. Again he listened, and again the night lay frozen in silence. He dropped flat, lifted the wire closest to the ground, and dragged his way past the wire entanglements. He stayed low. There were no bushes about him. He crawled along open ground, using his elbows and his hands, sliding his body in snakelike convolutions to make progress. The low grass helped to ease his way and reduce whatever sound he might make in his weary clumsiness. It was slow going. Before he moved his body, he extended one hand, fingers outstretched, to feel his way.

It saved his life. He felt a small peg in the ground. Then a wire extending away from the peg. He needed no light to reveal the danger. He followed along the wire, touching it with infinite gentleness. Twenty feet from the peg the wire disappeared into the ground. A trip-wire mine. He nodded in satisfaction to himself. He had expected this. Minefields spread before barbed wire were common enough. He wormed past the point of danger. As a sapper he knew how such fields were laid out and where to expect the next mine. All about him was death, but weariness and the depression were gone.

Now he was in his own element. He needed no light to know what was about him. He had moved through such fields many times before. Experience was all on his side. He moved cautiously, every gesture calculated not to commit the single error that could be so fatal. His fingers preceded his body, and he found another peg with its deadly wire. He followed the wire to where it went beneath the ground and then went back to the peg. There; he knew it now. Finally he moved one leg over the wire, and then the other. He crouched, moved on his knees, and then dropped to his belly again to continue crawling.

Life and his men were ahead of him. Time faded from reality. His whole world was the field of explosive hell along which he moved like a lizard. There could be no thought of anything save what was about him. The first wrong movement and everything would disappear in a blinding flash. The slow, painstaking movement across the field took him the rest of the night, a fact he learned only when his left eye saw the horizon beginning to lighten. Looming before him were

dark bushes. Any further movement would be disastrous. The Germans could hardly miss his crawling body through the field separating them from the Russians. Shershavin crawled into the bushes and made himself comfortable. He planned to sleep. A moment later he opened his eyes. The bushes . . . wouldn't they conceal him from view of the Germans? It was worth the risk. He could make better time in daylight.

Another twenty minutes of crawling. Perhaps longer; it didn't matter. A foxhole appeared on the edge of his limited world of vision. The walls had been smoothed down with a shovel. Wooden logs covered half the shelter. It showed signs of recent occupancy. Then . . . why was it empty? He strained to see better, but his eye refused to give up details. Shershavin crawled about the foxhole, leading to a deeper trench, feeling with his hands. He stopped and broke into a huge grin that cracked his lips even wider than before. It was his own foxhole!

Almost there. Still not out of danger, but he was also on the verge of safety. He dare not make a single slip now. The outposts he needed so desperately to reach lay not far beyond the bushes. He needed to find the telephone cable. It should be nearby. After several minutes he found it, barely visible in the grass. Back to his belly, back to crawling like a lizard, his fingers using the cable for guidance. He knew the lay of the land here. Another seventy or eighty feet and he would be safe.

He couldn't move. It took a long time for the realization to get through his brain. His body was giving out on him. So long without food, barely a sip of water, his injuries, the long period without sleep. It all rushed upon him, and he found his body refusing to obey his urge to move on. He railed and cursed, beat with his fist against his legs. He gritted his teeth, sought pain, anything to get his numbed body to move. He tried to climb to his feet, but wobbled like a wild man and collapsed. He cursed himself and dragged his body across the ground, his fingers digging into the grass and dirt, dragging him along. Tears coursed down his cheeks. Still a few feet more. Sobbing for the strength his body refused him, he crawled and scraped his way along the uneven earth.

A sudden sound. Even as he tried to identify the hollow cry above

him, his instincts took over and flattened him to the ground. A mortar shell, nearly at the end of its trajectory. A sound he had heard thousands of times, which brought him to react without thinking, made him hug the ground for survival. Seconds later the crash of the exploding shell swept over him, showering him with clumps of dirt. He recognized the soft whistling sound of shell fragments directly above the ground. If he had been standing, he would have been cut down without a chance.

Another shell arced from the sky and exploded. Then a third, the last shell exploding with a deep coughing roar somewhere ahead of him. Shershavin lay prone, his face in the grass, covering the back of his head with his hands as if those soft hands could stop fire and steel. Another shell exploded, this time closer, heaping earth, grass, twigs, and stones onto him. Shershavin felt no fear. He had come so far for *this!* Rage swept through him.

Two more shells exploded. One in the distance. Another close enough to shake his body, hurling debris across him. The sapper knew nothing of the last two explosions. He was fast asleep.

They found him with his head resting in the palm of his hand, his face showing utter exhaustion and a strange sense of peace.

One week later the Germans struck from their positions to begin the Battle of Kursk. Armored units pounded against the Russian lines. They fell back slowly.

Then began the counterattack. Russian forces threw back the Germans. One of the men who pushed back toward Kharkov had been awarded the title of Hero of the Soviet Union.

He was one of the few men ever to have been accorded so high an honor.

Posthumously.

For a man who is alive today.

Actually, the award was given when Shershavin was still behind German lines and presumed to be dead.

5

THE DEBATE OVER KURSK'S
ROLE IN HISTORY

If you are a Russian, there are two wars to remember from the period of 1941 to May 1945.

The first is one with which all the world is familiar: World War II.

But there is another, and it is known as the Great Patriotic War. It involves the same span of time, from June 1941 to that day in May 1945 when what was left of Germany's armed forces was bludgeoned to final helplessness.

The Russians make a clear and bitter distinction between those two conflicts. World War II was, of course, the entire struggle by the Allies against the Axis powers, involving as the main combatants the United Kingdom, the United States, and the Soviet Union arrayed against Nazi Germany and the Japanese Empire.

But what of the Great Patriotic War? This conflict, involving only the struggle between Russia and Germany, the Russians consider to be the mainstream of the massive fighting of World War II. It is kept distinct from all else. Where official history is concerned, as that his-

tory was compiled within the Soviet Union, whatever else happened in the world depended wholly and completely upon what happened between the two military giants of the European continent.

It is a Russian conviction (which disregards such factors as the atomic bomb) that if the Great Patriotic War had been lost to the Nazis, the Allies could never have seen a victorious conclusion to World War II. At worst the Germans and the Japanese would have triumphed throughout the globe. At best, behind its barriers of ocean distance, the United States would have had to negotiate for a peace that left it an island in a world ruled by her enemies.

And in the Great Patriotic War it was the Battle of Kursk on which everything else swung.

It would be impossible to place Kursk in its proper perspective, at least from the viewpoint of understanding what it all appeared to be from the Russian side of the line, without at least listening to the Russian argument, which is that historians of the United States and England have done everything in their power deliberately to falsify the record of World War II and, more specifically, to downgrade the achievements of the Soviet army. If these convictions are true, then we have been misled as to the contributions of the Russians to *our* emergence as victors from the war. If they are not true, it would certainly help to explain the bitterness of Soviet historians toward their contemporaries in the Western world. Because true or not, if the Russians *believe* their viewpoint is correct, they will act accordingly.

G. Koltunov and B. Solovyov, research associates at the Institute of Military History of the U.S.S.R. Ministry of Defense, in 1970 completed an exhaustive study of the Battle of Kursk, a work written on the basis of vast documentary material that included the personal reminiscences of participants and availability of all known Russian and German records.

"In the battle at Kursk," state Koltunov and Solovyov, "a shattering blow was delivered at the Nazi war machine, as a result of which the enemy was forced to relinquish his offensive strategy for good and revert to defense on the entire Soviet-German front and other fronts of the Second World War." The two historians insist that "not only

the offensive but the defensive strategy of the Wehrmacht was defeated" in the raging fight of the Kursk salient.

Colonel V. Sekistov lauds the work of Koltunov and Solovyov and
remarks that

> Soviet historians show that the Soviet victory and the Nazi defeat
> at Kursk exerted a tremendous influence on the morale of the troops
> and population in Germany and her allies, as well as on develop-
> ments in Europe. Disbelief in victory started spreading not only
> among soldiers but also among officers and even generals of the
> Wehrmacht. The Resistance movement intensified in France, Nor-
> way and Bulgaria, and especially in Yugoslavia and Albania.

There seems to be a tendency on the part of the Russians to insist
that the shock waves of the fighting at Kursk extended to distances,
with immediate results, that would be questioned by most impartial
observers of the history of the war. This does little more, on the part
of the writer, than to raise a questioning brow, but did the Resistance
movement in France *really* intensify so quickly, so greatly, so specifically, as a result of the Battle of Kursk? Or are the Russians, even
those in the history chairs of their universities, wound up so tightly
that they must attribute distant events (which were supported by the
Americans and British, in the case of the French underground, especially in support of the anticipated invasion less than a year later)
as relating to Kursk and *only* to Kursk?

In another reference to the relationship between Allied war leaders
and the Kursk fighting, Colonel Sekistov makes this illuminating
statement:

> The great impact of the Soviet Army's victory at Kursk on the course
> of the Second World War was admitted by F. D. Roosevelt, Presi-
> dent of the United States. In a special address to the Head of the
> Soviet Government he wrote on August 6, 1943, that during a month
> of giant battles the Soviet Armed Forces, by their skill, courage, self-
> lessness and tenacity, had not only stopped the long contemplated
> German offensive but also launched a successful counteroffensive with
> far-reaching consequences.

Sekistov, continuing his references to comments in the United States during the war, adds:

> At that time the American press commented that the Soviet Army's victory at Kursk opened up a "new phase" of the war, whose focal point was "Russia's action as a powerful military force."

Well, all this hardly seems to justify the Russian claims that Western historians sold the Soviet accomplishments at Kursk down the nearest river. Indeed, the comment attributed to the president of the United States was actually made while the battle still raged.

One begins to sense an element of paranoia in the Russian complaints that they have not been afforded their due when it comes to their contributions to the war. The reference to Roosevelt as having *admitted* the Russians had turned an enormous point in the war at Kursk certainly strains the issue. Roosevelt was not admitting anything, in the sense that admission comes begrudgingly or only after specific pressure to wrest from some recalcitrant an admission of one sort or another. A point of semantics? Of course, but the irritation of the Soviets on the historical weight of Kursk is riddled with such semantic barbs. And when a Russian is irritated, most especially when he feels his country has been shortchanged in the history books, he falls back on the tried-and-true system of lofty ideological mutterings. A shame, for there is no need for such antics. However, the issue here is not so much *our* claim to a logical understanding of the place of Kursk in the war, but how the Russians feel they have been so sorely mistreated by the bulk of those who recorded the war for the readers of much of the world beyond the borders of the Soviet Union.

Writing in the *Soviet Military Review* (August 1971), Colonel Sekistov (who is also a professor of history) first notes that the great fight at Kursk

> occupies a definite place also in the postwar writings of bourgeois historians. For instance, in the U.S. there recently appeared a book *Kursk: The Clash of Armor* by G. Jukes, who admits, among other things, that the Kursk Bulge witnessed the biggest tank engagement. For his part, H. Baldwin points out that in that period the Russian

front pinned down a considerable part of the German Air Force, owing to which the Allies received absolute air supremacy over the Mediterranean, whereas the Anglo-American Allied operations did not lead to weakening Germany at sea or in the air, nor did they weaken the German forces on land.

Now, let's hold it right *there*.

This writer has no intention of drawing away from the main issue, which is the Battle of Kursk, of course, and not the somewhat myopic (and paranoid-tinged) viewpoint of Colonel Sekistov, who seems unable to avoid a smattering of party line in his protests. Once again he has grasped the term "admit," in reference to Geoffrey Jukes, who labored through an entire book specifically to lay the credit for one of the great turning points of the war right where it belongs—at the feet of the Russians.

Sekistov's remarks concerning "admissions" of Hanson Baldwin leave much to be desired where accuracy of major events in the war is concerned. For the good colonel-professor to so neatly "accept" that air supremacy over the Mediterranean was due to events in Russia is to apply extraordinary flexibility to the facts at hand. One might assume that the tremendous air power assembled against the German air force in the Mediterranean had virtually nothing to do with that air supremacy. Nor might there be any effect from the destruction of the German air units in North Africa. Nor is there any effect from the great assembly of German fighters thrown against the Allied bomber streams from England.

If we were to accept at face value the contentions of Sekistov, would it not be fair to state that without the great numbers of aircraft tied down against the American and British air fleets, the thousands of additional aircraft the Germans would have had available would have produced a different result at Kursk? How badly would the balance of power have tipped had the ground units, infantry, tanks, armored vehicles, and supplies used on other fronts against Britain and the United States been thrown into the cauldron in central Russia?

Despite these quite obvious circumstances that directly or indirectly helped the Russians smash the Nazi juggernaut, Colonel Sekis-

tov goes even further in his attribution about the long-range implications of that titanic armored engagement when he adds:

> . . . not a single other battle has been the object of such deliberate falsification as the Kursk battle. And this is not accidental. It was the Soviet Army's victory at Kursk that *completed the turn of the tide* in the Second World War and brought Nazi Germany to the brink of catastrophe. It also played havoc with the hopes of the reactionary imperialist circles that they would be able to dictate their will to the Soviet Union which, they reckoned, would be weakened by the war.

The foregoing statement provides one of the prime examples of why researching a major Russian event is so often a maddening effort. Where do we separate specifics—hard facts and hard military judgment—from the impromptu, unexpected trumpeting of the party line? There is no escaping this intrusion in almost anything the Russians provide for perusal. It lurks behind every page, insinuates its discord from almost every line.

Is there validity in the Russian claim that the Battle of Kursk was downplayed *deliberately?* Is there some manner of plot that crosses oceans and to which most of us must confess to be members? I, for one, am unaware of any such machinations, and I find that Colonel Sekistov and his colleagues do themselves harm in attempting to correct the record by such foolish accusations.

But are these accusations completely unwarranted? That is entirely another question, and we are here to permit the colonel to have his say. He continues:

> The falsifiers' favorite method is to hush over this mammoth battle. For instance, such publications on the history of the Second World War as *The American Heritage Picture History of World War II*, by C. Sulzberger, and, *Hitler and Russia*, by T. Higgins, abound in references to battles at El Alamein and Midway, in Tunisia and Sicily, in Southern Italy and the Pacific islands, but do not contain a single word about the battle of Kursk. A number of bourgeois historians keep repeating the version that the German offensive did not hold any great place in the plans of the German High Command, and, we are told, pursued "limited aims."

Facts, however, testify to the contrary. Indeed, it is hardly possible to commit to action the best formations, a great part of the forces, as Hitler did in the summer of 1943 at Kursk, merely to achieve "limited aims." Over 100 German divisions—nearly one-half of the Wehrmacht's divisions operating on the Soviet-German front at the time—were thrown one after another into that battle. Incidentally, most of these divisions, the Soviet historians G. Koltunov and B. Solovyov emphasize, were specially prepared for a decisive blow and were the most battle-worthy formations.

Colonel Sekistov then rallies to his argument the admissions of the enemy. This is an about-face from the usual Soviet attitude to anything claimed, admitted, or otherwise stated by German officers and officials, but in this instance it provides an obvious value to the colonel's argument:

The Nazi forces suffered heavy losses. Even according to the minimized figures of the Nazi Command, in the fifty days of fighting the Nazis lost 500,000 men killed, missing and severely wounded, up to 1,500 tanks, 3,000 guns and over 3,700 aircraft. Nazi General [F. W. von] Mellinthin was forced to admit that "in the Kursk battle, in which the troops were attacking with the desperate determination to win or die, the best units of the German army were wiped out." Another Nazi general, H[einz] Guderian . . . pointed out: "As a result of the failure of Operation Citadel, we suffered a devastating defeat. . . . The initiative passed over completely to the enemy." At Kursk, in the opinion of the West German historian [Walter] Görlitz, "the last formations capable of conducting offensive operations were burnt, reduced to ashes, and the German armored forces had their neck broken." That, as Marshal of the Soviet Union I. Konev correctly pointed out, was the "swan song" of Nazi Germany's armored forces.

Colonel Sekistov gets down to numbers comparisons:

Understanding the importance of the Soviet Army's victory in the battle of Kursk, won in the absence of a second front in Europe, some bourgeois historians, to minimize its significance, search for various circumstances which, they claim, were "favorable" for the Soviet

forces. Some of them have gone to such lengths as to ascribe this victory . . . to the success of the Anglo-American armies in the Mediterranean theater. Thus, the American historian R. Leckie maintains
that in the summer and autumn of 1943 the main events unfolded
in the Mediterranean, on which the attention of the whole world
was focused. Without minimizing the significance of the Allied
operations in the above-mentioned theater, we should like to note
that the Kursk battle started earlier (July 5) than the Allied landing
in Sicily (July 10). This simple arithmetic comparison is also rather
convincing: 50 of the best German divisions, including 16 tank and
motorized divisions, were concentrated near Kursk in the areas of the
forthcoming offensive, whereas in Sicily the Allies were opposed by
nine Italian and only two German divisions. . . .

Now that he has momentum, Colonel Sekistov winds it up:

It is perfectly obvious that, as compared with the mammoth battle of
Kursk, the limited successes of the Anglo-American forces in the Medi-
terranean could not seriously affect the course of the Second World
War. In the Mediterranean theater of operations the actions of the
Anglo-American forces did not divert considerable German forces.
General D. Eisenhower, Supreme Commander-in-Chief of the Allied Forces, had to admit [there it is again!] that the combat actions in
the Mediterranean turned into an auxiliary operation. The main
operations, as W. Churchill pointed out, unfolded on the Soviet-
German front, where three huge engagements—for Kursk, Orel, and
Kharkov—all carried out in the course of two months, signified the
collapse of the German army. These *admissions* [emphasis mine]
of prominent U.S. and British statesmen fully expose the concoctions
of the falsifiers of the history of the Second World War, who are trying in vain to minimize the Soviet people's contribution to the rout of
Nazi Germany—the shock detachment of world imperialism.

Have we really done it up so badly? There are points of validity in
Sekistov's remarks, especially in his reference to histories that purport
to cover the entire Second World War and that, in fact, present a dis-
torted view of the weight of operations between the different Allied
powers. There is no question that much of the story on the Russian
front failed to reach the writers, the editors, and the publishers who
were responsible for historical volumes.

Right there is one of the problems. Too bad that Sekistov is not on *this* side of the fence. Too bad that he hasn't spent years as a bourgeois writer fighting the futile battle of trying to extricate even accurate historical information from the Soviet Union. It is no small wonder that there has been as much as has been printed to emphasize the enormous contribution of the Russians to the defeat of Germany. There is a towering wall to be scaled, a maze to be run, in attempting to gain the cooperation, the willing assistance, of Soviet authorities, even for the telling of the *Russian* story.

And when liaison is established finally, there is the bog to traverse, one slow sucking step after the other, of the strident cries of the party line, which, for all their importance to the Russians, present little interest to the researcher of specific facts. It has made the attempt to portray the Russian side of the ledger a frustrating experience.

From the protests of Sekistov, one might assume that Soviet authorities have always been ready to step forward with accurate accounts of forces involved, of losses suffered and inflicted. Such assumption would be greatly in error, for in the years-long effort to draw attention to their prowess and their accomplishments, the Russians have seldom stopped to provide accurate figures rather than blatant, unsupportable propaganda.

One item suffices for this point. During and shortly after the Battle of Kursk, the Russians claimed that for the eighteen days between July 5 and 23, 1943, their aircraft supporting the Kursk operation shot down in air battles no fewer than 1,392 German aircraft. This adds up to 70 percent of *all* the German aircraft available for first-line combat duty at Kursk. The claim was so patently ridiculous that the Russians saw fit simply to delete the figures from later histories of the Great Patriotic War.

They did not correct. They simply deleted.

For this same period of eighteen days, the Russian high command insisted that their forces destroyed 2,900 German tanks in battle. This is destroyed; not "destroyed and damaged."

It is an interesting figure, when one considers the total German strength in tanks at the time, in the area involved, was fewer than 2,700.

One regrets such problems in trying to assess so mighty a battle as Kursk, for what did take place needs only the truth, not false claims, not the strident finger-pointing of Soviet historians obsessed with the notion that there exists a huge and deliberate plot to deprive the Russians of the credit due them for their monumental share in destroying the German army.

Part II

Operation Citadel

6

DISSENSION IN THE
GERMAN HIGH COMMAND

Like any major military operation, Citadel was handmaiden of the plans, directives, manipulations, and machinations of many high-ranking officials and military officers of wartime Germany. But in the battle that emerged finally as the greatest armored clash of history, there was an extraordinary difference in the direction and control of the German forces involved.

Only one man was thoroughly in touch with all top elements. Only one man had the absolute authority to countermand, to override, and to direct all those about him. That man was the absolute leader of the Third Reich—Adolf Hitler. Thus any measure of the Battle of Kursk, especially from the viewpoint of German participation, must take into account the individual touch (or meddling) of this one man. It is the sort of situation where schisms develop swiftly and to preposterous and dangerous extremes, and this is precisely what happened. The high staff of Germany was also a house divided.

There's an old axiom that what you don't know can't hurt you. There should be another axiom that the foregoing has to be one of

the more ridiculous statements ever made, and especially does this apply to military adventures. In anything so complex and intricate as a major battle, unseen factors often play a greater role than what is clearly visible directly before the participants.

The fighting that was to take place in the Kursk area during the summer of 1943 inevitably had to evolve from past experiences. The affairs of men are filled with axioms, and there is the one that insists that history always repeats itself. There is also the hasty appendage that history may always repeat itself, but never in quite the same way.

Considering the opening phase of the German invasion of Russia in the summer of 1941 and the events that took place in the Kursk area of central Russia in 1943, one wonders at the repetition of certain elements of the fighting. Sir Basil Liddell Hart, one of the more sharp-eyed historians of World War II, notes on page 174 of *The Other Side of the Hill* that the very nature of German field support might have been its greatest weakness in the Russian invasion. It is not enough for an armored striking force to be able to pierce deeply into enemy territory *unless* that armored force can be kept supplied with the fuel, ammunition, spare parts, and replacements it requires to sustain its strength and mobility. The Germans prided themselves on their panzers, and with good reason as they rolled back and cut to pieces the defending Russians.

But they were moving into a country with crude and almost ancient communications, with roads that made a mockery of the term and that became impassable quagmires when the skies turned dark and rain covered the countryside.

The panzers were tracked armor, of course—tanks, self-propelled guns, and the like. *But* the transport to support the German advances was motorized. And that was literally the undoing of the far-reaching invasion. As Liddell Hart points out:

If the Soviet regime had given her [Russia] a road system comparable to that of the western countries, she would probably have been overrun in quick time. The German mechanized forces were balked by the badness of her roads.

But this conclusion has a converse. The Germans lost the chance of victory because they had based their mobility on wheels instead of

tracks. On these mud-roads the wheeled transport was bogged when the tanks could move on.

Panzer forces with *tracked* transport might have overrun Russia's vital centers long before the autumn, despite the bad roads.

It was a lesson taught with bitterness to the Germans. Yet the planners of the fighting at Kursk, including Hitler, appeared to have forgotten the impact of the crude Russian road system. They were soon to remember.

Earlier we mentioned that Operation Citadel did not spring fullgrown from the fertile mind of either Hitler or any of his generals. Instead, it came into existence in fits and starts, was hobbled from the beginning by constant changes in plan, the latter brought on by a bewildering multiplicity of factors that seemed to change from week to week. The one ingredient entirely on the side of the German army —time—was thus frittered away in these fitful exercises of delay, all to the advantage of the Russians.

We have also seen that in March 1943 the Russians were forced to yield (for the third time) the great city of Kharkov. Not even the last-minute intervention of Zhukov, with all his brilliance, could avert that loss. Thus Kharkov was yielded, and it was at this point that continued operations against the Russians began to bog down in German indecision and the conflict amid the military hierarchy surrounding Hitler.

Field Marshal Erich von Manstein was the victor in the fighting at Kharkov. One of the demonstrably more brilliant Nazi generals, he wanted nothing more than to keep up the pressure against the Russian forces he had just thrown out of Kharkov, and he fought for this advance. Other factors prevailed. The only way Manstein could push far beyond Kharkov with the results he sought would be if Field Marshal Günther von Kluge, commanding German forces to the north, would also bring hammerlike pressure against the Russians he faced. Kluge could then prevent exceptionally heavy Russian reserves being thrown against Manstein. Without that pressure, Manstein's chances of shattering the Kursk salient would be greatly reduced. But no matter what the considerations, delay could be crippling.

In Berlin, where the general staff considered the issue, the prevailing opinion was against the plans offered by Manstein. His Operations Panther and Hawk, felt Berlin, could not succeed without Kluge in the north, and, equally important, the central front in the Kursk region was just coming into the spring thaw. No one wanted to face an offensive at this particular time, for it was that period when the ground turned from frozen hardness to sucking mud and bog that could cripple an offensive.

Just as quickly as Manstein ended his advance, the front bogged down. Active operations, in the sense of major assaults against the Russians with the intent to pierce the enemy defenses and take ground, died away almost overnight. It was time to tidy up. The Germans moved all their panzer divisions back from the front lines. Where possible the infantry that had fought the longest and the hardest also was pulled back from the front lines.

In the Kharkov area all armored forces were brought together under the XLVIII Panzer Corps. The German commanders immediately began a thorough training program to assure that replacements would fit in well with the seasoned veterans. This was no idle effort, for the training ran from the smallest units all the way to divisional maneuvers. The front—although major struggle with the Russians was avoided—echoed with the thunder of small and heavy guns as the Germans intensified the training program. Major General F. W. von Mellinthin, who commanded armored forces in the Kharkov area, was determined to keep his men sharply honed for a swift resumption of fighting.

As it turned out, the training was about all the combat his men would know for some time.

Hitler and his staff were being forced by the changing pressures of the war to adapt their strategy to the harsh facts of life. There was general agreement among all concerned that Germany no longer had available the power to mount a strategic offensive in Russia. Hitler, whose hopes and dreams seemed to vacilate from one week to another, would exult in the possibilities of smashing into Moscow, but for the moment, in March 1943, he was more concerned with the problems of establishing the future avenues the German army would take.

For a start there had to be a broad general agreement as to Germany's situation. It was not hard to come by, for the facts of life were distressingly apparent to all involved. First, the Americans and the British were channeling all their energy into the invasion of Europe. When that invasion would come was a point leading to argument, but whether it was 1943 or 1944 was really not the issue. The invasion would surely take place, and it would require enormous effort on the part of the German army and air force to resist the assault.

If the continent was to be invaded, then, could Germany dare to remove a substantial part of its forces along the west, and transfer these to the Russian front in order to inflict a crippling blow against the Russian army? Some generals were of the opinion that were these forces to be made available, then the German army would be within reach of a stupendous victory against the Soviets.

But did Germany risk weakening itself along the Atlantic Wall? The situation did not look promising. Japan had shot its best arrows in the Pacific war. Despite the Japanese occupation of vast areas of territory, the war in the Pacific was primarily being fought by the navy and air forces of the United States, and they had clearly wrested the initiative from the Japanese. With the Japanese essentially on the defensive, and the Americans building an overwhelming air and naval force against them, Germany could not count on any help from its ally.

Italy was a bad joke in Berlin. In fact, the Italian government was willing to pay almost any price to withdraw from the terrible meat grinder of the Russian front. As for Germany's other allies, or, if not allies, those governments that had sent divisions to the Russian front, the only direction of interest to those troops was the nearest exit from Russia.

No matter how they turned the situation for study, Hitler and the top staffs of OKW (armed forces high command) and OKH (army high command) found general agreement on two points. One, that the Allies were determined to invade the Continent from England and, two, that 1943 was a year in which it would be impossible for the German army to force a favorable decision on the eastern front.

This seemed to be the only area of general agreement, and one step beyond found the hierarchy in a deep split. One group, led by Field

Marshal Alfred Jodl and the armed forces high command, recommended strongly that Hitler remove much of the strength from the Russian front to bolster German forces both in the Mediterranean and along the Atlantic Wall. The Russian front was best held static.

The army high command raised immediate and strenuous objections to such a move. In truth, this OKH group cared little about problems beyond Russia. They were responsible for the eastern front, and it was obvious they should concentrate both their interest and their efforts toward the problem of fighting the Russians.

Besides, they argued, the situation was worsening. By the end of January 1943 the OKH could argue with telling effect that they were short of 487,000 men necessary to fulfill their responsibilities. They pointed to the appalling casualties suffered in armor; Germany invaded Russia in the summer of 1941 with superbly equipped armored divisions, and at their disposal was a total force of 3,300 tanks. But as the last week of January 1943 rolled around, there was a total along the entire Russian front of only 495 tanks that were considered fit for immediate combat. Hundreds more were in repair depots. New replacements were needed desperately, and although they were being shipped, their effect at the front would be nil until they were integrated into the combat units. There were shortages of aircraft, trucks, and even horses.

They presented a convincing argument. The Russians were far from the technical equal in the air of the German planes and pilots, but the numbers of Russian aircraft were increasing at a frightening rate. Equally important, their quality was improving just as quickly. The Russians were upgrading the quality of their armored vehicles, and they were turning them out in staggering numbers.

When the Russian production of new tanks—at a rate many times that of German industry—was questioned, the OKH answer was that the situation had to a great extent been brought about by the extremely heavy aid from the United States to the Russians. The Russians were in desperate need of rugged, reliable transport. They needed trucks by the tens of thousands, and they were getting these from the United States, thereby leaving Russian industry free to concentrate on the production of tanks. It also gave the Soviets an unprecedented mobility to support fast-moving armies.

The presentation of such facts did not mend the schism between the groups, of course, but it did lend credence to the OKH argument that they would consent to the weakening of German forces on the Russian front only if certain conditions were met. These demanded that the size of the front itself be reduced, in some cases greatly, so that the army could withdraw to the most favorable defensive positions. At the same time, many of the requirements that Hitler had placed upon the army on the eastern front must be removed. It would be a matter of withdrawal, defensive fighting only, and no hopes to exploit whatever weaknesses in the Russian line that might be discovered.

Hitler refused. To him, continued withdrawals on the Russian front spelled a disastrous loss of prestige among his allies, which also meant increased difficulties in keeping them in line. He also contended that if this plan were to be followed, Germany would lose critically needed resources in the areas presently occupied. Prestige and economy—reasons that would later prove to be specious—formed the basis of his refusal to "tighten up" along the huge Russian front.

Yet not even Hitler could avoid the harsh reality that the German army was no longer capable of a strategic offensive in Russia, and this conviction was shared by his entire staff. There was only one way to go, then, and that was on the defensive. But there are different ways to do this, and it was in the search for the method best meeting Germany's needs that attention began to focus on Kursk.

General Kurt Zeitzler, chief of the army general staff, agreed fully with Hitler that the best means of defending the long front line in Russia was to mount a campaign of limited offensive against selected areas of the front. This would keep the Soviets off balance, accomplish the destruction of their military forces, and also reduce German losses to an absolute minimum.

The limited offensive would begin as soon as the spring thaw had passed through its worst period and the roads were considered suitable for wheeled transport needed to support advanced operations. If the army moved the moment the roads were ready, reasoned Hitler, again with Zeitzler's full support, the Russians would never have time to prepare any offensive of their own. This would accomplish a whole

string of goals Hitler had in mind. The offensive capability of the Russian army would be severely blunted. There would be no need to reduce the strength of German forces on any other front. Germany's allies would be greatly impressed with the striking force of the Wehrmacht at a time when many questioned its continued capabilities in the field.

These goals, it must be remembered, were considerably less than the hopes Hitler eventually placed in Citadel at its height. But Citadel began in a comparatively modest way, and despite bickering and backbiting among the top German military staffs and an almost leaden atmosphere in which it stumbled from one week to the next, the offensive began to contain hopes for Hitler that were far beyond what any of his staff saw in the operation.

Nevertheless, in his initial instructions to his commanders, Hitler was uncharacteristically hesitant. On March 13, 1943, he outlined his strategic plan:

> It is to be expected that the Russians will continue their attacks at the end of the winter and the muddy season and after they have rehabilitated and reinforced their forces to some extent.
> Therefore, it is important for us to take the initiative at certain sectors of the front if possible before they do, so as to be able to dictate their actions at least at one sector. . . .
> At other sectors we must ward off the Russian attacks until they have spent their strength. In these places our defenses must be made especially strong by means of heavy defense weapons, additional fortifications, strategic minefields, supporting positions, and mobile reserves.

It was at this point that whatever offensive Hitler had in mind began to stumble in its preparatory phase. The reasons were convoluted, and Hitler's own capacity for rendering firm decisions was sorely undermined by the constant bickering about him, to say nothing of valid reasons advanced by his generals, all of which were not always in agreement, but still were possessed of sufficient validity to keep postponing the launching of Citadel.

Among his generals, Field Marshal Walter Model was one in whom Hitler had great confidence, and when Model raised serious objec-

tions about the starting date of the offensive, Hitler had little choice but to heed the general's advice. Model insisted that opening the attack on the Russians would leave the infantry forces critically short of necessary troops in their proper positions. He must have time, he insisted, to carry out the needed movement and disposition of the front-line combat units, as well as those making up the immediate reserves.

No sooner did he receive a postponement on these grounds when Model insisted (with valid reasoning, it turned out) that his troops must be heavily augmented. Model went about his objections with thoroughness. He produced extensive intelligence reports. He had prepared hundreds of aerial photographs proving the staggering depth and complexity of defenses the Russians were creating in the Kursk area. These were only the beginnings of his basic complaint that the Soviets would far outnumber the German army, and that unless this disparity in troop strength, armor, artillery, and supporting units was corrected before the attack, Kursk could become a great disaster for the Wehrmacht. Hitler accepted these arguments as sufficient cause to give his commanders more time. Citadel began slipping again.

There was the matter of Manstein who fairly chafed at the bit to be off and running after the Russians. The Kursk salient, he insisted, was perfect for an immediate strike. It bulged into the German lines like an immense fist 70 miles across at its base. Along its entire frontage it spanned 250 miles. Within that salient were Russian troops worn to a thin shell of their former fighting abilities, claimed Manstein. They had been fighting steadily for months. Their strength was sapped. They were low on equipment, fuel, supplies, and replacements. If the Wehrmacht struck swiftly, the Russian lines would melt away like soft dough under hot knives. An immediate strike could bring in great numbers of prisoners and large quantities of captured armor and supplies, and break the back of any offensive hopes nurtured by the Russians. Such an attack must be launched early in May, he said, when the sucking ground of the spring thaw would largely be gone. The panzers could strike with deadly effect. It would be a narrow period in which to carry out the operation—immediately after the worst effects of the thaw were ended and just before the Russians could move in sufficient replacements to regain their strength.

The reasoning was sound. But despite his proven brilliance and successes in battle, Manstein lacked the full support of his fellow generals, whose doubts so disturbed Hitler that he rejected Manstein's pleas for a swift strike in early May.

Again Citadel bogged deeper in passing time. Hitler had become irritated with the matter of German armor needed for the strike he contemplated. Intelligence reported Russian production of tanks soaring to astronomical numbers. Even if these reports were considerably watered down, they were still reason for great concern. Hitler wanted not only more Tiger tanks in the battle, but also the new Panther—lighter and faster than the Tiger, but just as deadly in its main firepower.

Unfortunately for Hitler's hopes, the Panther was wallowing through a sea of teething troubles, driving its engineers and test crews to distraction as they sought to bring the desperately needed tank to operational status. Where the attack on Kursk would require thousands of tanks, and at least several hundred of the best armor for the most critical parts of the front, the best that German industry could manage with the Panther was a meager trickle of twelve tanks per week—hardly enough to bring on more than a sorry groan from the men trying to equip the panzer divisions with the necessary weight of matériel to shatter the Russian defenses.

As the delays continued, the conflicts between the generals deepened, and the cohesion and efficiency of the German high command began to disintegrate as dissension constantly flared between opposing factions. The month of April saw even greater strife and argument spreading its poison through the ranks of the general staff. The effects became so pronounced that many generals and their immediate staffs began to despair of success with any form of attack launched against the Russians that summer.

Jodl, chief of staff of OKW, wanted Hitler to abandon completely all plans for an offensive move against the Russians. To mount such a strike, at Kursk or elsewhere, he argued, the Wehrmacht would have to be stripped of its strategic reserve. Such a move might be nothing more than the answer to the prayers of the enemy, who was making such heavy commitments in the Mediterranean.

Zeitzler, chief of staff of OKH, was openly scornful of the old-

woman attitude of Jodl. But in his presentation in favor of carrying out the strikes against the Russians, Zeitzler wandered so aimlessly that he evoked whispered questions as to his mental acuity.

He insisted that the German army was so disastrously weak along the entire Russian front that it could not hold its own against the enemy. Therefore, to solve this problem, the Wehrmacht must not stand still. Aggressive action was needed. Its purpose? To bring the Russians into close battle as quickly as possible.

But, argued his staff among themselves, if the army was so weak it could not withstand a major struggle with the enemy, what was the purpose in forcing the issue on the battlefield?

Zeitzler brushed aside any objections to his views. He also turned a cold shoulder to the members of the high staff when they emphasized serious problems in other sectors of the war. Zeitzler's position as chief of staff, in respect to all save the Russian front, was a constant affront and source of irritation to him, because he felt he lacked authority over the general staff. No one on the staff sought his opinion, and those who received it without such a request were disposed to ignore his remarks. It boded little good for cooperation among the generals.

On the other side of the fence, adding to the split that seemed to widen every day, was the fact that OKW was all but told to keep its nose out of the Russian front. The German table of organization called for OKW not to be fully conversant with all theaters of war but to play an active role in the conduct of such theater operations. It was an idealistic breakdown of authority, to be sure, for OKW found itself rebuffed at every turn when matters involving the Russian front were brought before Hitler.

More than a mere division of opinion separated Jodl and Zeitzler. Actual hostility had erupted between the two men, thus rendering even more difficult the smooth and coordinated functioning of the two high commands directly beneath Hitler. But whatever burned between Jodl and Zeitzler was pleasant enough compared to the undisguised hatred that marked the relationship of Field Marshal Kluge and Colonel General Heinz Guderian. The latter had virtually been sacked after the German army was beaten off from the gates of Moscow. Guderian remained in disgrace until the shocking reverses of

the Russian front convinced even Hitler that the genius of this man must be brought back into the fold.

He appointed Guderian, one of the great armored strategists of all time, as the inspector general of armored troops, with sweeping new powers to return to the panzer forces the dash, skill, and effectiveness with which they had opened the Russian front. This move by Hitler, welcomed by those who knew just how desperately Germany needed Guderian, failed to please a certain clique within the high command, notably Kluge.

The hatred—and it was nothing less—between the two men became so heated that in May, as the Germans stumbled and lurched toward a final commitment with Citadel, Kluge contacted Hitler with a request that he be allowed to challenge Guderian to a duel. What effect this request may have had on Hitler's attitude is not too difficult to imagine, for no matter what strange whims Hitler might display, he was still wrestling with the single greatest problem of his career—stopping the Russian army in its tracks and dealing the Soviets a crippling blow. And here were two of his top men, Guderian, whom he needed so crucially to rebuild the shattered panzer forces, and Kluge, commander of Army Group Center on the Russian front, having at one another with blood in their eyes.

History is unfortunately the servant to a host of emotions, the more prominent among them being ego, and ego is translated as "my point of view is the only real point of view." Emotion plays an intrinsic role in any historical study, if only for the fact that history doesn't record itself. The participants, of course, make up the ranks of the historians, and the historians are often notoriously prejudiced. In studying the records of events and of those involved in the Battle of Kursk and its far-reaching peripheries, it is impossible to avoid having to wade through startling conflicts of opinion. Certainly Jodl did not see eye to eye with Manstein, and Kluge could differ greatly from Mellinthin, and what Hitler thought or said or did depends upon who is reporting these events concerning Hitler.

There does not exist a hard-and-fast, specific record of the machinations of the German high command, leading up to the Battle of Kursk. Official reports of the German army are exactly that—official reports.

All too often they are doctored and altered to reflect in the best light the individual officer who passed final judgment on the preparation of those reports. Many times one general would comment emphatically on the conduct or feelings of another general, while a third officer would have something entirely different to say on the same matter which, of course, reflected *his* point of view.

Distressingly, this often carried over into the area of specific numbers. Thus if one spoke of the number of tanks in a panzer (armored) division, it was necessary to question the time period of that reference. A "Guderian division" of armor was *not* the same thing as a "Hitler division" of armor, and if one wishes to translate the tanks in a number of panzer divisions, it is necessary to specify the time.

When Guderian set up his panzer divisions in 1940, the order of battle for each division called for four battalions, each with 100 tanks. Every division thus had at least 400 tanks. But when Hitler (after ousting Guderian until the beginning of 1943) rearranged the panzer divisions, he diluted the strength of the panzers to a figure of 200 tanks and one battalion of self-propelled guns. It was hardly the same thing, of course. But even this was misleading, for with Guderian out of the picture the watering down of the panzer forces became almost disastrous.

As 1943 opened, there were eighteen panzer divisions on the Russian front. Under the 1940 order of battle this meant a total of 7,200 tanks. Admittedly this was an idealistic figure, but even with the dilution (during 1941 and 1942) to 200 tanks and 100 self-propelled guns, this meant that the eighteen divisions on the Russian front should have been able to muster 3,600 tanks and 1,800 self-propelled guns. In truth, when 1943 came around, there was a total of only 495 battle-worthy tanks for *all* eighteen divisions—or 27 tanks per division.

When Guderian was plucked from disgrace, he came roaring back into the midst of the German high command with tremendous new power and prestige placed on his shoulders by Hitler. Guderian's enemies, notably Kluge, viewed this triumphant return with undisguised distaste and no little hatred for the man. When Guderian laid the facts before Hitler, the latter had little choice but to yield to the reality of such numbers. He also found himself constrained to heed Guderian's insistence that all possible time must be spent in reequip-

ping and revitalizing the panzer forces. To do this, any offensive operations must be delayed—and such delays ran counter to the desires of many generals, including among them a number who flatly refused to believe Guderian's figures concerning the paucity of German armor.

One general who disagreed with Guderian in terms of delaying operations, but who apparently held the panzer leader in respect, was Manstein. He wanted nothing more than to break out of Kharkov and continue his pursuit of Russian forces that had recently taken a severe beating from his own divisions. But Manstein's great urge to renew the battle, as we have seen, went for naught.

So Hitler, where just these two men were involved, was directly in the center of opposing recommendations, Manstein wanting nothing more than to get on with the fighting and Guderian pointing out that if Manstein had his way in a local sector of the front lines, the Wehrmacht would be stripped of all ability to counter any Russian offensives.

The later subject created its own festering boil beneath Hitler's skin. Before he could commit, with proper planning, to his own offensive, he needed to have some idea of what the Russians planned, for any huge offensive on the part of the Red Army would require proper countermeasures by the Wehrmacht. But no one could reach conclusions about the Russian forces except on the basis of careful guesswork. The vaunted German intelligence system had run a cropper where the Russians were concerned. As Geoffrey Jukes states so well in his book *Kursk: The Clash of Armor,* "Soviet security was absolute, and there were consequently no German spies in the Soviet High Command."

Guesswork, no matter how educated and skillful, is still something on the order of crystal gazing. In Hitler's case this seemed more applicable than otherwise, for Hitler could not separate the personalities of the men with whom he met from their capabilities.

Guderian, in his new role of inspector general of armored troops, was on a whirlwind tour of army installations at that time when Kursk was being considered as the site for the major German offensive of the summer, and on March 29 Guderian met with Manstein and General Hermann Hoth (who commanded the Fourth Panzer

Army). The meeting was at Manstein's headquarters of Army Group South at Zaporozhye in Russia. When he later recalled that meeting, Guderian commented what a great pity it was that Hitler had to judge his men on personal issues. Indeed, Hitler had become almost blind to the brilliance of Manstein and, according to Guderian, could not even "tolerate the presence of so capable and soldierly a person as Manstein in his environment."

As Guderian emphasized, Hitler placed a great emphasis on personal magnetism. He was a man of extraordinary willpower, whose thoughts leaped to and fro through a fiery imagination. Not so Manstein, described by Guderian as "a man of most distinguished military talents, a product of the German General Staff Corps, with a sensible, cool understanding, who was our finest operational brain."

(Later in the war, when Guderian had become the chief of the army general staff, he pressed Hitler to place Manstein in the position of chief of the armed forces general staff. This would replace Field Marshal Wilhelm Keitel, a man who was quick to anticipate Hitler's moods and thoughts and was, of course, immensely satisfying on a personal level to the Reich leader. Hitler refused the suggestion by Guderian and offered an explanation that has elicited repeated adverse comments for many years since then. "Manstein," said Hitler, "is perhaps the best brain that the General Staff Corps has produced. But he can only operate with fresh, good divisions and not with the remnants of divisions which are all that is now available to us. Since I can't find him any fresh, operationally capable formations, there's no point in giving him the job.")

Guderian was fighting a series of personal battles on all sides in his attempts to revitalize the panzer divisions. On April 13 he was back in Berlin after his extensive tour and meetings with army and air force leaders. German hopes in Africa were being shredded before American and British firepower, and Guderian was extremely anxious to remove from Africa the tank crews who were left without weapons. To the old master of tank warfare, these men were even more important than the tanks, for they boasted many years' experience.

Hitler refused to authorize the mass evacuation of these crews for reasons of prestige, which no one really defined. Guderian argued that irreplaceable crews were being wiped out and that transport

aircraft were returning from Africa with empty holds. No argument would sway Hitler, and Guderian was to watch these outstanding men, whom he considered the finest armored fighting teams in the world, swallowed up in a war that was hopelessly lost—a debacle, Guderian was convinced, that could have made an enormous difference at Kursk.

Two days later Hitler issued his Operations Order Number Six. Germany was committed to massive confrontation with the Russians in the Kursk salient.

7

HITLER'S PLAN OF ATTACK

Operations Order Number Six, code name Citadel, dated April 15, 1943, carrying the signature of Adolf Hitler:

I have decided to undertake as the first priority offensive of this year the Citadel offensive, as soon as the weather permits. This offensive is of decisive importance. It must be carried out quickly and shatteringly. It *must* give us the initiative for the spring and summer of this year. Therefore all preparations are to be carried through with the greatest care and energy. The best formations, the best armies, the best leaders, great stocks of ammunition are to be placed at the decisive points. Every officer and every man must be indoctrinated with the decisive significance of this offensive. The victory of Kursk must be a signal to the world.

To this end I order:

1. The aim of the offensive is to encircle the enemy forces deployed in the Kursk area by means of incisive, coordinated, forward looking and quickly conducted advances by one attacking army each from the area of Belgorod and south of Orel, and annihilate them

through a concentric attack. In the course of the offensive a shortened front, which will liberate forces for use elsewhere, is to be gained along the line Neshega-Korocha (exclusive)-Skorodnoye-Tim-east of Shchigry-Sosna (exclusive).

2a. It follows from this that surprise must be maintained as far as possible and above all the enemy must be kept in doubt as to the time of the offensive.

2b. The offensive forces are to be centered on as narrow fronts as possible, so that with overwhelming local support in all means of attack (tanks, assorted guns, artillery, rocket mortars, etc.) they can smash through the enemy in one blow with both armies, and thus close the cauldron on him.

2c. To cover the strike forces as quickly as possible, forces are to be brought up for flank cover from the depth, so that the strike forces themselves need only to push *forwards*.

2d. By pushing in quickly from all sides *into the cauldron*, the enemy must be given no rest and his destruction hastened.

2e. The attack must be carried through *so fast* that the enemy is unable to break contact or to bring strong reserves from other fronts.

2f. Through speedy *construction of the new front*, to liberate forces, especially mobile formations, for further operations in quick time.

3. Army Group South is to break through the Belgorod-Tomarovka line . . . head eastwards and establish contact with the attacking arm of Army Centre near Kursk. To cover this attack from the east the line Neshega-Korocha exclusive-Skorodyne-Tim is to be reached as soon as possible . . . to cover the attack from the west, forces are to be allocated with the task of immediately pushing in to the cauldron as it is built up.

4. Army Group Center attacks . . . on the line Trosna-north of Maloarkhangelsk . . . to break through and establish contact with the attacking arm of Army Group South, near, and east of, Kursk. To cover the attack from the east, the line Tim-east of Shegreya-Sosna (exclusive) is to be reached as soon as possible provided that the forward impetus and concentration of force is not imperiled. Forces are to be allocated to cover the attack from the west.

The forces of Army Group Center operating from west of Trosna to the boundary of Army Group South are to tie up the enemy's strike forces from the moment the offensive begins, by means of local attacks, and then to push on into the cauldron in good time. Constant air and ground reconnaissance is to ensure that the enemy cannot disengage

without being noticed. If he does, a general offensive is to be mounted immediately along the whole front.

5. The preparation of forces of both Army Groups must utilize all possible means of camouflage, deception, and misinformation, so that from the 28th April on, an offensive can be undertaken within six days of receipt of an order from OKH. The earliest date for the offensive will be 3rd May. The march to the start line must be carried out only at night, and every possible means of camouflage is to be used.

6. To deceive the enemy the preparations for "Panther" are to go ahead in the area of Army Group South. They are to be strengthened by every means . . . and to be kept going as long as possible. These deception measures will be carried out in addition to those already in progress to increase the defensive capability of the front on the Donets. In the area of Army Group Center no large scale deception measures are to be carried out, but the enemy is to be given a confused picture of the situation in every way possible (by back and fore movements, by false movements, movement of transport by day and dissemination of false information suggesting that an attack is to take place no earlier than June).

In both Army Groups the formations newly brought up to reinforce the attack armies are to observe radio silence.

7. To preserve secrecy only essential personalities are to be identified, so that enemy espionage can be fought constantly.

8. Because of the reduced scale compared with earlier operations . . . the attack forces are to leave behind all vehicles and impedimenta which are not absolutely necessary . . . every commander must see that he takes with him all that is absolutely essential for battle. Commanding generals and divisional commanders must keep a strict and sharp control over this. Strict traffic control is to be established. They must push through without a backward look. . . .

10. The air force will concentrate all usable forces at the decisive points. Conferences with the command organizations of the air forces must begin at once. Special care will be taken to preserve secrecy.

11. For the success of the offensive, it is decisively important that the enemy does not succeed on other sectors of Army Groups South and Center, in nullifying Citadel, or compelling the attack formations to be withdrawn before time. Therefore, both Army Groups must, in addition to the Citadel offensive battle, prepare for a defensive battle on the remaining sectors of the front by the end of the

month. It is of primary importance here that sectors be made safe by all means, that those who are vulnerable to tank attack be well supplied with anti-tank defense, that local reserves be made ready, and that enemy preparations be learned in good time through ample reconnaissance of especially strong points.

12. It is envisaged as the final aim at the close of the operation that:

a. the boundary between Army Groups South and Center run on the general line Konotop (South)-Kursk (South)-Dolgoye (Center);

b. that Second Army with three general headquarters and nine infantry divisions plus troops of army subordination be transferred from Army Group Center to Army Group South;

c. that three further infantry divisions of Army Group Center be placed at OKH disposal in the area northwest of Kursk;

d. that the most mobile formations be withdrawn from the front for deployment elsewhere;

e. the movements, especially of formations of Second Army, are to be conducted with these views in mind. It is envisaged that in the course of the operation the units and staffs of various formations will be subordinated to Army Group South. I also envisage that if the operation turns out as planned the operation to the southeast (Panther) will be set in motion as soon as possible, to exploit the enemy's confusion.

13. The Army Groups will report what steps they have taken for attack and defense on the basis of this order, using the one in 300,000 maps. . . .

> [Signed]   *Adolf Hitler*
> Certified authentic: *Lieutenant-General Heusinger*

There was a terrible flaw in Operations Order Number Six. In reality, there were a number of grievous weaknesses, but one of these was so extraordinary as to make a major intent of the operational order an incredible mockery.

Item Number Seven stated: *"To preserve secrecy only essential personalities are to be identified, so that enemy espionage can be fought constantly."*

From almost the moment that the operations order began its dissemination to those units involved with the planned attack on the salient of Kursk, *Russian intelligence was aware of almost every*

detail, and Moscow was fully informed of the machinery already grinding its gears for the critical offensive.

Germany had no agents in the high command of Stalin, but the reverse situation existed. The Russians had available to them an extraordinary secret agent who provided Moscow with what amounted to a direct pipeline to Hitler's headquarters.

Lucy, the code name for the agent, kept the Russians on top of the situation almost as quickly as the Germans ended their staff conferences. The Russians knew so much about the German plans that even their most gifted general, Manstein, was wildly wrong in his assessments of what the Russians might attempt in the way of offensive operations in the Kursk area. Manstein was convinced that as soon as they were ready, the Russians would launch a major assault against German lines.

The Russians had, in fact, begun preparations for just such a move. Up to this point Manstein was proving himself once more the brilliant leader earned by his reputation in battle. But genius on the battlefield can sometimes be reduced to impotency by other factors, and this was indeed the case with the building clash at Kursk.

When the Russians learned through their secret agent that Operation Citadel was under way, they immediately abandoned their own plans for an offensive. They had intended to strike out against the Germans to eliminate *their* salient—the Donets bulge—but now found such a move far less appealing than to sit back and wait. Manstein and other battle commanders would be coming to them. The Germans would strike against the Kursk salient. Knowing well ahead of time the planned German moves, the Soviets would sit back and wait.

Lucy was, of course, a code name, the secret cover for a man named Rudolph Rossler. These pages are not the place for a detailed review of this incredible man, but suffice to say he was a German veteran of World War I who found Nazism revolting and felt that the only true service a German could offer to his country was to do everything possible to rid Germany of this dreadful force. Rossler and ten other Germans, also veterans of the war, were in unique, extraordinary positions to do something about their convictions. Rossler and his colleagues had remained in the skeleton military forces existing in Germany after their country's defeat in 1918. Of the ten men, eight

rose to vital positions in the armed forces high command (five of them were generals!), and the remaining two became high-ranking officers in the Luftwaffe.

Every one of these men never abandoned his hatred of the Nazis. Every one was determined to rid Germany of the foul touch of Adolf Hitler and his band of savages. Throughout the war they worked actively to destroy the Nazi regime. And they provided their impressive intelligence service directly from Berlin (through Rossler in Switzerland) to Moscow.

It would be impossible to overestimate the value of the Lucy Ring to the Soviet high command.

Two weeks before Hitler signed Operations Order Number Six, the top generals of the Soviet command were fully informed of the planning details of the forthcoming German offensive at Kursk. The Russians knew the particular divisions and units, the commanders, the planned number of weapons, and the anticipated dates of movement of German forces. Details of supply units, locations of airfields, quantities of ammunition—it was all there in a series of messages from Lucy.

Copies of Operations Order Number Six reached Zhukov and other Russian leaders before the same operations order was received by German army field commanders.

If the German staff in Berlin had known of the extent of Russian knowledge of their plans for Citadel, and especially had they known of the extraordinary defenses being prepared to meet their every move, there is no question that Hitler would have canceled Citadel before he sent the finest units remaining in the German army into the terrible holocaust Zhukov was preparing for the Wehrmacht.

8

THE INVASION DATE IS SET

On May 4, nearly three weeks after he issued his operational order for Citadel, Adolf Hitler convened a meeting in Munich with many of his top leaders to thrash out final problems of the attack against the Kursk salient.

Once again the historical events reflect individual attitudes, and the official papers and the memoirs of many of the German leaders attending this meeting are often in serious conflict with one another. Most records indicate quite clearly that the Munich assembly was called for the purpose of thrashing out final details of Operation Citadel. One key man who did not appear at the meeting was Model, but he was represented by a detailed letter in which he raised serious objections to the forthcoming attack on Kursk.

The gist of Model's argument was that Citadel was most likely doomed to failure before it started. Model quoted chapter and verse in terms of the formidable defenses being established in the Kursk salient by the Russians. He insisted that the German army divisions along that front were suffering from inequality in numbers. The

Russians were already so strong, he indicated, that they would be able to contain the best advances of the Wehrmacht and react quickly enough to rush in powerful reserves that could smash the German panzers and infantry divisions.

Manstein and Kluge took a divergent view. Citadel could be successful, they said, but only if the attack were begun at once. Further postponements inevitably shifted the balance of power to the Soviets, for Zhukov clearly was using every available day to gather more reinforcements.

What the official records (and some participants) state as the purpose of the meeting is strangely in variance with the personal memoirs of Guderian, who claims he did not come to the meeting to discuss the how and why of Citadel, but, as he says in his own words, "the problem under discussion was the extremely important one of whether Army Group Center and South would be in a position to launch an offensive on the Eastern Front in the foreseeable future—that is to say, during the coming summer of 1943." This is remarkable for its omission of any statement about the specifics to which the other participants make such clear reference.

According to Guderian—or at least this is the impression he gives—everyone concerned knew and accepted the fact that because of the Stalingrad disaster, and the "consequent defeat to the whole southern flank of the German front in the East, large-scale offensive operations seemed scarcely possible at this time." Guderian makes it clear that the meeting of May 4 was to decide whether or not Citadel would be carried out, and not (as most of the others stated) to wrap up final details.

Hitler opened the meeting with an uninterrupted speech of forty-five minutes which even his critics report was thorough, factual, and realistic as to the situation on the Russian front, and then threw open the conference for all possible considerations. Model, through his letter, was dead set against the Kursk attack. Kluge and Manstein hedged with the warning that the attack *could* be successful if it was started without further delay. Manstein, in fact, said the delay had already cost them dearly in the growth in Russian defense systems and that to carry out his part of the offensive with Army Group South he would

need two full-strength infantry divisions in addition to his forces already assembled.

As usual, Manstein was far from his best in a face-to-face meeting with Hitler, and received the curt reply that two more divisions simply were not available and that Manstein must perform with what he had. After his perfunctory reply, Hitler again put to Manstein the question of the Kursk attack. From the reports of those at the conference, Manstein mumbled more than answered, and Hitler went on to the others.

Keitel voted for the strike. Jodl insisted it was foolhardy. Zeitzler sensed that Hitler wanted the attack to take place, and he cast his recommendation to roll the tanks. Kluge went along with Hitler and Zeitzler.

Model in absentia voted against the Kursk offensive, so that Guderian was the only one in actual attendance who was unquestionably opposed to Citadel. Guderian told Hitler that the attack was "pointless" and that the German army was "certain to suffer heavy tank casualties, which we would not be in a position to replace. . . ." Guderian adds in his memoirs that only he and Albert Speer, the reichminister of armaments, were "bluntly opposed" to Citadel. The weight of the officials present, however, swung to supporting the attack.

Yet Hitler did not set a specific date. There was the serious matter of building the attack forces' strength in tanks, which everyone recognized had been seriously deficient. Hitler, as everyone knew, was entranced with numbers and with technology. Long before Kursk he had placed enormous faith in a new antitank shell with a hollow charge, which produced the Munroe jet effect by concentrating the explosive energy of the shell at a single point so that it could penetrate thick armor. It was much like the American bazooka, and Hitler believed it would give the German foot soldier and light mechanized units a powerful killing force against Russian tanks. Unfortunately for those who counted on high performance by the new projectile, it failed to live up to expectations. Yet those who knew Hitler recognized the symptoms. What Hitler now wanted was technological superiority in new tanks, for those tanks, he insisted, could turn the tide at Kursk and rout the Russians.

The führer's constant meddling in weapons systems was a thorn in the side of German production staffs and military commanders. Rather than leaving the field to the true experts, Hitler disdained the readily available advice of his engineers and technicians and chose to decide for himself what path would be followed in the manufacture of tanks and related weapons.

This was no idle matter, for it affected most seriously the plans for the Kursk battle and, indeed, was one of the prime factors in inducing Hitler to repeatedly delay the anticipated starting date of the offensive. Whatever he may have gained in increasing the available number of tanks for his forces on the front, he more than lost in handing to Zhukov the priceless gift of two months for the Russians to build up *their* strength. (With the Russians turning out approximately two thousand medium and heavy tanks every month, it is rather obvious what these delays meant in terms of the steady buildup of Soviet defenses in the Kursk salient.)

In the last months of 1942 German factories were turning out one hundred Pzkw IV tanks every month. Increased production of this tank was assured, but to no one's great joy, because the Pzkw IV was a weapon that was sorely deficient in terms of performance. Except for the increased firepower of the latest version, the Pzkw IV was inferior in handling, maneuverability, reliability, defense, and speed to the Russian T-34 tank.

New tanks were, of course, of the utmost priority for the German army, but management problems, arguments over varying engineering techniques, and Hitler's constant interference in even the smallest details of tank design, modification, testing, and manufacture slowed down production. More distressing to his generals who desperately wanted more and better tanks was Hitler's insistence that many engineers spend their time in devising new superweapons of which he was so fond.

Hitler was obsessed with tanks of massive weight and had ordered the rapid development of one-hundred-ton tanks. What drove his armored commanders to distraction was that his frenzied support for tanks could evaporate overnight as a result of some unexpected influence, such as the army had experienced early in 1942.

At that time a group of key artillery officers had gained Hitler's con-

fidence and convinced him that self-propelled guns—great artillery pieces mounted on tank bodies (but without the complicated turret mechanism)—were far superior to the standard tank. Hitler personally stepped into the production end of things. He ordered a number of production lines to convert from tanks to these self-propelled guns. At the same time, recognizing the need for tanks as well, he issued a directive that tank production be stepped up to six hundred units per month.

By the summer of 1942, just one year before Kursk would dominate Hitler's thinking, the matter of tank design, development, and production had degenerated into utter confusion. The factories were turning out tanks the armored commanders were discovering to be inferior to the Russian T-34. They needed better tanks, and they needed them quickly and in quantity.

Instead, much of the effort of those responsible for the new tanks was expended in meeting Hitler's constantly changing demands. In the advanced development stage were three new main designs—a heavy tank, the famed Tiger; a medium tank known as Panther; and a light reconnaissance tank called Leopard, which never made it out of the testing grounds, thus leaving the new heavy and medium tanks, the Tiger and the Panther.

Each tank existed in two competitive versions. While hair-splitting at this moment may seem to beggar the issue of the Battle of Kursk, the competitive aspects of the German tanks turned out to be critical because no one seemed able to decide which of the competing designs (for the heavy and medium class) should be rushed into production.

The Mark VI Tiger existed in two versions—Porsche and Henschel. The Porsche version, known as Tiger P, was actually produced by the Krupp Company and was immediately branded a loser by tank experts and crews because it was difficult to maneuver under rough field conditions. It also suffered from a disastrous error in design, as has been noted, in that it lacked secondary (machine gun) armament, being equipped solely with its main cannon.

Adding to the confusion was the fact that many of the Krupp-manufactured (Porsche) Tigers were kept from entering active service. Their shortcomings as a tank were considered so severe that the vehicles were drastically modified into a tank destroyer with no turret,

and an exposed long-barrel L71 88-mm. gun. These models were known as the Ferdinand. What is so difficult to understand is that the serious weakness of the Porsche Tiger—the lack of secondary armament—was repeated in the Ferdinand!

The Tiger produced by Henschel was clearly a better weapon than its competitor manufactured by Krupp. The Henschel Mark VI was almost invulnerable to attack from the front because of its heavy armor; it maneuvered well, its main armament was an L56 88-mm. converted flak gun (probably the best weapon of its type and size produced by any country during the entire war), and it had two machine guns as secondary armament.

But the bright and shining light held aloft by the panzer leaders was the new Panther, the Panzerkampfwagen V. The Panther (described as both a medium and a heavy tank, depending upon the source) weighed some forty-five tons in combat dress, had a most effective 75-mm. gun as well as three machine guns, and was considered by the army general staff as the finest weapon of its type ever produced. The truth of the matter was that the best characteristics of the finest German *and* Russian tanks had gone into the Panther, which fitted into the category of a "second generation" weapon.

But the Panthers failed to materialize in numbers sufficient to affect the projected fighting in the Kursk area. At the meeting of May Hitler learned that despite all the great promises from his production experts, no more than 130 Panthers had been produced, and of the number fewer than 100 had actually been delivered to army units. Hitler was infuriated by this news, for he had been promised that at least 250 tanks would be in the hands of combat crews by the end of May.

The critical decisions affecting tank production and delivery—and consequently the fixed date for opening the Battle for Kursk—appear to have been made on May 10 in Berlin. At this meeting, which included Guderian, Speer explained to Hitler that early production difficulties with the Panther had been overcome. Not only would the original target date of the end of May, with its 250 tanks, be met, but no fewer than 324 Panthers would be delivered. All well and good, for the Kursk offensive needed the Panthers desperately. But again time was being eaten away. For the Panthers to be included in the battle, they must be rushed to the front and placed in combat units.

That meant another two weeks after delivery, so Hitler established a tentative date of June 13 for the Kursk offensive.

There was a separate issue to be decided involving Hitler and Guderian—and Kursk. On May 1, ten days before the convocation in Berlin, Guderian incurred Hitler's wrath because of a technical decision he had made. Hitler had gone to the Krupp works to inspect a wooden mockup of a new tank called the Mouse, a massive creation of Professor Porsche that was to weigh 175 tons and mount a huge 150-mm. cannon. Those present at the inspection waxed enthusiastic about the gigantic Mouse. All except Guderian, that is. He spoke of the tank with derision. It had the same fatal weakness of other Porsche designs—no secondary armament.

Guderian exercised his authority and ordered that the Mouse not be allowed into further development, let alone production. He left that meeting as the unquestioned subject of bitterness and even open hatred, for he had assailed Porsche for stupidity in planning tanks and self-propelled guns that were helpless without secondary armament.

But the issue of the tanks was still not settled. At the Berlin meeting of May 10 Guderian waited until the conference ended to have a discussion with Hitler. He urged the German leader "to give up the plan for an attack on the Eastern Front." Guderian spelled out his reasons for branding the Citadel offensive as a programmed disaster for Germany and asked Hitler directly: "Why do you want to attack in the East at all this year?"

The answer came, not from Hitler, but from Keitel. "We must attack for political reasons."

Guderian was incredulous and made no attempt to disguise his reaction. "How many people do you think even know where Kursk is?" he demanded. "It's a matter of profound indifference to the world whether we hold Kursk or not."

Guderian turned from Keitel to address Hitler, and again he asked: "Why do we want to attack in the East at all this year?"

Keitel kept his silence as Hitler looked directly at Guderian. "You're quite right," he told Guderian. "Whenever I think of this attack my stomach turns over."

"In that case," Guderian said quickly, "your reaction to the problem is the correct one. Leave it alone!"

The Panther tank had problems other than those connected with production. Any new weapon is plagued by development bugs during its early months of operation, and the Panther was no exception. Some of the problems, as detailed by Guderian, concerned unsatisfactory performance of the track suspension and the drive. The optics systems also were faulty. All would be worked out in good time, but the ensuing interval would be too great to permit the inclusion of the Panther as a *reliable* weapon for the Kursk offensive.

June 13 came and went, and still the offensive was put off. Guderian (and other experts) did their best to persuade Hitler not to commit untested equipment to battle. Not only were the Panthers giving their crews headaches, but there were also serious problems with the Porsche-designed Tiger tanks and Ferdinand self-propelled guns.

None of these three weapons—Panther, Tiger P, or Ferdinand—had even completed its acceptance tests by the German army. Nevertheless, Hitler's final decision was to commit every piece of armor to the fight. Everything Guderian had tried to do went for naught.

One would expect that after his comment to Guderian on May 10 that even the thought of the Kursk offensive made him ill, Hitler might well have decided, because of all the serious complications surrounding the operation, to cancel the long-planned attack. Such was not the case. Mellinthin, a capable, even gifted armored leader, states emphatically that it was the pressure of Keitel and Zeitzler that brought Hitler to override all other considerations and commit Germany to the awesome gamble of Citadel.

Mellinthin reports that for the two months before it was finally committed to opening its first barrage, Operation Citadel was a pall that affected everything the combat leaders had to do on the eastern front. Mellinthin offers an unusual explanation for some of the machinations behind Citadel to the effect that Hitler never really believed in the operation, that his intuition warned him to stop the attack before it ever started. Somewhat dryly, Mellinthin adds that this was one time Hitler's "intuition did not play him false."

By the middle of June, the invasion hour having come and gone, Hitler established another "firm" date to open Citadel—on July 4. It was to be a date, remarked the chief of staff of the XLVIII Panzer

Corps in a blunt appreciation of what Citadel was all about, that was "Independence Day for America and the beginning of the end for Germany."

The "beginning of the end," however, was to be launched with a combination of finely honed German steel and the mumbling of the supreme leader in the background. On July 1 Hitler brought together the senior commanders who would be directly involved in Citadel, so that they could thrash out any final problems. Nothing was to be left to chance. Rather than the intense strategic and tactical discussions one would expect on the eve of such a battle—then only three days away—Hitler wandered off into one of the monologues for which he had gained no little ill fame among his subordinates.

His audience heard that Citadel was not merely the product of the military situation, but rather the inevitable result of failure on the part of so many surrounding him. The war situation had deteriorated because the Italians had eroded the solid foundation of all his plans, and they, in truth, were responsible for almost every misfortune that had befallen Germany. As Hitler rambled on, he decided to include in his list of the damned Romania and Hungary as well, which had turned out to be unspeakably unreliable and therefore never to be trusted. Finland was another matter, since that small country was almost totally exhausted and no longer could be relied upon to provide its share of the fighting along its front with the Russians. All about him, Hitler grumbled, Germany was being denied the support of its "friends."

Hitler emphasized that "at all costs" Germany must not yield an inch of the conquered territory, for the Reich could not exist without this land and its resources, both physical and human. Every German soldier must know that it was for these reasons he was fighting and that where he now faced the enemy, that is where he must remain without retreating. To give up the Balkans was something he would not countenance, and the worthless Italian troops there must be replaced with German forces. Under no circumstances would Crete be yielded so that the enemy could turn it into another huge air base from which to send bombers to strike at German industry.

Russia, he warned his leaders, held many grave problems in store for them. But the time was ripe for Citadel, and in what came as a

shock to all present, Hitler seemed totally unaware of all the warnings he had received about growing Russian strength and said that the Red Army would lie dormant through the summer, biding its time, preparing for a major offensive in the winter. Thus, *now* was the time to smash the enemy.

Orel was a salient deep in the Russian line (the reverse of Kursk being a salient deep in the German line), and there was no intention of relinquishing this ground to the Red Army. The Reich had the advantage in the Orel salient of tying up a great force of the Russians. The Russians did not know how to conduct an orderly retreat, and therefore they must be hit immediately. In the rout that would follow the German attack, the panzers could utterly destroy the fleeing enemy forces.

Yet, Hitler admitted, the Russians possessed great strength, and Citadel was a gamble. Suddenly the führer seemed to be fully aware of all the dire warnings from many of his generals that Citadel constituted a grave risk. But such warnings were based on paper studies and on numbers, he said, and it was his belief in victory that would make all the difference. He reminded those present that it was against all military advice and the findings of the general staff that he had made the decision to envelop Austria, to sweep into Czechoslovakia, to smash Poland, and to crush the Russian army.

On the afternoon of July 4 the Wehrmacht would strike. The whole world would once again be taught the power of the German army.

9

THE GERMANS MASS
FOR THE ATTACK

Let none of the behind-the-scenes machinations of the Reich cloud
the issue.

Operation Citadel was no military pauper. The Wehrmacht had
been badly mauled in two years of fighting with the Russians, but
there remained a tremendous cutting edge of German steel for the
offensive against the Kursk salient.

It is also true that compared to the major offensives of 1941 and
1942, Citadel appears to represent only a nominal effort on the part
of Germany to destroy the enemy arrayed against its armored divisions. On paper especially does this seem valid, for in 1941 the Nazis
invaded Russia with eleven armies spread along a front of 1,200
miles, and in 1942 they used six armies to strike along a front of 450
miles. Citadel, in 1943, encompassed three armies prepared to thrust
forward along a front of only 150 miles.

Such numbers can be deceiving. Citadel represented an enormous
reduction in the combat area—and especially the distance of the front
line—from former offensives, and this very fact enhanced the striking

power of the divisions involved. They would be able to concentrate their firepower by massing heavy weapons along a lesser front. Supply lines would be shorter, easier to protect. Any unfavorable situation stood a better chance of being speedily corrected because of the shorter distances involved.

The final delay—from June 13 to July 4—enabled the Germans to rush an additional two battalions of Panther tanks to Model's divisions along the northern front, as well as the Panthers that had been assigned to the southern sectors.

In its broadest sense, Army Group A in the Crimea and Army Group North were to remain on the strategic defensive. All possible forces were to be concentrated on the left of Army Group South and the right of Army Group Center for a converging assault on the Kursk salient.

The attack was to be made by Fourth Panzer Army from the south. In the north would be Ninth Army; the two forces were to strike out toward one another and meet east of Kursk, thus cutting off the city from Soviet reinforcements and trapping a huge force of the Red Army within the closed pincers.

The Fourth Panzer Army would deliver its main thrust on both sides of Tomarovka, with a strike on the left by the XLVIII Panzer Corps and a strike on the right by the S.S. Panzer Corps. The latter force had been supplied with three panzer divisions—Leibstandarte, Totenkopf, and Das Reich. There would also be the effect of Army Detachment Kempf, with a single panzer corps and two infantry corps at its disposal; Kempf was to move in a northeasterly direction toward Belgorod and provide flanking cover for the main assault. Included in the XLVIII Panzer Corps were the 3d and 11th panzer divisions and P.G.D. Gross Deutschland.

Gross Deutschland provides an excellent look at a key German force that dismisses any nonsense that the German units had been scraped from the bottom of some mythical barrel. General Mellinthin makes special note of this organization, which included some 180 tanks. These were not the familiar vehicles, but 80 new Panthers in a single strike force, with the remaining 100 tanks assigned to the panzer regiment. An indication of what such an organization involves is pro-

vided by a breakdown of the remaining units, which included an artillery regiment with four detachments, an antitank detachment, an assault gun detachment, an engineer battalion, and a scattering of units through the main organization made up of communications, transport, supply, maintenance, administrative, and similar services.

A special study of the Kursk operation, carried out by the United States Army, shows for the summer of 1943 the following order of battle of German forces on the Russian front:

| ARMY GROUPS | DIVISIONS | | |
	Panzer	Other Types	Total
ARMY GROUP NORTH (Kuechler)			
Reserve	1		1
Eighteenth Army (Lindemann)		24	24
Sixteenth Army (Busch)		12	12
Total Divisions/Army Group North	1	36	37
ARMY GROUP CENTER (Kluge)			
Reserve	5	2	7
Third Panzer Army (Reinhardt)	1	6	7
Fourth Army (Heinrici)		18	18
Second Panzer Army (Schmidt)	1	13	14
Ninth Army (Model)	4	14	18
Second Army (Weiss)		7	7
Total Divisions/Army Group Center	11	60	71
ARMY GROUP SOUTH (Manstein)			
Fourth Panzer Army (Hoth)	6	4	10
Army Kempf (Kempf)	3	6	9
First Panzer Army (Mackensen)	3	9	12
Sixth Army (Hollidt)	1	9	10
Total Divisions/Army Group South	13	28	41
ARMY GROUP A (Kleist)			
Reserve	1	1	2
Seventeenth Army (Hoeppner)		10	10
Total Divisions/Army Group A	1	11	12
TOTAL DIVISIONS/EASTERN FRONT	26	135	161

German divisions in other theaters of war in July 1943 included seven in Finland, twelve in Norway and Denmark, twenty-five in France and the Low Countries, three in Sicily and Italy, and eight in the Balkans.

The divisions on the eastern front in July 1943, then, represented approximately 75 percent of the total strength of the German army, which lends hard credence to the insistence of the Russians that *they* were carrying the brunt of the land war against the common enemy.

Figures taken from Russian forces provide still another indicator of the awesome power assembled by the Germans for their attack on the Kursk salient.

In the north the Ninth Army, with 1,500 tanks and 3,000 pieces of artillery, was able to concentrate 4,500 troops, 40 to 50 tanks, and 70 to 80 pieces of artillery for each kilometer of its forty-kilometer attack zone. (One kilometer is approximately 6/10 of one mile.)

The Fourth Panzer Army, deployed on an eighty-kilometer front north of Kharkov, had some 1,700 tanks and 2,000 pieces of artillery, with 3,000 men, 40 tanks, and 50 pieces of artillery per kilometer of front in the zone of its main effort.

The total assembly of Nazi forces assigned specifically for the attack on the Kursk salient, and scheduled to strike hard along some sixty miles of front lines (with each main force having as its goal an advance of thirty-five miles, which would let them close the pincers on the salient), added up to thirty-five divisions equipped with 2,700 tanks and self-propelled guns.

The total involvement of manpower breaks down into two groups —570,000 men were involved in the main combat assault force, and 230,000 troops were aligned within the so-called quiet sectors of the front—for a German manpower force of 900,000.

In addition to the 2,700 tanks and self-propelled guns, these divisions had 10,000 pieces of artillery poised to open the battle.

Two German air fleets would cover the immediate battlefront, with approximately 2,050 fighters and bombers between them. Another 500 aircraft were available for support and replacement.

These are only numbers. The status of the men and their conditions as soldiers is as vital as the columns of figures. Mellinthin makes this

Soviet troops attacking in the region of Kazachyi Lisitsy in 1943. *(Novosti Press Agency)*

Soviet soldiers on the front roads during the Battle of Kursk. *(Photo by B. Kudoyarov, Novosti Press Agency)*

From Belgorod to the Carpathians. After forcing the Dniester, tankmen fight their way forward. *(Photo by Pedkin, Sovfoto)*

Soviet troops fighting German tanks near a Russian village. German tank on fire is seen at left. *(Sovfoto)*

Lieutenant F. Loginov (foreground) commanded an antitank rifle platoon. His unit destroyed two medium tanks, two antitank guns, three machine guns, and killed twenty-five German officers and men. *(Novosti Press Agency)*

Combined attack of Soviet tanks and planes. *(Sovfoto)*

Soviet Katyusha rocket launchers at firing positions. *(Novosti Press Agency)*

Soviet self-propelled guns and tanks in battle-scarred town. *(Novosti Press Agency)*

Soviet infantry and tanks in action against the enemy. *(Sovfoto)*

Russian Stormovik ground-attack planes strike hard at German supply con voys with clear results (left) on road leading to Kursk salient. *(Novosti Press Agency)*

Ilyushin-2 assault planes on an attack assignment.
(Novosti Press Agency)

Russian self-propelled artillery during barrage of German lines. *(Novosti Press Agency)*

Russian troops breaking from cover to attack German strongholds. *(Novosti Press Agency)*

clear when he states that many groups prepared for the struggle had "a striking power [they were] never to see again." He points out, as well, that "for the first and last time during the Russian campaign the divisions enjoyed a few weeks' rest before the attack, and were up to full strength in personnel and equipment."

On July 2 Russian units across the lines from the German forces gathering their strength for the assault were alerted for possible attack by the enemy. The Soviet high command estimated that the Germans would most likely make their move sometime between July 3 and 6 and sent appropriate warnings to the Russian front lines.

Small events make for great battles. And it was on the night of July 3 that such an event unleashed a tremendous artillery bombardment along the Kursk front.

The incident involved one man. He was a specialist with an engineer battalion of the Nazi LII Army Corps. He was a Czech, and he seized an opportunity to desert the companionship of his German "friends." Not too rare an incident, except that this particular man had a small tale to tell that was of enormous consequence. The German troops, said the Czech, had just received a special issue of rations and schnapps to last them for five days without resupply.

That information was enough for the Soviet command to break its battle silence. Medium artillery units received their orders to open fire, and for four hours they poured a hellish barrage against the German lines. It was significant that the Russians ordered all antitank units to remain silent.

The German troops dug deeper and held on while the sky turned savagely red all about them. Sometime during the night they were alerted for a special message from Adolf Hitler:

> Soldiers of the Reich!
> This day you are to take part in an offensive of such importance that the whole future of the war may depend on its outcome. More than anything else, your victory will show the whole world that resistance to the power of the German Army is hopeless.

Was Hitler whistling in the dark?

A study of the final disposition of forces indicates otherwise, that Hitler had come to believe, *along with many of his generals,* that

the German army stood an excellent chance of achieving its main objective at Kursk—to cut off the Russian forces in the salient and decimate them.

Mellinthin has stressed the high morale of the German soldier, the fact that he was properly equipped, that he was well rested and fit for the operation. Mellinthin also represents a group of German combat leaders who continued to state, even after the war (and this is against the tide of their contemporaries), that the Tiger tank and the new Panther were unquestionably the qualitative superior of the Russian tanks they opposed. There is another point to be made. Despite the enormous Russian gains in numbers of weapons, the Germans entered the Kursk battle with near parity in numbers of tanks and self-propelled guns.

That parity was even closer in aircraft, the difference in numbers being 2,500 German to an admitted Russian force of 2,650. And there wasn't a German flying who didn't know that his equipment was superior to that of the Russian and that the average German pilot could fly rings around his Soviet opponents.

Even the attitude of local commanders was such as to give the German troops confidence that they would emerge the victor in the Kursk fighting. The Germans were so determined to press home their attacks and close the pincers that they accepted before the battle the risk of heavy losses in armor. The tankers had received sobering orders that

> . . . *in no circumstances* will tanks be stopped to render assistance to those which have been disabled. Recovery is the responsibility of engineer units *only*. Tank commanders are to press on to their objective as long as they retain mobility. Where a tank is rendered immobile but the gun is in working order (e.g., from mechanical failure or track damage), the crew will continue to give fire support from a static position.

Consider, his generals told Hitler, the special circumstances of this battle. Never in the war so far had German armored forces failed to penetrate Russian lines at the very outset of combat. Every time the panzers had struck they had succeeded in their objectives—punching a gaping hole in the Russian lines. The problems suffered by the

Wehrmacht had never resulted from the panzers. It was long after a battle had been joined, and the German army was in hot pursuit, that they ran into their terrible difficulties. The fields and steppes of Russia were so enormous, and the advances made by the panzers and supporting divisions so great, that the Wehrmacht had literally outrun its ability to keep itself supplied.

But the important thing to remember, Hitler was told again and again, was that the panzers had *never* failed to crack the Russian lines. This time, at Kursk, there would be no danger of the advancing Wehrmacht running out of steam, for there would be no long-distance advance, no perilously stretched supply lines, no thin flanks for the Russians to pierce. This time the whole mighty blow of the army would be kept to no more than seventy miles, and the maneuver could be accomplished, as it had always been, in a swift, devastating march of unstoppable power.

Until the final moment, with the only break in their preparations the savage pummeling by Russian artillery the night of July 3–4, German troopers readied themselves. The soldiers in the field were of course completely unaware of the effectiveness of Soviet intelligence as to Citadel (as was Hitler and his staff), and every man in the front lines attended to his duties with the strictest adherence to orders. All panzer officers, as they had been directed, discarded their easily identified black uniforms before moving anywhere near the front. Anyone who went to the most forward positions did so with every effort bent to avoid identification of his particular unit by the enemy. What the Germans saw in this forward reconnaissance was not endearing to them, for out from their trenches there extended

a far-flung plain, broken by numerous valleys, small copses, irregularly laid out villages with thatched roofs, and some rivers and brooks; of these the Pena ran with a swift current between steep banks. The ground rose slightly to the north, thus favoring the defender. Large cornfields covered the landscape, making visibility difficult.

Panzer commanders wished fervently for clear, dry weather, for the area on which the battle would be fought counted its roads as little

more than rutted tracks through sand. As Mellinthin emphasized, it was far from even passable tank country, but it certainly was not "tank proof." German hopes were raised when the weather teams predicted excellent weather for the opening day of the assault.

The Germans, with the delays brought on by Hitler's repeated postponement of Citadel, put to excellent use the unexpected two months of front-line preparation. Not a single detail had been omitted in getting set for the assault. Every square yard of the Kursk salient had been photographed by German reconnaissance planes, and the prints were distributed throughout the forces of Citadel. Infantry and armor officers had spent days in studying with field glasses every detail of the land before them. They had marked on their charts trenches, strongpoints, armor—everything. German officers were brought to the most forward positions in order that they might personally scan the Russian terrain.

By day German transport and armor lay quiescent beneath camouflage. The land was still. The nights were a different matter, and through every available hour of darkness the Wehrmacht shifted and moved and readied itself.

No detail was left wanting in the preparations for air-ground cooperation. Wherever it was possible to do so, the Luftwaffe stripped its other fronts of fighters and bombers and moved them into the area where Citadel would be fought. In the south, in the area of Belgorod, General Hans Seidmann had an outstanding front-line combat force of one thousand fighters, bombers, ground-attack and antitank planes. This force would support Hoth's Fourth Panzer Army, now bristling with greater armor and firepower than any German force had ever known. Model's Ninth Army in the north was covered by Major General Paul Deichmann's 1st Air Division, stationed in the Orel area, with a front-line force (exclusive of reserves) of seven hundred aircraft of all combat types.

When the attack signal was given, *all* seventeen hundred planes were to be in the air, sweeping across the Russian defenses from directly ahead of the advancing German troops to the full limit of the defense systems of the Red Army.

The main headquarters for the fighting in the Belgorod area was at Mikoyanovka, only twenty miles from the front lines. Five airfields

in the Kharkov region were jammed with planes, and their crews were ready to start rolling within minutes of the signal to fly.

There was nothing left to do in the way of preparing for the attack. Never had there been a major combat operation, states Mellinthin, that "could have been better prepared than this one. . . . The morale of the attacking troops was of the highest; they were prepared to endure any losses and carry out every task given them."

Citadel was ready.

Part III

The Russians

10

SOVIET DEFENSE PREPARATIONS

No one ever said he was kind. He was never known for anything that remotely touched on consideration. Indeed, he had always seemed more machine than man, a being dedicated totally to what he felt must be done. He seemed to be oblivious to death on even a staggering scale, no matter if those who died were his own men or the enemy. Only one thing mattered to Marshal Georgi Zhukov, and that was the objective.

He acknowledged only one god—unflinching devotion to duty. Anything less deserved even worse than his contempt—the firing squad. He accepted no excuses, nor did he ever offer any. He was above all else severely meticulous in all his actions. He left nothing to chance, and he punished, often with fatal results, those who failed him.

Yet he was responsible for more German fatalities than any other man or group of men in World War II. He was responsible for breaking the German wherever he met him. He may never have inspired the adulation of his men, but he earned their fierce respect. He was brutal, gifted, brilliant.

We too have our ranks of military greats. General George Patton springs to mind. There is Field Marshal Bernard L. Montgomery and General Douglas MacArthur. Guderian is considered one of the great masters in armored warfare. So is General Erwin Rommel. There are other military giants. Admiral Chester W. Nimitz, General Dwight D. Eisenhower, Lieutenant Colonel James H. Doolittle. How many students, to whom World War II is now musty history, recognize at once the name of Georgi Zhukov? How many know who he was, what he did? How many are aware that this is the man, best described by Harrison E. Salisbury, who "will stand above all others as the master of the art of mass warfare in the twentieth century."

Zhukov's extraordinary record against the best that Nazi Germany could throw against the Russians is all the more astounding when the battles fought under his command are studied. For Zhukov rarely enjoyed the advantage in any given situation. Indeed, he was the true "fireman" of the Russian front in that when all else had failed, when the other generals were being beaten, when disaster rose from the battlefield to drown the defenders, that is when Stalin called for Zhukov. He came to such arenas with his military genius, his iron temper, his determination that never accepted any but his own will—and he transformed disaster into checkmate, and salvation into thundering victory.

In the final days of August and the early days of September 1941, when the German war machine pulverized all before its mighty armored divisions, it was Zhukov who gave the Russians their first bright moment of victory in a sea that held only dark and terrible defeat. The Battle of Yelnya, a savage, clawing struggle fought 220 miles west of Moscow and fifty miles southeast of Smolensk, was the handwork of Zhukov. For the first time the Germans were stopped in their tracks and mauled by the Russian defenders.

But it was the next towering struggle that was to cement this man as perhaps the greatest expert of all time in mass war. From October 1941 into January 1942, when all the world expected the Russians to go down to bloody defeat at the hand of the German invaders, Zhukov directed the Battle of Moscow.

Then came the Battle of Stalingrad, from August 1942 into February 1943. After this savage engagement the Germans prepared for

the blow they needed so desperately to regain the initiative—the Battle of Kursk. And once again it would be the heavy, unstoppable, merciless hand of Zhukov that would be felt all across the battlefield.

Each of these enormous conflicts represents a pattern that seems almost unbroken from one to the other. In each battle Zhukov commanded more than a million men, usually twenty armies or more at a single time. The numbers of tanks are legendary. Starting with Kursk, he had at his disposal the first Russian self-propelled guns. He was not simply excessive with his use of massed artillery; he believed in the dense, shattering effect of firepower overkill. Every manner of long-range weapon was brought into his battles, from mortars to massed rocket assault.

More than numbers, he believed in concentrations of firepower. He assembled every machine that could fly and was combat-worthy for his air cover. He used land mines by the tens of thousands for limited areas. And men were the same as the weapons with which they fought; they were simply another weapon. They were to be honed to the finest degree possible, they were given the best equipment, and they were sent en masse onto the field of combat. They were ciphers. Zhukov had no compunction about Russian casualties in any struggle —just so long as the objective was reached, the enemy was crushed, the battle was won.

It is difficult to argue with this reasoning. Had Zhukov not been the man he is, had Zhukov not acted as he did, it is likely that the crucial battles that Russia fought and won might have been lost—and with the loss of Russia we could well have counted the loss of *all* Europe.

Zhukov was no latecomer to war when finally he was sent to extricate his country from a Germany determined to crush the Soviet Union. His family counted professional soldiers as far back as anyone could remember. In World War I he fought bravely and brilliantly and emerged with not one, but two, of the highest decorations for valor under combat to be awarded by the czarist government. In 1919 as a member of the Bolshevik party he fought fierce battles against the White Russians at Tsaritsyn. Wounded, already earning the attention of his superiors, he was sent after the civil war to a series of special military schools and academies.

Zhukov was no stranger to the Germans—from either side. Early in the 1930s he went secretly to Germany with a select group of officers from the Red Army to learn advanced tactics and doctrine under General Hans von Seeckt. School was one thing; Spain was another. The armored battles fought by the Germans, Italians, and Russians were observed closely by Zhukov.

After Spain there came special duty with a military mission in China. This brought exposure to, and observation of, the Kwantung Army of Japan, which stood him in good stead when he fought the Japanese in 1939 and virtually disemboweled the enemy. Mongolia cost the Russians dearly in losses incurred under Zhukov. But no one really complained. The Japanese had been routed and they left the field of battle with the shock waves reaching all the way to Tokyo.

Zhukov had been questioned about the tremendous losses of his own men. The question to him seemed specious. How does one win battles and a war without casualties?

"If we come to a mine field," he once told Eisenhower, "our infantry attack exactly as if it were not there. The losses we get from personnel mines we consider only equal to those we would have gotten from machine guns and artillery if the Germans had chosen to defend the area with strong bodies of troops instead of mine fields."

The philosophy of the man who would command the Soviet forces in the Battle of Kursk was crystal clear well before the Germans launched their attack. Zhukov's presence significantly influenced the nature of the struggle. This was one of the primary reasons why Manstein was finally so adamant against the German army continuing with Operation Citadel. Manstein knew that with Zhukov in the picture, most especially with the dividend of two months given to him by Hitler's procrastination, the Red Army defenses would be impossible to overwhelm. But by then it was too late, and Manstein fatalistically went into the horrendous assault.

On page 13 of his introduction to *Marshal Zhukov's Greatest Battles* (Harper & Row, 1969), Harrison Salisbury provides the incisive summation of how Zhukov fought:

Zhukov's way of fighting a battle—and it may have been a way dictated as much by necessity as design—was to let the enemy extend

himself, to wait until the last moment of the German offensive momentum, and then to grind the Nazis down in terrible bloody exchanges as they drove in for their objective. Meanwhile, despite fearful Russian losses and the dangerous German penetration, Zhukov cautiously, carefully, and painstakingly massed reserve armies which he refused to commit to action, no matter what the peril at the front. Then, at the moment when the German strength was spent he would unleash his counterblow with dramatic rapidity—often within forty-eight hours of a German pause and before the Nazis were able to establish a reliable defense.

Earlier we saw the contents of Hitler's Operations Order Number Six, which was issued to German commanders on April 15, 1943; this operations order, as was also noted, reached the Soviet high command through its Lucy espionage contact in Switzerland. But no Russian in his right mind could accept verbatim the material being delivered from Berlin. There was always the chance that such material was being sent deliberately and that the Russians might be drawn into a trap of monumental proportions. The high command acted in the only sensible manner. Everything from Lucy was considered, and then intensive reconnaissance of the German lines and rear areas was begun.

Through the study of the Russian preparations for the Battle of Kursk one point becomes clear. The Germans have long held the reputation for being methodical, for efficiency, for leaving nothing undone in their preparations for combat. All this is true enough, but what is not evident is that the Russians exceeded their enemies in detail and thoroughness of preparation.

With the information from Lucy fed into the hopper with reconnaissance and intelligence reports from the front, Zhukov was able by April 8—one week *before* Operations Order Number Six went out from Berlin—to provide a careful assessment of the growing assembly of the Wehrmacht for its Citadel offensive. This is the message sent by Zhukov to Stalin:

1. Because of their losses during the winter of 1942–43 the Germans will be unable to make another attempt at seizing the Caucasus, or advancing to the Volga with the aim of encircling Moscow. The

state of their reserves is such that they will require the whole of the spring and the first half of the summer to assemble forces large enough for an attack on Moscow by the shortest possible route.

2. In the first stage they will probably attack with maximum forces, including thirteen to fifteen Panzer divisions, against the Kursk salient, attempting to pinch it off with an attack from the Orel-Kromy area north of the salient, and from Belgorod to the south of it. A secondary attack, aimed at splitting the South-West Front, can be expected from the Vorozhba direction, coming up between the Seym and Psel Rivers, to aim at Kursk from the southwest. The object of this first stage offensive will be to defeat and encircle the Soviet Thirteenth, Twenty-First, Thirty-Eighth, Sixtieth, Sixty-Fifth and Seventieth Armies.

3. In the second stage the Germans will attempt to get behind the flank and rear of South-West Front by moving along a line through Valuyki and Urazovo, and attacking northwards from Lisichansk.

4. In the third stage the Germans will regroup, then probably try to advance to the Liski-Voronezh-Yelets line, cover themselves against attack from the southeast and organize a strike to outflank Moscow from the southeast through Ranenburg, Ryazhsk and Ryazan.

5. Because of the losses in infantry trained for offensive operations, the main weight of attack will be borne by tanks and aircraft. A total of 2,500 tanks will probably be employed.

6. In these circumstances it is essential to reinforce the Soviet defenses by transferring large numbers of anti-tank forces from quiet sectors and GHQ Reserve to the Kursk salient.

The Zhukov technique of preparing to the utmost, and then drawing in the enemy for his destruction, was evident in the closing paragraph of his message:

I consider that it would be pointless for our forces to go over to the offensive in the near future in order to pre-empt the enemy. It would be better for us to wear out the enemy on our defense, to smash his tanks and then by introducing fresh reserves and going over to a general offensive to beat the main enemy force once and for all.

At the time that Zhukov sent his report off to Stalin, the front lines of the Kursk salient, and the area north and south of Kursk, had

been held for some weeks in a stabilized condition. The area involved was broken into several fronts. The northern half of the Kursk salient was made up of the central front, under the command of Marshal Konstantin Rokossovsky, and the Voronezh front (covering the southern flank of the salient), commanded by General Nikolai F. Vatutin (Nikita Khrushchev was on this front as the political member of the military council).

North of the central front was General M. M. Popov's Bryansk front. The west front was under command of General V. Sokolovsky. And south of the Voronezh front was the southwest front.

It was Rokossovsky (central front) who made the initial recommendations that a huge reserve be established directly east of the Kursk salient. This main strategic reserve was identified as the reserve front (the name was later changed to steppe front) and placed under the command of Marshal Ivan S. Konev, with five armies at his disposal.

Konev's five armies included one tank army and one tank, one mechanized, and three cavalry corps. Rokossovsky's central front had six armies that included one tank army and two independent tank corps. Vatutin's Voronezh front had four armies in the front lines, and in reserve counted one rifle and one tank army and two tank and one rifle corps.

There is a great deal of controversy surrounding the forces assembled by the Russians for the Battle of Kursk, and at times it appears that accuracy in numbers depends upon belief in the integrity of the source. The "official figures" as released by the Soviet government include 1,337,000 men, 20,220 pieces of artillery, 3,306 tanks and assault guns, and 2,650 combat aircraft.

Zhukov states his supply problems had to be solved for 1,300,000 men, a total of 3,600 tanks, 20,000 guns, and 3,130 combat aircraft (including long-range bombers).

Rokossovsky lists a force of 1,300,000 officers and men, approximately 20,000 artillery pieces and mortars, "at least 3,600 tanks and self-propelled guns (among them 2,535 heavy and medium tanks and self-propelled guns)," and about 3,130 aircraft. Rokossovsky adds the interesting figures that the Russians were "1.4 times superior to the enemy in men, 1.9 times in artillery and mortars, 1.3 times in tanks and nearly 1.6 times in aircraft."

Alan Clark in *Barbarossa* states that Rokossovsky's central front "by the end of June" was equipped with more artillery than infantry regiments. Clark also applies to Rokossovsky's forces a total of "over 20,000 pieces" of artillery and specifies that of this number no fewer than 6,000 were deadly 76.2-mm. antitank guns as well as 920 Katyusha rocket launchers (each launcher containing up to several layers of launching racks). Clark adds that the central front was laid down with an incredibly dense carpet of more than four thousand antipersonnel and antitank mines *for every mile of front*.

Zhukov states that for the Thirteenth Army front, where the Germans were expected to strike in their greatest strength, the lines facing the enemy were equipped with "up to 148 guns and mortars per mile of front line." Zhukov adds:

> The most powerful antitank defenses on the Central Front were concentrated in the sector of the Thirteenth Army and the adjoining flanks of the Forty-Eighth and Seventieth Armies, and on the Voronezh Front in the sector of the Sixth and Seventh Guards Armies. There the density was 25 guns per mile and, counting the second line of defense, as many as 48 guns per mile. The antitank defenses in this sector were further reinforced by two tank regiments and one tank brigade. The density of antitank artillery in the Thirteenth Army sector was more than 48 guns per mile.

Two days after Zhukov sent his preliminary report and assessment of the situation to Stalin, another report arrived in Moscow, this time from the central front (Rokossovsky):

> . . . bearing in mind what forces and supplies are available, and above all the results of offensive operations during 1941–42 and the spring and summer of 1943, an enemy offensive can be expected only on the Kursk-Voronezh operational axis. On the other axes an enemy offensive is hardly likely.
>
> Given the strategic situation as it is at this stage of the war, it would from the German point of view be useful to secure firmly for themselves the Crimea, Donbass and Ukraine, and to do this they must advance their front to the line Shterovka-Starobelsk-Rovenki-Liski-Voronezh-Livny-Novosil. To accomplish this task the enemy will re-

quire not less than sixty infantry divisions with appropriate air, armor and artillery reinforcement. The enemy is able to concentrate this amount of forces and equipment on the axis in question. Therefore the Kursk-Voronezh operational axis is of primary importance.

If these operational premises are accepted, we must expect the directions of the main enemy efforts simultaneously on inner and outer radii of action to be:

1. On the inner radius—from the Orel area through Livny to Kastornoye and from the Belgorod area to Kursk via Oboyan.

2. On the outer radius—from the Orel area via Kromny to Kursk and from the Belgorod area via Stary Oskol to Kastornoye.

If we take no counteraction . . . enemy success on these axes could lead to the defeat of Central and Voronezh Fronts' forces, with seizure by the enemy of the very important Orel-Kursk-Kharkov railroad, and would bring his forces out on a line advantageous to him, ensuring firm retention of the Crimea, Donbass and Ukraine.

The enemy can begin regrouping and concentrating forces on the probably axes of attack, and also accumulating the necessary stores once the spring thaw and floods have ended. Consequently the enemy can be expected to launch a decisive offensive approximately in the second half of May.

Given the present operational situation, I consider it logical to propose the following measures:

a. To destroy the enemy force at Orel by the combined efforts of West, Bryansk and Central Fronts, and thus to deprive him of the ability to strike from the Orel area via Livny to Kastornoye, to seize the most important. Mtsensk-Orel-Kursk railroad which we need, and to deprive the enemy of the possibility of using the Bryansk network of railroads and dirt roads.

b. To disrupt the enemy offensive operations, Central and Voronezh Fronts must be strengthened with air forces, above all fighters, and with not less than ten regiments of antitank artillery per front.

c. For the same purpose it is desirable to have strong Stavka reserves in the Livny, Kastornoye, Liski, Voronezh and Yelets areas.

Two days later, on April 12, after completing a detailed report of German forces arrayed in their area, the staff of the Voronezh front headquarters submitted its report to Moscow:

... we should expect that the enemy can create an assault group facing Voronezh Front with up to ten panzer divisions and not less than six infantry divisions, altogether with up to 1,500 tanks, and these should be expected to concentrate in the area Borisovka-Belgorod-Murom-Kazachya Lopan. This assault group may be supported by strong air forces numbering up to about 500 bombers and not less than 300 fighters.

The enemy's intentions are to strike concentric blows from the Belgorod area to the northeast and from the Orel area to the southeast, so as to surround our forces deployed west of the line Belgorod-Kursk.

Afterwards the enemy should be expected to strike southeastwards into the flank and rear of South-West Front, so as subsequently to operate on a northerly axis. However we cannot exclude the possibility that this year the enemy will reject the plan, namely that after concentric blows from the Belgorod and Orel areas, he intends to attack northeast to outflank Moscow. This possibility must be taken into account and reserves made ready accordingly.

Thus against Voronezh Front the enemy will most likely strike his main blow from the Borisovka-Belgorod area towards Stary Oskol, and with part of his forces towards Oboyan and Kursk.

Rokossovsky on the central front clearly wanted to move immediately against the Germans facing his own forces. Vatutin on the Voronezh front came to a different conclusion, namely, that the most effective way of dealing with the ominous German buildup and plans for a major offensive was to lie back and wait for the Germans to impale themselves on the thickly strewn Russian defenses.

At first glance this seems a divisive chasm between the thinking of the two Russian commanders, but each man was reacting specifically to the situation on *his* front and drawing up recommendations for the best means to solve that military problem as quickly and as effectively as possible.

The Germans facing Rokossovsky were still in the throes of supply difficulties. They were having fits with transport bogging down in the spring thaw. The special organization for a major offensive, reckoned Rokossovsky, was still far from complete. He reckoned that the Ger-

mans needed at least five weeks before they would be in a position to attack.

By this reasoning—and by any measure of logic it was wholly valid —the best means of attending to the growing Nazi force on the central front was to strike immediately and catch the enemy at his lowest ebb in strength. It was the time-honored instance of the best defense being a good offense.

But what was so valid for Rokossovsky did not apply to the situation on the Voronezh front faced by Vatutin. There the Germans had been entrenched for some time. There they were in strength, and their supply problems were far fewer than those judged by Rokossovsky in his sector. According to Vatutin's estimate, the Germans would be ready for a massive offensive in three weeks or less.

Another reason for the discrepancy in situations was geographical. In the south (Vatutin) the thaw would end much sooner than would be the case in the north (Rokossovsky), and the Germans therefore, would be ready that much earlier for any offensive.

What stands out like a beacon from the reports and recommendations of the two Soviet officers is that despite different problems and conditions—and the fact that Hitler had still to issue his Operations Order Number Six—both Rokossovsky and Vatutin had formulated a brilliant assessment of the capabilities of the enemy facing them. As events would have it, the needs of the Soviets called for a waiting game rather than a preemptive strike, and Rokossovsky was denied his recommended assault (to be carried out at once) against the enemy arrayed against him.

Of course, as the reports indicate, there didn't seem to be a Russian officer of any rank who did not believe the Germans would launch their offensive no later than May. Who could anticipate the thorny problems facing Hitler, let alone those he created by his own procrastination? Nowhere in the Russian plans, in the judgment of enemy capabilities, is there any mention that the Germans would be so incredibly "generous" as to afford the Red Army a minimum of six to seven weeks *beyond* any estimated date for the offensive against the Kursk salient.

This makes for an interesting point, because the Russian high com-

mand seemed perfectly convinced that if the German attack did indeed take place in May, it would still be defeated.

Zhukov arrived in Moscow the night of April 11 and spent the entire next day working with General Alexander Vasilievsky and General A. I. Antonov of headquarters staff to prepare a current situation map and recommendations for the coming months for the Red Army. The three men formed a conclusion that was exactly the same as that advanced by Hitler—the Germans must hold the front line from the Gulf of Finland southward to the Sea of Azov, and to do this and secure their entire front they must carry out a major assault against the Kursk salient.

The evening of April 12 was spent with Stalin, drawing the final decisions necessary to commit the Red Army to a definite line of action. Agreement was reached that the Kursk sector must receive the bulk of strength of the army, although Stalin had never quite yielded his deep concern for the safety of Moscow. He would continue to press for protection for the Soviet capital, but his gnawing fears would subside steadily.

By the middle of April the front-line commanders received their orders to prepare an intensive defense in depth for the attack the Russians knew was coming. The orders girding the Russian forces for such battle were actually issued *before* Hitler released the operations order that would officially create Operation Citadel. Under Zhukov's firm direction the Russians worked day and night, pouring men and matériel into the Kursk salient, but always holding open the options to modify their main strategy should new events so dictate.

Two main points had to be reached and passed: the last week of May and the first week of June. By this time, Zhukov relates, "we knew virtually all the details of the enemy's plan to strike against the Voronezh and Central Fronts with major tank forces, using the new Tiger tanks and Ferdinand self-propelled guns."

The defensive preparations represented a staggering effort by the Russians. In the salient itself the defense lines were laid down one after the other. Across—or through—a line that extended for 110 miles from west to east, the Russians prepared six lethal belts through which the Germans must pass. Each belt was a hell of fortifications,

and should the Wehrmacht somehow smash through the bristling defenses, the massed power of the steppe front would be waiting for them, and beyond *that*, another deep belt of fortifications along the east bank of the Don River.

Lying before, and extending between, each belt of fortifications were some of the most intensive minefields ever laid, averaging more than five thousand antitank and antipersonnel mines *for each mile* of defensive zone. This is four times heavier than the bristling defenses used at Stalingrad and six times heavier than the minefields sowed at Moscow.

Hundreds of miles of deep antitank ditches were gouged in the earth. In the central front alone the Russians dug more than three thousand *miles* of trenches. The same was done along the Voronezh front, so that on these two fronts alone the Russians dug the equal to a trench that would extend from the west coast of the United States all the way to England. Much of this work was carried out by Russian troops, but the commanders recognized the need for direct military work as well, and impressed into service every able-bodied citizen from Kursk who could be spared for the laborious task. By mid-April of 1943 the Russians had moved more than 100,000 civilians into the salient to hack the trenches from the hard earth, and within the next sixty days they swelled this number to 300,000 civilians.

As the work continued, the Russians honed their own forces by means of constant training and preparation for the titanic struggle. Nothing was left to chance, and a Soviet army captain describes that his brigade

anticipated five possible places where the Germans may strike and at each of them we know alongside whom we shall be fighting, our replacements and command posts. The brigade is stationed in the rear, but our trenches and shelters are ready up in front, and the routes by which we are to get there are marked out.

The ground, of which we have made a topographical survey, has been provided with guide marks. The depths of fords, the maximum loads of bridges are known to us. Liaisons with division have been doubled, codes and signals are arranged. Often alerted by day or night, our men are familiarized with their task in any eventuality. . . .

11

ZHUKOV'S BATTLE PLAN

Zhukov's basic plan for the coming battle in the Kursk salient would be an extraordinary refinement of those measures he had found most effective in the violent clashes for Moscow and Stalingrad. Everything centered about his intention to permit the German army to open the fight and to extend itself all across its line of action—and so reveal its most vulnerable points as swiftly as the battle was joined.

In Moscow, Stalin gave his approval to the basic course of action that would be pursued by the many armies preparing for the battle, and Zhukov relayed to the field commanders their responsibilities in meeting the attack. The Russians would hold back any commitment of firepower until the Germans were clearly on the move. Then, as quickly as "the enemy's main concentrations in the jumping-off areas for the offensive were identified," everything the Russians had available in artillery and mortars, as well as ground-attack aircraft, was to pour its fire into these German concentrations.

Air units were assigned two specific roles; they were to afford all possible assistance in the defensive actions of the Red Army, and

fighters were to concentrate (in addition to long-range bombers brought in from other commands) on wiping out the German air force.

The Russians would yield ground only when it was patently impossible to hold their positions any longer, but such retreat would be strictly in accordance with the plans laid down before the battle, and only with the assurance of crippling losses to the Germans.

Then, in the classic manner of Zhukov's operations, as the German thrust lost steam, as enemy units were decimated by the superiority of Russian firepower, the momentum of the battlefield would change. With Zhukov studying every detail of the fighting, he would know when the German offensive began to flag. At that moment he would hurl his armies against the Wehrmacht hordes along the Voronezh, central, steppe, and Bryansk fronts, along the left wing of the western front and the right wing of the southwest front.

The central front, as has been evident through this review of Russian preparations for the fighting, was perhaps the single most critical area of the battle. On the twenty-fifth anniversary of that battle, Marshal of the Soviet Union Rokossovsky, twice hero of the Soviet Union, prepared for the *Soviet Military Review* a special study of those events, which follows:

> The Soviet Supreme Command, having superiority over the enemy in men and matériel, chose the most rational method of action [for the Kursk battle]—to wear out the enemy forces and bleed them white in deliberate defensive battles and then to strike a blow with powerful reserve forces and launch an offensive on a wide sector of the front. The defensive operation at the Kursk bulge was to be carried out mainly by the troops of the Central and Voronezh Fronts. But in view of the fact that the enemy was preparing powerful blows with decisive aims, the General Headquarters massed big reserves east of the Kursk bulge, forming the Reserve Front (which was later named Stepnoy Front). This Front was the most powerful strategic reserve of the General Headquarters ever formed during the Great Patriotic War.
>
> While preparing for the defense on the Central Front we took into consideration the following factors: the most dangerous for us was the right flank—the foot of the bulge, for a breakthrough at this

sector would enable the enemy to penetrate into the rear of our entire defense, whereas a blow from the height of the bulge could at the worst only press our troops from the depth of the bulge without creating any special threat.

It was decided to set up the densest grouping of forces on the right flank at the foot of the bulge, the most probable sector of the enemy's main attack. The bulk of the Front reserves was to be concentrated on this direction. Our decision was approved by the Supreme Command.

Taking into consideration the presumed time of the enemy's probable offensive and the fact that the blow would be delivered with large forces, as early as the end of March the Front Command gave in its orders and directives, concrete instructions concerning the preparation of defense zones.

While beginning to organize our defense, we drew on our previously gained experience. The main idea of all the orders and directives of Front Headquarters was to create a strong, deeply-echeloned, multi-zone field defense with the utmost development of engineer fortifications throughout its whole operational depth.

At first it was planned to build up five defense zones 120–130 kilometers in depth. But, in the course of the preparation, the depth of the defense was increased to 150–190 kilometers along separate, most vital directions. Between April and June, the Front built up six main defense zones. Besides this, intermediate zones and cutting-off positions stretching for hundreds of kilometers were also built up. Communication trenches were designed for use as cutting-off positions if necessary. Battalion resistance centers, as a rule, were prepared for perimeter defense. Special attention was paid to protecting the limiting points, to artillery maneuvering by trajectory and wheels, and to troop maneuvers along the front line and in depth.

Between April and June, the Front troops dug about 5,000 kilometers of trenches, laid about 400,000 mines and land charges. On the sector of the 13th and 70th Armies alone, 112 kilometers of wire entanglements, with 10.7 kilometers of live wire entanglements, were built and over 170,000 mines laid.

A number of strong antitank zones with powerful antitank strong points, saturated to the maximum with antitank artillery, were prepared along directions of tank danger. In order the better to organize cooperation and coordination, strong points were combined to form antitank areas. It was decided to concentrate all the artillery of the

Front, antiaircraft artillery included, in the defense zone of the 13th and 70th Armies to repulse the enemy's tanks along the probable direction of his main attack.

By July 4th, 1943, the depth of the antitank defense on the right wing reached 30–35 kilometers. The first defense zone of the 13th Army had thirteen antitank areas with 44 antitank strong points; the second defense zone had nine antitank areas with 34 antitank strong points, and the third—fifteen antitank areas with 60 antitank strong points.

A dense zone of antitank obstacles was set up before the forward defensive line and in the depth of the defense in the areas accessible to tanks. Besides a large number of mine fields, the troops dug antitank ditches, set up dragon teeth, built dams to flood certain areas, and prepared slashlings.

To fight enemy tanks which might pierce our defense, mobile antitank detachments were formed. In divisions these detachments consisted of one or two sapper companies; in armies, one engineer battalion reinforced by submachine gunners. These detachments were to lay mines, antitank charges and set up portable obstacles along the directions of enemy tanks. Besides mobile detachments, artillery antitank reserves were formed in divisions, armies and the Front.

Special attention was paid to the fire system. Fire means were echeloned on the whole army depth. Fire maneuver and concentration were provided for along dangerous directions. To simplify fire control and make it more reliable, a ramified network of observation posts with permanent communication was established. It should be pointed out that, while forming battle formations in company defense areas, we were guided above all by the need to set up an impregnable curtain of fire.

According to the terrain, units took either forward wedge or back wedge formations to provide fire within the whole of the battalion area and to conduct flank and slanting fire. Practically all the battalions prepared barrage and concentrated fire of mounted machine guns both before the forward edge of defense and in the depth of the battalion and regiment areas.

Mortar companies prepared adjustment fire beforehand at areas and lines. Antitank rifle companies were concentrated in platoon or squad formations in areas inaccessible to tanks.

The infantry small arms system of fire on the second and rear army defense zones was built according to the same principle. As far as

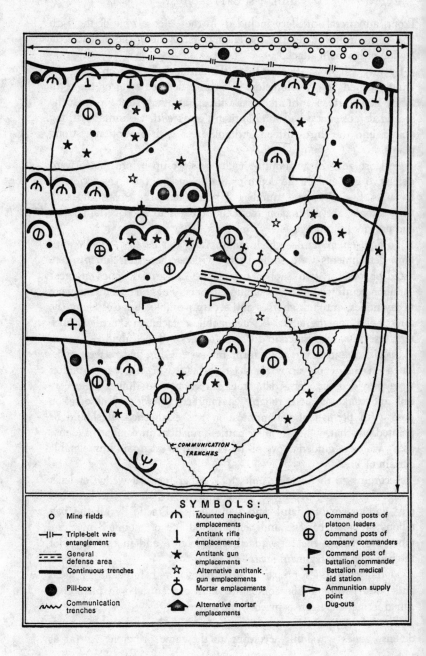

S Y M B O L S :

○	Mine fields	⋔	Mounted machine-gun emplacements	◐ Command posts of platoon leaders
‖‖‖	Triple-belt wire entanglement	⊥	Antitank rifle emplacements	⊕ Command posts of company commanders
▭▭	General defense area	★	Antitank gun emplacements	▷ Command post of battalion commander
▬	Continuous trenches	☆	Alternative antitank gun emplacements	+ Battalion medical aid station
●	Pill-box	⚲	Mortar emplacements	▷ Ammunition supply point
∿	Communication trenches	⬟	Alternative mortar emplacements	• Dug-outs

fire means were concerned, the second defense zone was practically not inferior to the main defense zone and the fire density of the rear defense zone of the 13th Army was even higher than that of the main and second defense zones.

Powerful artillery forces were concentrated along probable directions of enemy action. The total artillery density of the Front was 35 artillery pieces and mortars, including 10.2 antitank guns, per kilometer of frontage, and in the defense zone of the 13th Army it was far higher.

Thus the Front's antitank means and the rational planning of their utilization provided a reliable antitank defense. Along with the measures for organizing defense, the troops, profiting by a temporary lull, had been undergoing intense combat training since April. At least one-third of all the exercises were carried out at night.

Staffs at all levels engaged regularly in special training. The combat readiness of artillery was checked directly on the positions. On arrival at an observation post of the artillery commander, the inspector would show the commander the area of enemy concentration in accordance with the plan of defense. In less than a minute the artillery would open fire at the area.

The Command and Staff of the Front considered it their duty to become personally acquainted on the ground with the defense system of each army. All possible variants of the battle were thoroughly discussed and worked out on the spot. We attentively considered all the proposals of commanders of units and formations and made the corresponding corrections in the system of defense. The Front Command together with commanders of the Armies and fighting arms worked out cooperation at junction points between the armies. Cooperation was also organized at the junction point between the Central and Voronezh Fronts. We maintained close contact with the Voronezh Front, whose Commander, N. Vatutin, I knew personally in peacetime. We realized that the main enemy blows would be against the troops of our front.

Close attention was paid to political work before the operation. Political bodies, Party organizations and all Party members took an active part in preparing the troops for the forthcoming actions and in explaining to them the combat tasks to be fulfilled by the units. Political bodies and Party organizations, using the experience of political work gained during previous operations, planned practical measures to improve Party political work. We did a lot to instill in officers

and men unshakable staunchness and a sense of responsibility for defending the positions of their units.

Widely using visual aids, political workers discussed with soldiers the ways and means of fighting new enemy tanks and self-propelled guns. . . .

Considerable aid was rendered to the Front by the Bryansk partisans. At our request, they collected information on the movement of German troops, their disposition, armaments and airfields, destroyed enemy communications, hindering the concentration of enemy troops. On information from the partisans, our aviation struck at important objectives and targets. They also helped us to ascertain the effectiveness of our bomber raids on railway junctions, bridges, depots and communication centers.

Thousands of people from liberated towns and villages strove to render our troops all necessary assistance. Local Party organizations headed this patriotic movement of the Soviet people. They did their utmost to accelerate the building of defense zones, restore communication lines, roads, set up hospitals, and enlarge airfields. The population worked selflessly often under bombing and shelling by the enemy, who tried by all means to hamper the building of our defenses.

In June, enemy bombers started night raids on railway stations, junctions and bridges. The enemy decided to paralyze transportation of everything our troops were in need of, and they were in need of many things, ammunition in particular.

Our command post was also hit from the air. During one of the night raids, the house I lived in was destroyed by a bomb. I had a narrow escape. At that time, I usually used to read ciphergrams, but then I decided to go to the messroom and called the cipherman there. That saved us.

From the second half of June, the Nazis started bombing raids not only at night but in daytime, too. The actions of bombers were covered by fighters. Bitter air fights began with a large number of aircraft on both sides. The enemy suffered considerable losses and withdrew. Our aviation gained air supremacy. . . .

Having at its disposal intelligence data concerning the enemy intentions, the General Headquarters warned us on July 2nd of a probable enemy offensive between July 3 and 6. Closely watching the enemy, we noticed that all of his radio means kept silent, which had never happened before. Usually we got information about the movement of Nazi troops from our radio intelligence service. This fact

made our Headquarters pay more attention to other intelligence services, organize additional observation posts, ambushes, searches.

On the night of July 5th, our active reconnaissance located a group of Nazi sappers preparing lanes in the mine fields of the defense zone of 13th and 48th Armies. During the fighting some enemy sappers were killed, two escaped and one was taken prisoner. At the interrogation he told us that at three A.M. on July 5th the Germans would start the offensive and that their troops had already taken up assault positions. The Military Council of the Front was informed at about two A.M.

The dilemma was whether to believe this testimony or not. On this depended the vital decision to start artillery counterpreparation during which we had to spend about half of ammunition establishment of shells and mines. We had no time to consult General Headquarters since the situation was such that delay could be fraught with extremely grave consequences. This ruled out any vacillation. I ordered the Front artillery commander to start artillery counterpreparation.

There have been several references to the capture and/or defection of men from the German lines that enabled the Russians to obtain immediate information about the impending German attack. Several of these references are a matter of crossed lines, and it seems appropriate to bring them back into focus.

The first "capture" took place on July 4 in the Belgorod sector. There a Slovene sapper managed to work his way free of the German forces to which he was attached and reach the Soviet lines, where he surrendered. It was his report that contained the news that the German troops had been issued rations and brandy (actually vodka) for five days. He also stated that his unit was involved in clearing the minefields and barbed wire that infested the area in front of the German lines and that their work had to be completed in time for the German troops to start moving by 3:00 A.M. on July 5.

A second incident occurred to lend credence to the first. On the night of July 4–5 the Thirteenth Army of the central front received a special alert. A patrol moving out from the 15th Rifle Division encountered a group of German sappers marking clear lanes through the minefields (obviously the group to which Rokossovsky refers). The captured trooper, a Private Fermello attached to the sapper force of

the 6th Infantry Division, sang a song with a loud and clear message to the Russians. Fermello (perhaps with some prompting by his hosts) told the Russians that the attack was set definitely for 3:00 A.M. on July 5 and that advance units were already at their jumping-off points.

That made two very clear, remote, unrelated incidents, and others began to trickle in from other units. The time of attack had emerged from the unknown, and the Russians prepared themselves accordingly.

It was a time of anticipation before a battle never before experienced by the Soviets. In many ways it was a struggle to which the Russians looked forward. For the first time the shoe was really on the other foot.

"At the beginning of the war," said a captain of the armored forces, "everything was done in a hurry, and time was always lacking. Now we go calmly into action."

One thing was certain: The Germans were encountering what many of them considered to be a new breed of Russian soldier.

Time, then, for us to take a closer look at "Ivan."

12

ANATOMY OF THE
RUSSIAN SOLDIER

Every war has its own sounds. They're different from one battlefield to the other. Russian shells have a sound all their own, a characteristic that separates them from the artillery rounds fired by guns of other manufacture. When you're on the receiving end of such things, as were the Germans in the Kursk area, you learn instinctively to listen, to recognize the acoustic signature of death cracking the air.

"Ever hear a door slam? A door well up in the sky? That," wrote a German trooper to his family, "is what the Russian shells sound like. A door slamming shut. When they fire their barrages it's like insanity is everywhere. One door slams, and then another, then a dozen, and there's nothing else to hear but that sudden sound. Then the shells are coming in so thick and fast the sound blends together into the dull crackling explosions, except for those that come closer and closer and the noise becomes a crackling, banging thunder that drowns out the world. . . ."

The sounds of weapons. Even in the dark the seasoned veterans can tell the difference between "ours" and "theirs." Hear that?

Machine-gun fire. That wind-sound. A whipping sound, really, higher-pitched. A deep hissing crack. That's a German machine gun.

Then there's the rougher noise. Rough like a rasp. The dull, coughing-burp sound of the Russian machine guns. Unmistakable.

But there is one weapon whose sound is different from all others. In the German lines it is known as Nebelwerfer—a rocket projectile held in racks, many of them with bulbous explosive charges. They smoke like mad. When they fire, a great ripping sound is produced. Dark flame explodes back, but you must watch closely, for in an instant after the flame appears the smoke is everywhere, a huge boiling cloud, rushing back from the rocket. To see it clearly you can't look at the rocket because in that split second of ignition there is the slashing flame and the smoke that appears *at once*. You look ahead, where the rocket will be—where the many rockets will be after the salvo is fired —and there, leaping forward from the dirty smoke drifting before the wind, is the blurred shape of the explosive charge on its way to the Russians. Later, there comes the dull booming *whump* of the shells exploding.

The Russian Katyushas are different in a terrifying way. To the men in the field they are known as the Stalin Organ, a bullwhip of rocket fire that lays down a wicked barrage. The rockets are fired from launching racks anchored on trucks. The Russians line up the trucks by the dozens, one row after the other. Atop each truck is either a single tier of launching racks or racks placed one atop the other so that one truck may mount two, three, or even four such layered racks, and the firepower from a single truck is devastating, equal to or in excess of the full broadside from a cruiser on the high seas.

When they fire in massed salvos, the flame appears at once—rippling spears of eye-stabbing fire slashing upward from each truck, running up and down the line, until all the visible world is a mass of fire leaping upward and piercing the thick rolling smoke of its own making. It could be compared to the noise produced by tearing a bed sheet in half if the sheet were the size of the entire heavens. The flame does not last long, only what is needed to get the explosive charge moving. But it is ten thousand heavy guns firing all within the space of seconds. The sound tears and rips and gashes the sky, the flame is everywhere, the smoke pours forth acrid and thick.

At the receiving end the rocket shells arrive like a plague of biblical times, but far more terrible, for thousands of stones shriek down from the heavens, and wherever they strike the world goes mad. Thousands of blasts of flame, bright and angry, geysering up from the earth until the world, even in daylight, becomes a maddened rippling of flickering fire sheaves as far as the eye can see. It is an instant, dense carpet of fire, concussion, and destruction.

There is still another distinctive sound—a sound no German who fought the Soviets will ever forget, a roar from a human throat, the battle cry of the Russian soldier. At times he becomes incensed with his role in the attack, and as he and his fellow soldiers come running over the edge of the trenches, leaping from their foxholes, they shout "Hurrah!" Again and again they shout this crazy, impossible Hurrah! in a ragged, defiant chorus. Some of them die with the shout gurgling in their throats, but others pick it up as they rush into withering fire.

The Russian soldier, explains General Mellinthin, is unique, a fighting man who "has an almost incredible ability to stand up to the heaviest artillery fire and air bombardment." It is an ability that is recognized as much by the Russian commanders as it is by those who fire desperately at Ivan in his entrenchments, waiting to leave the safety of bunkers and trenches and foxholes and begin the lethal march straight into the German guns. And straight into those guns they come—human waves, roaring and bellowing as they move. If one is to believe both the Russians and their enemies, they are soldiers who do not yield under the kind of fire that would send the men of other armies staggering for safety.

"The stoicism of the majority of Russian soldiers and their mental sluggishness," Mellinthin relates, "make them quite insensible to losses."

Can this really be? We used to hear of how the Japanese had so little value for individual life. We had it drummed into our heads that the Japanese cared not a whit for themselves, that they would gladly throw themselves before American guns. Was it possible we were confusing blind dedication to duty for lack of concern for life? Was it possible we failed to understand this total commitment to the nation and that we were regarding as suicidal what was possibly complete patriotism? After the war we found that the Japanese were really

no more insensitive to dying than were our own men. Were they, then, so fatalistic that they accepted their death on the battlefield as inevitable? Perhaps. One cannot argue fatalism in combat. What soldier in the thick of fighting lived without it?

But is it truly a total *lack of caring* about one's life? Might we go so far as to claim, as Mellinthin (and others) would have us believe, that the Russian soldier truly did not much give a damn, that his was the supreme stoicism?

"The Russian soldier," states Mellinthin in *Panzer Battles* (Norman, Okla.: University of Oklahoma Press, 1956), "values his own life no more than those of his comrades. To step on walls of dead, composed of the bodies of his former friends and companions, makes not the slightest impression on him and does not upset his equanimity at all; without so much as twinkling an eyelid he stolidly continues the attack or stays in the position he has been told to defend."

Mellinthin cuts to the core of the matter when he states of the Russian soldier: "Life is not precious to him. He is immune to the most incredible hardships, and does not even appear to notice them; he seems equally indifferent to bombs and shells."

One of the more remarkable documents researched for this book was one of a series of historical studies prepared by the U.S. Department of the Army, identified in the series as Number 20-230, titled *Russian Combat Methods in World War II,* and carrying the classification of *restricted.*

It is specified clearly in the preface that the publication "was prepared by a committee of former German officers" during their intensive interrogations in Neustadt, Germany, in late 1947 and early 1948. "All of these officers," explains the preface, "had extensive experience on the eastern front during the period 1941–45. The principal author, for example, commanded in succession a panzer division, a corps, a panzer army, and an army group."

A rather remarkable succession of commands, and so clearly stating what we may be forgiven as labeling tunnel vision, that the study repeats its cautionary note to remind the reader that "publications in the GERMAN REPORT SERIES were written by Germans from the German point of view."

It makes for fascinating study, and it is also perhaps the closest look we shall have of the Russian soldier who figured so prominently in the Battle of Kursk. To our everlasting dismay it continues to be impossible to obtain *from the Russians* a representation of their foot soldier without being forced to wade through a thick morass of utmost devotions and hysterical loyalty to the Communist party. Thus the excerpts following from Historical Study Number 20-230, with selections made specifically by the writer:

It is possible to predict from experience how virtually every soldier of the western world will behave in a given situation—but not the Russian. The characteristics of this semi-Asiatic, like those of his vast country, are strange and contradictory. During the last war there were units which one day repulsed a strong German attack with exemplary bravery, and on the next folded up completely. There were others which one day lost their nerve when the first shell exploded, and on the next day allowed themselves, man by man, literally to be cut to pieces. The Russian is generally impervious to crises, but he can also be very sensitive to them. Generally, he has no fear of a threat to his flanks, but at times he can be most touchy about flanks. He disregards many of the old established rules of tactics, but clings obstinately to his own methods.

The key to this odd behavior can be found in the native character of the Russian soldier who, as a fighter, possesses neither the judgment nor the ability to think independently. He is subject to moods which to a Westerner are incomprehensible; he acts by instinct. As a soldier, the Russian is primitive and unassuming, innately brave but morosely passive when in a group. These traits make him in many respects an adversary superior to the self-confident and more demanding soldiers of other armies. . . .

Disregard for human beings and contempt of death are other characteristics of the Russian soldier. He will climb with complete indifference and cold-bloodedness over the bodies of hundreds of fallen comrades, in order to take up the attack on the same spot. With the same apathy he will work all day burying his dead comrades after a battle. He looks toward his own death with the same resignation. Even severe wounds impress him comparatively little. For instance, a Russian, sitting upright at the side of the street, in spite of the fact that both lower legs were shot away, asked with a friendly smile for a

cigarette. He endures cold and heat, hunger and thirst, dampness and mud, sickness and vermin, with equanimity. Because of his simple and primitive nature, all sorts of hardships bring him but few emotional reactions. His emotions run the gamut from animal ferocity to the utmost kindliness; odious and cruel in a group, he can be friendly and ready to help as an individual.

In the attack the Russian fought unto death. Despite most thorough German defensive measures he would continue to go forward, completely disregarding losses. He was generally not subject to panic. For example, in the breakthrough of the fortifications before Bryansk in October 1941, Russian bunkers, which had long since been bypassed and which for days lay far behind the front, continued to be held when every hope of relief had vanished.

Following the German crossing of the Bug in July 1941, the fortifications which had originally been cleared of the enemy by the 167th Infantry Division were reoccupied a few days later by groups of Russian stragglers, and subsequently had to be painstakingly retaken by a division which followed in the rear. . . .

The sum of these diverse characteristics makes the Russian a superior soldier who, under the direction of understanding leadership, becomes a dangerous opponent. It would be a serious error to underestimate the Russian soldier, even though he does not quite fit the pattern of modern warfare and the educated fighting man. The strength of the Western soldier is conscious action, controlled by his own mind. Neither this action on his own, nor the consciousness which accompanies the action, is part of the mental make-up of the Russian.

In judging the basic qualities of the Russian it should be added that by nature he is brave, as he has well demonstrated in his history. In 1807 it was the Russian soldier who for the first time made a stand against Napoleon after his victorious march through Europe—a stand which may be called almost epic.

In line with this awakening, another determining factor has been introduced into the Red Army by the political commissar—unqualified obedience. Carried out to utter finality, it has made a raw mass of men a first-rate fighting machine. Systematic training, drill, disregard for one's own life, the natural inclination of the Russian soldier to uncompromising compliance and, not the least of all, the real disciplinary powers available to the commissar, are the foundations of this iron obedience. In this connection, it must be remembered that Russia is

an autocratically ruled state—an absolute dictatorship demanding and compelling the complete subordination of the individual. That blind obedience of the masses, the mainspring of the Red Army, is the triumph of communism and the explanation of its military success. . . .

It is no exaggeration to say that the Russian soldier is unaffected by season and terrain. This immunity gave him a decisive advantage over the Germans, especially in Russian territory where season, temperature, and terrain play a decisive role.

The problem of providing for the individual soldier in the Russian Army is of secondary importance, because the Russian soldier requires only very few provisions for his own use. The field kitchen, a sacred institution to other troops, is to the Russian soldier a pleasant surprise when it is available, but can be dispensed with for days and weeks without undue hardship.

During the winter campaign of 1941, a Russian regiment was surrounded in the woods along the Volkhov and, because of German weakness, had to be starved out. After one week, reconnaissance patrols met with the same resistance as on the first day; after another week only a few prisoners were taken, the majority having fought their way through to their own troops in spite of close encirclement. According to the prisoners, the Russians subsisted during those weeks on a few pieces of frozen bread, leaves and pine needles which they chewed, and some cigarettes. It had never occurred to anyone to throw in the sponge because of hunger, and the cold (thirty below zero Fahrenheit) had not affected them.

The kinship with nature, which the Russians have retained to a greater degree than the other peoples of Europe, is also responsible for the ability of the Russian soldier to adapt himself to terrain features, and actually to merge with them. He is a master of camouflage, entrenchment, and defense construction. . . .

The utmost caution is required when passing through unknown terrain. Even long and searching observation often does not reveal the excellently camouflaged Russian. Frequently, German reconnaissance patrols passed through the immediate vicinity of Russian positions or individual riflemen without noticing them, and were then taken under fire from behind. . . .

The Russian has mastered all new weapons and fighting equipment, all the requirements of machine warfare, with amazing rapidity. Soldiers trained in technical subjects were carefully distributed through the ranks where they taught the necessary rudiments to their

duller urban comrades, and to those who came from rural areas. The technical skill of the Russian was especially notable in the field of signal communications. The longer the war lasted, the better the Russians became at handling this type of equipment. . . .

In contrast to the good side of the Russian soldier there were bad military aspects of equal significance. To the Germans, it was one of the imponderables about each Russian unit whether the good or the bad would predominate. There still remained an appreciable residue of dullness, inflexibility, and apathy which had not yet been overcome, and which probably will not be overcome in the near future.

The unpredictability of the mood of the Russian soldier and his pronounced herd instinct at times brought on sudden panic in individual units. As inexplicable as the fanatic resistance of some units, was the mystery of their mass flights, or sudden wholesale surrender. The reason may have been an imperceptible fluctuation in morale. Its effect could not be countered by any commissar.

His emotions drive the Russian into the herd, which gives his strength and courage. The individual fighter created by modern warfare is rare among the Russians. Most of the time a Russian who has to stand on his own feet does not know what to do. During the war, however, this serious weakness was compensated for by the large mass of men available.

Referring to Russian command echelons, the study states, in part:

The higher echelons of Russian command proved capable from the very beginning of the war and learned a great deal more during its course. They were flexible, full of initiative, and energetic. However, they were unable to inspire the mass of Russian soldiers. Most of the commanders had advanced in peacetime to high positions at a very early age, although there were some older men among them. All social levels were represented, from the common laborer to the university professor of Mongolian languages and cultures. Of course, merit in the Revolution played a part, but a good choice was made with respect to character, military understanding, and intelligence. Purely party generals apparently got positions carrying little more than prestige. The extraordinary industry with which the commanders went about their duties was characteristic. Every day, and far into the night, they sat together to discuss and to record in writing what they had seen and heard during the day.

. . . the resources of their country and the large number of troops that were available gave the Soviet command an advantage over the Germans. Equipment, training, and physical and spiritual character of their armed forces all corresponded to the conditions in the East. For this reason the Germans had to contend with a great number of difficulties which simply did not exist for the Russian high command. In addition, the low valuation placed on human life freed the Soviet high command from moral inhibitions. Whether, for example, several divisions were lost in an encirclement, or whether a reindeer division on the Murmansk front perished in a snowstorm, was of no particular importance. Not until later did the long duration of the war and the extensive losses force the Red high command to greater economy of firepower.

The flexibility demonstrated by the higher commands (army and army group) was not evident at lower levels. The lower command echelons (echelons below division level) of the Russian Army, and for the most part also the intermediate echelons (generally division level), remained for a long period inflexible and indecisive, avoiding all personal responsibility. The rigid pattern of training and a too strict discipline so narrowly confined the lower command within a framework of existing regulations that the result was lethargy. . . . Russian elements that had broken through German lines could remain for days behind the front without recognizing their favorable position and taking advantage of it. The Russian small unit commander's fear of doing something wrong and being called to account for it was greater than the urge to take advantage of a situation.

The commanders of Russian combined arms units were often well trained along tactical lines, but to some extent they had not grasped the essence of tactical doctrines and therefore often acted according to set patterns, not according to circumstances. Also, there was the pronounced spirit of blind obedience which had perhaps carried over from their regimented civilian life into the military field.

No judgment of the Russian as a soldier can be complete without comment on the role played by the political commissar, excerpts of which are provided from the historical study:

The influence of the Communist Party and of its representatives in the Army—the commissars—was tremendous. The commissar was probably the most controversial man in the Russian Army. Even in the

Soviet Union opinions varied concerning his usefulness, his position, and his duties. He was the driving force of the Army, ruling with cunning and cold-bloodedness.

By means of a close-meshed network of especially chosen personalities, the commissars held the entire army machine under their control and in a tight grip. The commissars were to a preponderant degree real political fanatics. They came mostly from the working class, were almost without exception city people, brave, intelligent and unscrupulous. . . .

However, it is not true that the Russian soldier fought well only because of fear of the commissars. A soldier who is motivated solely by fear can never have the qualities that the Russian soldier of this war displayed. The motive of fear may often have been the final resort in difficult situations, but basically the Russian has no less national—as distinguished from political—patriotism than the soldier of western armies, and with it comes the same source of strength. . . .

Among the troops themselves the relationship of the soldier to the commissar apparently was endurable in spite of the commissar's uncompromising strictness and severity. The higher headquarters, on the other hand, appear to have regarded him with mistrust. . . .
compromising strictness and severity. The higher headquarters, on the tenacious resistance of the Russian soldier, even in hopeless situations. It is not wholly true that the German commissar order, directing that upon capture commissars be turned over to the SD (Security Service) for "special treatment," that is, execution, was wholly responsible for inciting the commissars to bitter last-ditch resistance; the impetus much rather was fanaticism together with soldierly qualities, and probably also the feeling of responsibility for the victory of the Soviet Union.

There was this comment on the matter of women in the fighting ranks:

The commissars found special support among the women who served within the framework of the Soviet Army. Russian women served in all-female units with the so-called partisan bands, individually as gunners in the artillery, as spies dropped by parachute, as medical corps aides with the fighting troops, and in the rear of the auxiliary services. They were political fanatics, filled with hate for

every opponent, cruel, and incorruptible. The women were enthusiastic Communists—and dangerous.

It was also not unusual for women to fight in the front lines. Thus, uniformed women took part in the final breakout struggle at Sevastopol in 1942; medical corps women in 1941 defended the last positions in front of Leningrad with pistols and hand grenades until they fell in the battle. In the fighting along the middle Donets in February 1943, a Russian tank was apparently rendered immobile by a direct hit. When German tanks approached, it suddenly reopened fire and attempted to break out. A second direct hit again brought it to a standstill, but in spite of its hopeless position it defended itself while a tankkiller team advanced on it. Finally it burst into flame from a demolition charge and only then did the turret hatch open. A woman in tanker uniform climbed out. She was the wife and cofighter of a tank company commander who, killed by the first hit, lay beside her in the turret. So far as Red soldiers were concerned, women in uniform were superiors or comrades to whom respect was paid.

13

RUSSIAN PARTISANS HARASS
GERMAN SUPPLY LINES

In his review of preparations for the forthcoming battle in the Kursk salient, Marshal Zhukov, referring to the period of April 1943, stated that more than 200,000 Russian guerrillas were operating far behind the front lines of the German army. This was no small force the purpose of which was simply to harry the Germans. Instead, they were a powerful extension of the Red Army and, as such, received their orders and support through the central headquarters of the guerrilla movement. Headquarters passed on its directives through underground and partisan units operating through the occupied cities, provinces, and districts.

Listing the various fronts established by supreme headquarters in Moscow for the Kursk battle, Zhukov identifies the central, Voronezh, steppe, Bryansk, and western fronts, and then states: "Central Headquarters of the Guerrilla Movement was instructed to organize massive diversive actions in the enemy rear against all major transport lines of Orel, Bryansk, Kharkov and other oblasts and to collect and deliver intelligence information."

The partisans were thus a major, even a critical element in the Battle of Kursk, and the role of these fast-moving forces behind the German lines is essential to the telling of this vast conflict. For whatever the Germans did or tried to do in their preparations for the coming fight was affected by the activities of the partisans operating behind their lines and often directly in the midst of powerful but widely spread German forces.

It was more than annoyance; the Russians so harried the Wehrmacht with their attacks from "nowhere" that a considerable percentage of the German army was dissipated in holding off or attacking the partisans. This effort seriously obstructed the army's ability to prepare for the advance into the Kursk salient. Also, very serious losses in men and matériel were incurred by the Germans in this series of increasingly savage assaults to the rear of their lines.

When one looked at a map of the areas of Russia under German occupation, the result was a deceptive understanding of the actual situation. An accurate representation would have indicated that although the Germans actually held many strongpoints, the vast territory seemingly under their control was often pitted with hotbeds of fierce resistance. In effect, the German occupation forces held only the larger administrative-transportation centers linking with the front. Vast districts in the rear of the German lines were burned out and uninhabited, the roads were too dangerous for maintenance, scarcely a bridge was left intact, and only those railroads provided with constant heavy guard by the Germans moved any trains. The others were simply abandoned by the victors.

Surrounding these German-held "oases" were huge wild forests and remote marshy regions which, one might think, had been swept clean of all opposition by the occupying Germans. The truth was grimly otherwise, for these distant areas teemed with life: angry, hating, dangerous life, the actual lords and kings of the forests, so feared and hated by the Germans—the Russian partisans.

Within these dense tracts of woodland and thick brush was a form of nocturnal life, for it was only when daylight faded and darkness covered the land that the partisans stirred. They would cut rail lines and destroy bridges only recently repaired by the Germans. They exploded mines in the path of trains or trucks or cars. They set fire to

fields so that the winds carried the flames into German encampments. They poisoned water supplies, fired every manner of weapon into barracks and other concentrations, and tried to blow storage dumps.

Even the night skies became the province of the partisans and those who supplied them from the other side of the German lines, for in the night the sky rumbled and thundered to the sound of Russian bombers and transport planes working their way down to cleared fields and isolated roads. Quickly they unloaded ammunition, fuel, explosives, weapons, and other supplies. The areas surrounding the night fields for supply were sure death for any German forces, for in such locales the partisan strength was overwhelming. This was their lifeline, and it could not be compromised.

There was plenty to occupy the Germans, anyway, to assure their interest elsewhere. Roadblocks, strongpoints, headquarters—any assembly of the hated Wehrmacht—became the target for rifles, mortars, high-velocity guns, sappers. The partisan country was a land of dull mushrooming sounds and sudden explosions of dazzling light as the Germans first one flare after the other to bring light to the sky, then to peer and squint into the wavering long shadows to discover their enemy.

The strongpoints were the partisan targets at night, for there was little else to draw their attention. The roads were abandoned, the railroad yards closed and heavily guarded. The separate garrisons closed themselves off from the outside world. And in each such strongpoint, free for the moment from the attention of the partisans, the men looking out into darkness could hear through the night the distant crackling explosions of other garrisons under attack.

Only with the first silent whisper of dawn would there come relief from the hidden dangers of partisan attacks. With daylight the guerrilla forces faded from all activity and vanished within their secret places of hiding. Only then would the Germans emerge from their fortified warrens and go about their business of making safe once again what they had to move. They searched for mines and explosive charges, repaired craters in roads, put out smoldering fires, searched for booby traps, replaced the ammunition they had used, and packed off their exhausted sentries to sleep. And every man knew that when

the sun slipped beneath the horizon and darkness fell, it would begin all over again.

The Germans, of course, did everything in their power to break this mind-bending assault on their position as conquerors. For the partisans did more than harry them; they undermined the whole fabric of rear-area security through all of Russia. There was only one way to strike back at the partisans in an occupied land, and that was with force, with weapons, with speed, with ruthlessness. So the Nazis brought together powerful mobile forces and linked them with expert communications. Bristling with firepower, they moved through those areas suspected to harbor the partisans intent on flushing out their quarry from concealment. If they lacked sufficient strength, they would even bring forces back from the front lines, and then, at what appeared to be the most propitious moment, the Germans would assail the area under suspicion.

It was impossible to hold the ranks tight, to sustain cohesiveness, once the German forces moved from the roads and level ground into the hills, the thick woods, the bogs and the marshes and the swamps. Before them, flushed indeed from their hiding places, the partisans were on the move. *Away* from the Germans until their ranks were thinned even more by the dangerous terrain. Away from the Germans until their vehicles were forced to grind slowly along narrow paths, until their very act of pursuit opened wide the seams of vulnerability.

What had begun as a concentric ring that the Germans tried to close on the elusive partisans became thin wavering lines, each more scattered than the other. And still the partisans remained invisible, content for the moment to let their invisible preparations work for them. A half-track would grind along a torturous path, and there would not be a partisan for miles. Then the vehicle would rumble over a mine concealed beneath the ground, and the shattering blast would set the vehicle aflame and kill several men and wound even more. And this is what the partisans wanted—not a showdown, but a steady eroding of Nazi strength. As the Germans continued their advance into the thick woodlands, their casualties increased with the explosions of mines and trip wires. The unseen presence of their enemy tightened tempers, made the Germans edgy, ready to fire at anything.

Actually the partisan movement went on around the clock; only

the nature of activity changed from day to night. There was constant reconnaissance by guerrillas to maintain an accurate assessment of German forces. Information of this nature sent back to intelligence was vital to the disposition and the movement of regular Red Army units. Terrorist strikes—sniping, exploding mines, and the like—were liable to come at any time of the day or night. Soviet agents working in German headquarters (and this was a problem faced by the Germans all through occupied Russia) were adept at dropping rumors that were often picked up as true information and led to much confusion and wasted energy on the part of the conquerors. There was constant sabotage, for an army of Russian laborers—cleaners, truck drivers, repairmen, carpenters and masons, electricians, interpreters—had been impressed into service by the occupying forces. Wherever they could, they cut lines, slashed tires, poured sand into fuel tanks; an unseen battle of such attrition went on all the time.

In German military offices Russian administrative and clerical assistants bided their time and when the moment was right either photographed or stole secret documents. Supply depots were set aflame, and no one was ever found who had carried out the work of arson. Arms caches were raided, and stores of weapons and ammunition vanished. Trucks were stolen wherever they were parked.

Any dwelling places that housed Russians who worked with the conquerors became a prime target for partisan assaults. The avowed policy was to kill the collaborators, their wives and children. It was terror at its worst, and sometimes it was pursued with a diligence characteristically Russian. Partisan agents went to work *for* the Germans. Their objective? To incite the Germans to hatred for the Russians so they would carry out vicious reprisals against the local populace—making life under the Germans unbearable and leading to stiffening of resistance to the enemy.

In the months-long preparations for the battle that would be fought in the area of the Kursk salient, the partisans, acting under direct orders from Moscow, intensified their activities against the German forces preparing to go on the offensive.

During the spring of 1943 the Second Panzer Army, comprising some thirty-five divisions, was engaged in heavy defensive operations

in the Orel-Bryansk sector. The great bulk of German supplies was carried by the double-track railroad line Gomel-Unecha-Bryansk-Orel, which also had to transport much of the supplies for the adjoining Second Army in the Kursk area. A single-track rail line running through Krichev-Surazh, which joined the main line at Unecha, was available for occasional use and provided some relief to the main line. Another single-track line that served as an additional supply route ran from Smolensk through Roslavl to Bryansk. In addition to train transport there was a main highway running through Smolensk-Roslavl-Byransk. A lesser road that led up from Gomel via Unecha was more frustration than anything else, because it ran through wide-open country and was in such terrible condition that the Germans felt it could be used only in the most dire emergency.

Strong partisan bands ruled the forests west of Lokot (south of Bryansk). These were not simple farmers, but groups of efficient killers that had been formed of Russian soldiers originally isolated from their main forces in a wild battle fought in the Vyazma-Bryansk area. Encircled by the Germans, lost to their main operational force, they were anything but removed from the field of conflict. They simply served in a new capacity—as partisans who received their instructions from guerrilla headquarters deep in the forests well behind the German lines. When Russian army forces pounded their way during the winter of 1942–43 into the Kursk area (to set up the salient), these partisans carried out constant attacks on the enemy and posed a serious menace to the deep flank and the rear of the Second Panzer Army.

They became so dangerous, and needed so much attention, that the Germans turned to recruiting Russians who lived in the area about Lokot; they were Russians sorely disaffected with the Stalin regime and willing to work as soldiers for the Germans against their own people. One may expect that after the Germans were driven from the area, particular attention was paid to these troops the Russians considered the most vile form of traitor.

The setting up of the Kursk salient also resulted in large numbers of Russian soldiers spread out as stragglers in the forests about Kletnya and Akulichi, west of Bryansk. They formed into new partisan bands, and in activity that laid to rest the German claims that they fully controlled their rear areas, the partisans actually took over control of

main sawmills and began shipping vitally needed lumber through the German lines—including some shipments at night by air!

These partisans were, of course, much more than lumberjacks and sawmill hands. They moved in powerful bands from the forests to strike at the highway and rail line leading to Roslavl, and for long periods of time stopped all moving transport. This proved vital to the Russians and gave the Red Army a distinct advantage in parrying before the Battle of Kursk.

To protect itself against the growing raids, the Second Panzer Army was forced to divert more and more strength into antipartisan combat. They removed from their front-line forces one entire security division to protect the communications lines running north and southwest of Bryansk and to attack the partisan bands in the forests north and northwest of the city and in the area around Kletnya. Several security battalions were assigned to guard the supply depots in the vicinity of Bryansk and to protect the road and railway line to Orel, as well as the connecting roads in the area of Zhisdra. The turncoat Russians employed by the Wehrmacht went into protective duty around the town of Trubchevsk (south of Bryansk).

Savage fighting erupted between the turncoats and the partisans, for the latter in the area of Zhisdra had made a major target of the Russian villages in the open country. These small communities were subjected to vicious attacks by the partisans who frantically sought food, supplies, and manpower. Apparently there was a personal element far beyond that to be expected in such pillaging, and the villagers banded together with open hatred against the partisans. So intense was this conflict between Russians that the villagers carried out forays of their own into the dangerous woodlands to gather what could be found of abandoned weapons and ammunition, in order that they might protect themselves, not against the German invaders, but against the partisans.

The antipartisan effort was a constant operation by day and by night. Nothing was safe from attack unless it was heavily guarded around the clock. The German security forces placed protective units at depots, bridges, headquarters, and barracks. Any train that moved through open country had to be accompanied by heavy security forces if it hoped to survive the trip. Virtually every truck convoy was es-

corted from one stronghold to the next. That the security efforts were, on the whole, generally ineffective is attested to by the heavy casualties and severe loss of supplies suffered by the German army. There was an ironic note about the area; it was in these same woods that bands of White Russians had held out until 1926 or 1927 without ever being captured by the Soviet government.

Of all the targets struck by the partisans the most important to the Germans *and* the Russians was the railway system. When the spring thaws came to Russia, only the rail lines could carry supplies and reinforcements from one area to another. The roads were impassable, and when they were restored to use, the Germans found thousands of their trucks in such poor mechanical condition that they had no choice but to resort to horse-drawn transport, in itself sadly vulnerable to partisan attack.

The partisans became experts in striking at the railway lines, and they varied their methods to meet particular goals. For daily interruption of rail traffic the partisans most often used different types of mines, the variety complicating German detection and disarming. Pressure and vibration mines were simple and effective and were timed to explode whenever the locomotive of a train passed overhead. But if the partisans wanted to do more than wreck a locomotive and stop movement, such as when they needed to destroy trainloads of supplies needed desperately by the German army (such as gasoline in tank cars), they sowed the tracks with mines fitted out with pull-type fuses that were detonated by remote control. The Nazis were aware that the railbeds had also been sown with mines by retreating Russian army units and that these mines had fuses that would remain quiet for as long as three months after they were buried beneath the tracks.

The Germans, of course, resorted to placing heavily loaded flatbed cars ahead of their locomotives. To counter this defense, the partisans turned to simple delayed-action fuses. The mines were activated by the pressure of the "safety cars" but did not explode for some seconds, so that they went off only after the locomotive or other cars were directly over the mines.

Nazi mine detectors were very efficient, but the most advanced equipment was often useless in the face of dogged Russian ingenuity.

Many of them were nothing more than explosives in a wooden box with a safety fuse. When the Germans shifted their detection efforts to concentrate on finding this type of mine, the Russians went to work with thousands of magnetic mines placed *on the trains* by saboteurs in workshops and stations; these magnetic mines had simple long-delay detonators.

(One of the most spectacular blows struck by the partisans took place within the Osipovichi railroad station. The destruction was so widespread that *all* operations stopped for weeks. A Russian saboteur attached a magnetic mine to a gasoline car of a tank train. The exploding mine sent a towering ball of fire outward from the car, and the secondary blast ripped open other tank cars, which immediately caught fire and exploded, soon engulfing the entire train.

(Alongside the tank train stood an ammunition train, and there was no time to move the long line of cars. The heat and continuing explosions from the gasoline cars finally set off the ammo train, which shattered the entire station. This, in turn, set ablaze almost every car of an adjacent forage train. The explosions and growing flames raged completely out of control, and they spread swiftly to encompass a fourth train loaded from one end to the other with brand-new Tiger tanks.)

Partisan intelligence was responsible for "uncanny knowledge" on the part of Russian headquarters for the location and contents of trains and supply depots on which the Germans counted heavily to outfit their armies arrayed for Operation Citadel. Again it is most important to mention that in every respect these activities were a part of the Battle of Kursk, for they influenced not only the operations leading to the battle but also its outcome. One may be led to wonder if the final results of Citadel might not have been different if the partisans had not acted so effectively and so closely in concert with (and under the orders of) the Russian high command.

Operating as highly coordinated teams, the partisans gathered extensive information on the rail system used by the Germans, and then directed strong formations of Russian bombers to their targets. In many instances the partisans remained in the target area to assure accuracy of bomb delivery. Until the spring of 1943 Russian air strikes against rail lines and supply centers had been largely ineffec-

tive. All that changed as Marshal Zhukov carried out his meticulous plans to destroy the backbone of German armored strength, and one of his major programs in preparing for the Battle of Kursk was to disrupt as much as possible the massive efforts of the Germans to bring to the front lines every weapon capable of being moved.

Red air power was now strong enough to mount heavy raids where German supplies were concentrated, and in the final months before Kursk became an open battleground, powerful attacks were carried out against the main railheads at Orel and Bryansk. These lines not only served the normal requirements for Second Panzer Army but also functioned as the main supply artery for Operation Citadel.

German historical records document that the effectiveness of the Russian air strikes was far beyond anything ever known before and did, in fact, slow drastically the preparations for Citadel. One air strike at Orel was particularly effective when the bombers scored a series of direct hits on a supply train, exploding the train and precipitating a conflagration that wiped out more than one million rations intended for the Citadel troops. The strike took place during the daytime and hurled sheets of fire into an army ration dump which had not yet had its contents placed in underground bunkers.

Along the eastern edge of Bryansk, Russian bombers went after a huge ammunition dump, the location of which had been marked by partisans. Everything went perfectly for the Red Air Force—more than twelve hundred tons of ammunition disappeared in a titanic salvo. Normally the Germans shut down train operations at night because of partisan activity, but the critical need for supplies for Citadel changed all that. The Russians threw hundreds of bombers into concentrated assaults on the rail centers, and Bryansk was often the target for raids that went on through the entire night.

The Wehrmacht resorted to desperate measures to get the needed supplies to the forces preparing for Citadel, and with the loss of trainloads of matériel and its attendant effect upon the front lines, they immediately separated all major supply dumps in the Bryansk area into scattered smaller dumps. The very act of this dispersion caused its own rash of severe problems. To have the smaller dumps function properly, the Germans needed to press into service everything that could roll on wheels. Corps and division vehicles were rushed back

from the front lines to the supply areas, and with them came thousands of security troops to guard the dispersed and highly vulnerable convoys.

Because the new dumps were so far removed from the main supply areas by the rail yards, they tied down every available vehicle and increased enormously the need for gasoline (which would have gone for tanks and armored vehicles). The strict orders for dispersion nearly wrecked the German attempt to move supplies to the intended objectives. Often supply trains were broken up before they reached the main unloading yards. Cars were moved individually to those corps that had their separate rail lines and unloading points. In this manner the Germans were able to clear by nightfall every last car from the vulnerable railroad stations.

The track system was subjected to constant attack by the partisans. Normally the Germans would keep an entire train waiting until the tracks were repaired. The pressure of time and partisan harassment forced a change in procedure, and they began to unload the supply trains right where they were. Thousands of troops fanned out on each side of the trains so that the supplies could be transferred directly to waiting trucks and other vehicles. The system worked to a degree, but it had its own failings in that it demanded even more trucks, more gasoline, more drivers, and more security troops. The Germans finally realized the futility of such a shredded effort and turned to rerouting their supplies for Citadel along the Roslavl-Bryansk line.

Immediately the partisans reported the shift in tactics to the Russian high command, and the Red Air Force turned its attention to the trains massing along the newly selected line.

Heavy, repeated, accurate air strikes completely destroyed the Seshchinskaya railroad station fifty-five miles northwest of Bryansk. Along this route the major highway paralleled the rail line, and the Russian bombers gave both the tracks and the road special attention, with the result that both were often rendered impassable. Desperate measures by the Germans brought them to halt the supply trains in Roslavl, where army group trucks waited to unload the trains and then fanned out to the front lines. When the Germans encountered the same problems as before, they brought in every available repair unit from throughout Russia to concentrate their efforts on this line.

There are certain basic shortcomings to air attacks against a determined ground supply effort. The long distances involved, the unpredictable weather that could ground the Red Air Force, and especially powerful German fighter cover made it clear that aerial strikes, even with partisan direction to targets, could not by itself isolate the front lines for Citadel. Orders went out from Moscow for the partisans to increase their unit strength and attack the German supply routes with the greatest force possible.

The first wave of partisan attacks resulted in dozens of track cuttings of the main line between Orel and Gomel, and the partisans kept up a ceaseless series of explosions that cut the lines as fast as the Germans repaired them. Now the Germans turned to the single-track line between Krichev and Unecha. But rear-area security for the line had become so thin as to be almost ineffective.

For a while the Russians managed to completely isolate their Orel salient in the Kursk area, along the main supply line. What the Russian bombers failed to do the partisans accomplished in a single bold act. The total break in the line occurred about fifteen miles southwest of Bryansk where a double-span railroad bridge crossed the Desna River. The bridge was the single most critical point of the line, and this fact had been impressed repeatedly on the Nazi commander of the area involved, who was told to keep the bridge intact and protected "at all costs." This meant a strong concentration of troops and above all a security platoon with antitank weapons.

Apparently the admonition of protection "at all costs" failed to work its way down through the ranks. Early one evening partisan lookouts studied the German relief force taking its position at the bridge and noticed that night fell before the individual sentries had reached their assigned posts. It was likely the German soldiers would prefer to stay grouped and under cover before moving about in darkness to be picked off by partisans. The Russians immediately assembled forces for their attack, and at the crack of dawn they struck. Partisans opened heavy fire on the bridge from the west and received immediate heavy counterfire from the defenders.

This is precisely what the partisans wanted. With the Germans blasting away on the western side of the bridge, a force of three hundred partisans raced in from the east, gunned down the German

guards, and under heavy covering fire laid heavy explosive charges along the main support beams. Moments later the blasts wrecked the bridge and closed the rail line completely.

The Germans rushed every available railway engineer and a strong maintenance force into the area. Under extra-heavy security cover they built crib piers of railroad ties to a height of sixty feet. Five days later, surrounded by the guns of their own troops, the German engineers were able to move a lone freight car across the bridge. But only one car at a time could make it across the improvised structure, and this had to be accomplished by hand. Several days later an entire train could be rolled across the bridge, but not with the locomotive. Each train had to be rolled onto the bridge by a locomotive pushing, and then removed from the other side by a locomotive waiting to pull the freight cars free.

In the meantime, the Germans had counted heavily on their relief rail line running from Krichev to Unecha. It was a hope that went up in a ragged series of explosions as the partisans cut the tracks in ninety places along a distance of sixty miles and knocked out the line for at least a week.

In January 1943 the Germans recorded 397 attacks on the railway system involving the Kursk area; these attacks damaged 112 locomotives and 22 bridges. It was only a small start to what would become an enormous effort, for records of the German general directorate of "Railways East" told the grim story that in February the number of attacks increased from 397 to more than 500, to 1,045 attacks by May, to 1,092 in June, and, in support of the active fighting in the Kursk salient, to 1,460 attacks in July.

A German soldier wrote home to his wife:

With us trains move for one day and three days have to be spent repairing the track, since the partisans blow everything up. The night before last they arranged a collision between an express train and a leave train, so that the trains aren't running . . . that's how we live in Russia.

Historical Study Number 20-230 (United States Army) makes reference to a German report that "unusual developments at the front

would immediately result in lively partisan activity, essentially aimed at the disruption and destruction of railroad lines." Referring to the opening stages of the Battle of Kursk, the report notes that "the main line of a railroad that had to handle the supplies for three German armies *was blasted at two thousand points in a single night* and so effectively disrupted that all traffic was stalled for several days."

The partisans at times showed great ingenuity in striking special targets. The same study refers to an incident in the summer of 1943 when a German-speaking Russian in the uniform of a German officer drove a truck directly into a military government detachment, where he then talked his way into an audience with the commanding general.

He managed to slug the general into unconsciousness and roll him tightly within a large carpet. In an incredible display of assurance as to what he was doing, he called the general's orderly into the room and enlisted the German's aid in carrying the heavy carpet out of the building and into the truck waiting outside. The German general was delivered neatly into the hands of partisans waiting in the woods beyond the town.

14

THE INCREDIBLE T-34 TANK

The driver sat in a padded armchair, his folding backrest locked securely behind him. No luxury there; a man needed all the "give" he could get against his frame when the going became so severe as to be violent. Lurching cross-country within the tight-fitting confines of a T-34 tank is not conducive to comfort. There are tanks and there are tanks, and the one thing its designers did not bother about in creating the Russian T-34 was anything more than a cursory consideration for the crew.

Four men rode to war in what was one of the truly great weapons of World War II. In the front left side of the tank hull, the driver controlled the T-34's track speeds with conventional steering levels. He had, as well, the usual tank controls of the clutch, foot brake, and accelerator, all placed in standard automobile alignment from left to right. Some tanks built during the war brought envy to other tankers' eyes in that every step was taken to assure maximum crew comfort along with as many controls and facilities as might be squeezed into the rolling fortress. Not so with the T-34.

Loaded for bear, the Russian tank as it went into the fighting at Kursk weighed between 54,000 and 56,000 pounds, the weight variations depending upon equipment and supplies to different situations. Measured from the muzzle of the 76.2-mm. cannon to the rear body, the T-34 had a length of not quite twenty-two feet. The tank stood eight feet high and moved on tracks each with a width of nineteen inches.

The heart of the T-34—and it was Guderian who had said long before the war that everybody thought too much about the guns and not about the engine—was one of its strongest points. The 12-cylinder engine was a partly aluminum diesel that ground out 500 horsepower at 1,800 rpm and performed with great reliability and exceptional economy. To monitor and control his engine, the T-34 driver had water temperature, oil temperature, and oil pressure gauges. To his left was a second instrument panel with a tachometer, speedometer, ammeter, voltmeter, and starter. The T-34 used in the summer of 1943 (improvements were made in the tank throughout the war) had a gearbox with three forward and one reverse gears.

To the right of the driver, in an identical padded seat with folding backrest, sat the hull-gunner, who fired a 76.2-mm. Degtyarev gas-operated machine gun. The weapon was fed through a drum-type magazine holding sixty rounds. Officially, the machine gun was capable of firing at a rate of 580 rounds per minute, but this was a grossly unrealistic figure (as are most firing rates for automatic weapons), and the combat firing rate was closer to a maximum of 150 rounds per minute.

The remaining two crewmen had even less room and considerably more discomfort than did the driver and hull-gunner; the tank commander and gun loader were forced to squeeze into the turret of the T-34. Considering that the commander had to operate in a space with only fifty-six inches of headroom—within which he commanded the tank's operation, laid and fired the heavy cannon, and coordinated his movements with the man who loaded the shells—crew performance in the T-34 demanded a great deal from Russian tankers.

The two men in the turret sat on padded seats secured to a tubular framework. Each man had a wide, thickly cushioned backrest that was permanently secured to the ring of the turret. The arrangement called

for some physical dexterity. In most tanks built by the United States or England, the crew seats were so fitted as to turn with the turret when the latter revolved. Not so the T-34 with its seats secured to the turret *ring*. When the turret traversed, it was up to the commander and the loader to shift their body position, turning physically on the non-moving seats, as they moved the turret to position the 76.2-mm. cannon.

That was only the start of the great skill and coordination needed for combat operations, when the world was a madhouse of screaming engine and gears, hammering machine guns, the crash of cannon, and the bone-bruising movement of the tank as it ground its way across inhospitable terrain.

The tank commander operated not only the high-velocity cannon but also a machine gun mounted beside the heavy weapon. He could activate the turret guns with the help of a periscope dial sight or through use of a cranked telescopic sight; in either case he did his sighting through an eyepiece with a rubber eye guard and a brow pad (with as much pressure as possible against this equipment to keep head-bashing to its minimum during severe maneuvering). The commander fired his weapons through his choice of hand or foot controls (the loader could also fire the machine gun through a separate hand trigger), and there were times when the ability to select one or the other was critical.

Few men in battle were ever busier than a T-34 tank commander. Below him the driver peered at the world through a distressingly limited field of view (much less than German tanks, for example). Unless the driver was on a straight course, he needed constant instruction from the tank commander, who passed on his orders by throat microphone. At the same time the commander was constantly shifting back and forth from driving commands to handling his weapon and seeing where his rounds had struck; the heavy cannon was completely under his control.

Accordingly, he needed to direct the forward movement of the tank through the driver, aim the heavy cannon (and often the machine gun), snap out orders to his loader for different types of ammunition, use his sighting equipment for range determination, sighting, and firing—and making *absolutely* certain he was clear of the cannon when

it fired, because it crashed back with lethal force a full fourteen inches of recoil on each firing. He also had to keep an eye peeled for signal flags from the troop commander for any special instructions; the Russians didn't bother with tank radio below troop commander rank (troop commanders had three tanks under direct control beside their own T-34).

The loader—in the turret with the commander—had his own headaches with which to contend. The heavy gun carried a total of seventy-seven rounds. Average ammunition loading (and it changed according to the expected combat requirements) came to nineteen rounds of armor-piercing, fifty-three rounds of high explosive, and five rounds of shrapnel. If the first engagement was short and swift, the loader could handle his job without much difficulty, but in any protracted battle he had to perform with almost physical legerdemain.

Of the seventy-seven rounds in the T-34, no more than nine were easily accessible—a wall rack on the left side of the turret held six rounds, and another rack on the right side held three rounds. At the bottom of the turret was a storage bin that held the remaining sixty-eight rounds. Fair enough, but the bin lay beneath a rubber matting that made up—physically—the floor of the turret. If the combat engagement promised to last for any length of time, the loader then had to get down to the turret floor and initiate an instant removal of the matting so that he might quickly (but never easily) reach the shells. And he had to do this (by agitated squirming) in a tank pitching and swerving violently, with his ears assailed by noise, in stifling heat— with a clanging, extremely hot shell casing dumped into the storage bin every time the gun fired.

Was this the same tank, then, that constituted the backbone of the Russian armored forces at Kursk? The tank the Germans considered so dangerous that they delayed the onset of Citadel for week after week in order to rush the new Panthers and Tigers to the front? This same T-34, with all its design shortcomings?

By every account the answer is yes. By every account the T-34 was *the* battlefield ruler, when all things are considered, of the fighting conditions on the eastern front.

Yet it was Mellinthin who stated flatly he considered the Panther and the Tiger Mark VI to be the superior to the T-34. It was Mellin-

thin, and others with him, who never considered the T-34 to be the armored ruler of the battlefield. The German tank experts who insisted upon *technical comparisons* almost always came up with a final evaluation that kept the T-34 from the head of the list.

But the Russians, ignoring such technicalities, went on to produce the T-34 in the greatest numbers possible and used the tank to crack wide open the shell of German panzers.

Was it sheer mass of numbers, then, that gained for the T-34 its accolades? Definitely no. Not that numbers were unimportant, but numbers alone could never account for the reputation and the battlefield record secured by the T-34.

This was the tank that Colonel General Heinz Guderian, at the time commanding Second Panzer Army, described as "very worrying . . . up to this time we had enjoyed tank superiority, but from now on the situation was reversed. The prospect of rapid, decisive victories was fading in consequence."

And to no less a figure than Field Marshal Ewald von Kleist of First Panzer Army, the T-34 "was the finest tank in the world."

All of which appears, at first blush, to be directly opposed to our brief review of some of the problems inherent in the design of the T-34. But there is a difference in such problems where armored vehicles are concerned, and it is a difference with a vengeance.

The problems of the T-34, insofar as this tank must be measured *as a weapon*, were minor.

Douglas Orgill, veteran tank commander of the British army in World War II, in his book *T-34: Russian Armor* takes careful note of the ultimate distinction in judging a tank. The T-34, states Orgill, "succeeded, in its day, in solving the basic equation which should be written in gold above every tank designer's desk: The effectiveness of a weapon is directly equal to its ability to get itself properly into position to deal decisive blows without being harmed by the blows it is itself receiving."

Orgill adds that the T-34 "was the production not of inspirational genius but of robust common sense. It owed its existence to men who could envisage a mid-century battlefield more clearly than anyone in the West, except for a handful of theorists, had been able to do. The work which the Koshkin design team carried out at the Kharkov loco-

motive works in 1939 was to change the history of the war, and thus of Europe and the world."

One final comment of Orgill's on the subject went a long way in establishing conclusively the efficacy of the Soviet behemoth on the great battlefield of Kursk: "The fundamentals of a tank are armament, armor, mobility. It is the degree of success in balancing these three factors which ultimately decides the fighting qualities of the tank. In each of these three factors, the T-34 offered the most formidable challenge of any tank in general service in its day."

The Russians massed two basic tanks for the struggle building in the Kursk salient. The T-34 was the main punch, and this may seem surprising because it was a medium tank rather than a heavy tank like the KV-1, which weighed nearly forty-four tons. Both tanks had the same basic engine, but because of the difference in weight, the T-34 had a top speed of 33 mph, whereas the KV-1 was restricted to 24 mph. The T-34 had its extremely effective 76.2-mm. cannon, as did the KV-1. The latter mounted three machine guns to the two of the T-34.

Many tanks had thicker or heavier armor than the T-34, but there was nothing like the T-34 armor *for its class of tank*. The armor plating (65 mm. on the turret and 47 mm. on the hull) was heavy enough, but for its thickness and weight it was far more effective than for any other tank in existence. The Russians paid the closest attention to getting the most for what they put into the protective design of the T-34, and in tests intended to produce armor that would best resist armor-piercing shells, they were fully aware that *sloping* armor is far more efficient as a defense than armor placed vertically about a tank. If 100-mm. armor plating is installed on a tank at an angle of sixty degrees, it will provide approximately the same protection as 300-mm. armor plating along a vertical plane.

Prior to the summer of 1943, when the Tigers and Panthers were rushed into service with Germany's armored forces, the principal opponent of the T-34 was the Mark IV tank. Originally this vehicle had a short-barreled 75-mm. gun, which proved woefully ineffective against the T-34, and was itself grimly vulnerable to the Russian tank. The short-barreled gun on the Mark IV had a muzzle velocity of only

1,300 feet per second as compared to 2,172 feet per second for the T-34, and the Russians took every advantage of the "can opener" effect of their tank.

The reaction on German morale was perhaps even greater than could be measured in losses on the battlefield, for here were the *Untermenschen*, the subhumans from Russia, with an armored weapon devastatingly superior to what had been the steel backbone of the Panzers.

"It is a wonder weapon," one German tanker wrote in his report, "that spreads terror and fear wherever it moves."

German antitank troops, armed with the Wehrmacht's 37-mm. cannon for destroying Russian armor, watched in amazement and growing fear as their shells bounced harmlessly away from the sloping armor plate of the T-34—and then ran for their lives as the Russian tanks advanced inexorably toward the helpless gun crews.

In a running engagement or a fast fire fight, or where cross-country speed and agility were vital, nothing could match the T-34. But there were many battles where the Russian KV-1 heavy tank showed a side that brought its own kind of despair to the Germans, as is recorded by the official history of the 1st Panzer Division after its initial contact with the KV-1:

> Our companies opened fire at about eight hundred yards but it was ineffective. We moved closer and closer to the enemy, who for his part continued to approach us unconcerned. Very soon we were facing each other at fifty to one hundred yards. A fantastic exchange of fire took place without any visible German success.
>
> The Russian tanks continued to advance and all armor-piercing shells simply bounced off them. Thus we were soon faced with the alarming situation of the Russian tanks driving through the tanks of First Panzer Regiment towards our own infantry and rear areas. Our panzer regiment therefore about-turned and drove back with the KV . . . roughly in line with them. In the course of that operation we succeeded in immobilizing some of them with special purpose shells at very close range—thirty to sixty yards.

A German sergeant tank-gunner of the 4th Panzer Division gave his report after an encounter with T-34 tanks:

. . . there is nothing more frightening than a tank battle against superior force. Numbers—they don't mean much, we were used to it. But better machines, that's terrible. You race the engine, but she responds too slowly. The Russian tanks are so agile, at close range they will climb a slope or cross a piece of swamp faster than you can traverse the turret. And through the noise and the vibration you keep hearing the clang of shot against armor. When they hit one of our panzers there is so often a deep long explosion, a roar as the fuel burns, a roar too loud, thank God, to let us hear the cries of the crew. . . .

But the Battle of Kursk would be fought with new armored weapons with which the Russians had never closed in combat. There would be, to be certain, many of the older Mark III tanks which the Germans would use away from the main clash of armor. The Mark IV's, especially those with heavier armor plating and with longer-barreled, high-velocity 75-mm. guns, would be in the thick of the fighting. Above all, there would be the new Panther and the Mark VI Tiger, thrown into the wedge-shaped shock fronts with which the Germans hoped to punch through the Russian defenses. There would also be the massive self-propelled Ferdinands, already dubbed *Elefants* by the German soldiers, to bring massive firepower to any point of the battle where it might be needed.

There is a note that must be added to this final preview before joining the open fighting that was to erupt in the Kursk salient. The word "Tiger" is synonymous with a brilliant, deadly armored weapon. It has emerged from World War II endowed with some magical quality of prowess possessed by no other weapon of its kind.

Where the Battle of Kursk is concerned, as the final days drew to their close, *there is no validity for such a belief.*

All one needs to do is to make a side-to-side comparison of the T-34 tank and the Tiger tank, as they were ready for battle in the summer of 1943, and an astonishing fact emerges—the T-34 was clearly the superior weapon. To be sure, the Tiger was more massive, carried thicker armor, and was armed with that splendid weapon—the 88-mm. gun.

But it was *not* the right weapon for the *offensive* in the Kursk sa-

lient. Moving across open countryside, it had barely half the speed of the T-34, being held to no more than 12 mph. Its range was barely more than sixty miles, and without fuel support in the field of battle, the Tigers soon ran out of fuel and became sitting ducks for Russian guns.

Another factor that was more than aggravating—to the point of producing overwhelming casualties—was that the Tiger tanks rushed to the Kursk front to launch Operation Citadel had the nasty habit of breaking down without warning. A tank that is crippled mechanically in combat is not a single loss.

It takes a Tiger to tow a Tiger. . . .

There was one incident many German officers kept in mind before the guns roared to open the Battle of Kursk; an incident that showed just how tough, tenacious, and deadly could be a single determined Russian tank crew. The following report of an astounding fight involving *one* Russian heavy tank, shortly after it made its first appearance in combat, is from German—not Russian—records. Were it a report by the Russians, there is no doubt few would believe its authenticity.

One of the KV-1's even managed to reach the only supply route of the German task force located in the northern bridgehead, and blocked it for several days. The first unsuspecting trucks to arrive with supplies were immediately shot afire by the tank. There were practically no means of eliminating the monster. It was impossible to bypass it because of the swampy surrounding terrain. Neither supplies nor ammunition could be brought up. The severely wounded could not be removed to the hospital for the necessary operations, so they died. The attempt to put the tank out of action with the 50-mm. antitank gun battery . . . at a range of 500 yards ended with heavy losses to crews and equipment of the battery.

The tank remained undamaged in spite of the fact that, as was later determined, it got fourteen direct hits. These merely produced blue spots on its armor. When a camouflaged 88-mm. gun was brought up, the tank calmly permitted it to be put into position at a distance of 700 yards, and then smashed it and its crew before it was

Lone German survivor of antitank unit virtually wiped out at Kursk.
(Novosti Press Agency)

Russian submachine gunners moving out against the enemy. *(Novosti Press Agency)*

When inhabitants of the city of Karachev came out to welcome their liberators, this soldier, Private Scherbakov, found his two sisters—"miraculously alive." *(Novosti Press Agency)*

Ferdinand self-propelled gun burning after direct hit by Russian tank at close quarters. *(Novosti Press Agency)*

Russian artillery firing at German tank concentrations. *(Novosti Press Agency)*

Seventy-ton Ferdinand self-propelled guns knocked out on the battlefield. *(Novosti Press Agency)*

Enemy equipment captured by Soviet troops. *(Sovfoto)*

Weapons deserted by the Hitlerites. *(Novosti Press Agency)*

German six-barrel mortars deserted during a retreat. *(Novosti Press Agency)*

even ready to fire. The attempt of engineers to blow it up at night likewise proved abortive.

To be sure, the engineers managed to get to the tank after midnight, and laid the prescribed demolition charge under the caterpillar tracks. The charge went off according to plan, but was insufficient for the oversized tracks. Pieces were broken off the tracks, but the tank remained mobile and continued to molest the rear of the front and to block all supplies.

At first it received supplies at night from scattered Russian groups and civilians, but the Germans later prevented this procedure by blocking off the surrounding area. However, even this isolation did not induce it to give up its favorable position. It finally became the victim of a German ruse. Fifty tanks were ordered to feign an attack from three sides and to fire on it so as to draw all of its attention in those directions. Under the protection of this feint it was possible to set up and camouflage another 88-mm. flak gun to the rear of the tank, so that this time it actually was able to fire. Of the twelve direct hits scored by this medium three pierced the tank and destroyed it.

And that was *one* Russian heavy tank.

Part IV

The Battle

15

THE NAZIS MOVE
TO THE ATTACK

Kursk was a nightmarish struggle that came alive in fits and starts. It progressed from dozens of small incidents into several major actions and then, full-blown, marched across the landscape of central Russia.

As we have seen, it was not planned that way. The German high command had intended that the Citadel offensive should begin with a devastating artillery and rocket barrage, supported by massive, repeated air strikes, in the dead of night. The concentration of firepower was expected to tear great holes in the thick defensive lines created by the Russians. As dawn broke on the morning of July 5, after hours of withering punishment being thrown against the Russian lines, the German troops would emerge from their fortifications and follow their tanks against the enemy. Above all, it was Model's Ninth Army that would carry the heaviest weight of the German attack, and it would be supported by the devastating punch of ninety of the massive Porsche Ferdinand self-propelled guns.

Well south of Kursk, in coordination with Model's forces, Hoth was scheduled to hurl his Fourth Panzer Army against the Voronezh

front commanded by Vatutin. Despite the great strength amassed by Model against Rokossovsky's central front, it was Hoth who commanded the preponderance of German armor, and it was to Hoth's panzers that the Germans had given the responsibility for breaking through to Kursk.

Zhukov, commanding the entire operation, was fully aware that no matter how extensive his secret intelligence data from Lucy or even his commanders' reconnaissance of the enemy plans, he was still involved in a huge gamble. A single wrong guess could open the lines to a German penetration behind their armor to Kursk.

To prevent the situation from getting out of hand—the Germans exploiting any breakthrough—Zhukov counted heavily on Marshal Ivan Koniev's powerful operational reserve. Koniev kept ready for immediate deployment to any danger area heavy armored forces, which included General Pavel A. Rotmistrov's Fifth Guards Tank Army, the I Guards Mechanized Corps, the IV Guards Tank Corps, and the X Tank Corps. Within that reserve force (and it was the Zhukov touch to keep the most powerful forces in reserve for his sudden counterblow) were the elite of Russian armor.

The German field commanders were far more knowledgeable about the thickly sowed Russian defenses than was their leader in Berlin, and well before the battle they abandoned the traditional offensive techniques formerly employed against the Russians. The "old" pattern of moving into the enemy lines had been conducted with the tanks and motorized infantry striking hard, fast, and for the greatest distance possible; behind them came the masses of infantry that would close the rings on the encircled enemy. It had worked in the past; it would not work now, and the Germans instead went over to the panzerkeil.

The panzerkeil was the armored wedge in its most potent sense. The point of the German attack would be a wedge made of heavy tanks, in this instance the new and massive Tigers. Behind these would be the new Panthers and the older Mark IV's. But there would be more than a single wedge; in fact, the panzerkeil called for a succession of wedges, one behind the other, fanning out in the rear, so that the thrust forward had the general appearance of a massive spear lance. Moving up behind the wedges, against what would be the base

of the blunt arrowhead, would be the infantry armed with automatic weapons and grenades. Directly behind this force were heavier combat elements consisting of armored personnel carriers, the troops within ready for overwhelming dense tactical fire from thousands of mortars.

The Germans hoped that not even the massive Russian defenses could stand up against a succession of these wedges, each theoretically capable of punching a disastrous hole in the Russian lines. Where one wedge ran out of forward momentum, another would already be in motion, and if a series of such wedges could be kept moving, then the Russians could possibly be wiped out to the last man or overrun in their most vital defense positions. The road to Kursk would then be wide open.

The Russians of course, could not be expected to be completely in the dark about the modified German tactics. But not even the best intelligence from Lucy, sappers, or aerial reconnaissance could provide Zhukov with the small details concerning the maneuvering of enemy units. There had to be a single modification to the systems employed by the Red Army in terms of defense that would meet *any* threat of an unexpected nature, and the Russians turned to their enemy for what they needed.

For their own defenses the Germans had long used what was known as a pakfront. Essential to the pakfront was the use of antitank weapons, and the major such Soviet weapon was their 76.2-mm. gun. This had proved devastatingly effective against the Mark III and Mark IV tanks, but the Tiger was wholly another matter, and the initial brushes with the fifty-six-ton tank had revealed to the Russian commanders that too often their shells would bounce from the thick armor of the new heavy tank. There was also the problem of the lumbering Ferdinands. The self-propelled guns were protected with 200-mm. armor, thicker than the armor plating of most battle cruisers at sea.

Accordingly, the pakfront was altered by the Russians in order to gain a torrent of heavy firepower where and when needed in the shortest possible time. One officer was given command of as many as ten antitank guns, the fire of which he could direct against a single target. Where one or two 76.2-mm. guns might be ineffective against a Tiger, ten such weapons were almost sure to have a can-opener effect or to

hit vital parts of the German tank. However, even more than this was needed, so the Russians surrounded each pakfront with a dense concentration of mines.

This served two purposes. First, it could damage or stop a tank dead in its tracks, leaving it open for savage firepower not only from the established pakfronts, but also from heavier artillery firing at point-blank range. Heavy artillery is notoriously ineffective against moving tanks—but the emphasis is on the word *moving*.

Thus the mines. Even if they failed to halt the tanks, they would slow their advance to a crawl, and *then* the artillery could be called on to hurl an overwhelming rain of shells directly against the tanks.

There was one further advantage to the pakfronts, which extended back for miles through the defensive system. They showed unprecedented care in their assembly, location, and entrenchment, and they lay concealed so effectively beneath camouflage that they blended into the earth to the point where German reconnaissance before the battle failed miserably in attempts to single them out. A typical panzer division report bears out the nature of the problems: "Neither mine-fields or pakfronts could be detected until the first tank blew up, or the first Russian antitank gun opened fire. . . ."

The orders to begin Operation Citadel called for the opening barrage of the battle to begin precisely at 2:30 A.M. on July 5. For thirty minutes German artillery, mortars, and rockets would pound the Russian lines. At 3:00 in the morning the first tanks would move forward, followed by infantry and the motorized units. They would thus be in position by first light of day for the German air force to assault the battlefield area directly and hit the first line of Russian defensive positions.

This was the plan, but it was destined not to function as outlined. Instead of Citadel being launched with this single massive blow all along the front that composed the Kursk salient, it got under way with a series of events, each larger than the other, some related, others carried out as separate actions, but each dictating in its own way the course of events that exploded fully on the morning of July 5.

Hoth had decided that his forces were at a disadvantage to initiate the full-scale attack of Citadel at the time ordered by Berlin—3:00 in

the morning of July 5. To his way of reckoning, if the Fourth Panzer Army could "reshape" the front lines prior to the attack, he could launch his major blow with forces arranged to his advantage. Twelve hours before the moment scheduled for Citadel to begin, German forces opposite Vatutin's Voronezh front plunged into action.

The day was hot and sultry, with threatening thunderclouds in the area—definitely not the best conditions for the strong aerial support and bombardment the Germans needed for the "line reshaping" attack. Despite the unfavorable cloud conditions, German bombers and fighter-bombers ripped the Russian lines, in concert with a short but extremely heavy artillery and rocket barrage. Moving quickly, armored and infantry spearheads lurched forward from the lines.

The attack appeared to have caught the Russians off balance. Scouting patrols of the LII Corps, moving quickly into Russian territory to provide both probing and diversionary action, were successful in penetrating the Russian defenses. At once, stronger elements of the XLVIII Panzer Corps broke from their lines and lunged against the defensive elements of the Sixth Guards Army. The Germans expected stiff resistance in these moves, for Sixth Guards Army was a strong and experienced force that had taken heavy casualties of the Germans when it routed the XLVIII Panzer Corps on the Don.

The German opinion that the Russians were caught by surprise was reinforced as the hours went by without any heavy counterfire from defending artillery. There was some fire, but it was sporadic and ineffective, and the Germans drew the conclusion that the commander of defending artillery was uncertain as to conditions along the front. XLVIII Panzer moved forward steadily along a line that extended about three miles south of the villages of Luchanino, Alexejewka, and Sawidowka. Heavy assault guns and engineer detachments provided direct, heavy, and effective support for the grenadiers and riflemen of XLVIII Panzer, the units keeping tight so they might exploit any breaks in the defending lines as they occurred.

The German attack proceeded with excellent results for the day. By nightfall, the probing forces had covered enough ground for the division to have improved greatly its positioning for the major offensive the next day as part of Citadel. As quickly as darkness fell, the Gross Deutschland division moved forward with its heavy tanks to

ready them for the main blow later that night (the morning of July 5). II S.S. Panzer Corps advanced into the newly occupied area and sent out strong patrols to further probe the Russian lines in preparation for the main attack.

The Germans were more than satisfied. The entire front line had been shoved back in the area west of Dragunskoye, and the main armored forces were in position to exploit their advantage. The frontline units received their orders: Early July 5 Gross Deutschland would strike with all available strength between Ssyrzew and Luchanino. The 3d and 11th panzer divisions would make their advance along the flanks of Gross Deutschland, enabling the central force to use its panzerkeil wedges to crack the Russian lines.

Unfortunately for the Wehrmacht, neither the Russians nor the weather offered any cooperation for such plans.

First, the Russians were proving to be singularly unalarmed by the German advance. It had not been, to their way of thinking, any indication of how the future fighting would go. The Germans had made progress, but what good it would do them when they encountered the main Russian defense lines was questionable.

On the situation maps the Germans had strengthened their own lines, but the advance was restricted generally to a width of about two and a half miles. The small Russian hamlets occupied by the Germans were of little consequence to the main defensive systems, and the Russians in command headquarters watched with interest as the Germans fought well into the night to clear individual houses in the hamlets. The interest was not so much for the fighting of the small combat units, but for the heavy tanks and other forces the Germans were moving up under cover of darkness.

To Vatutin, the Germans had played their roles well. With the advance to strengthen their own lines, after which reinforcements were moved closer to the Russian defense system, the Germans had, in effect, told the Russians precisely where their main forces were located. Russian artillery fire had been sporadic and of generally little effect on the battlefield during the afternoon and early evening of July 4, but Vatutin was about to change that story. He had been informed by Stavka (Russian supreme headquarters) that the main

attack would come the night of July 4–5, and now he had the opportunity to turn the tables on the enemy.

German troops, meanwhile, were hard at work against Russian diehards in the small hamlets taken as prizes in the German advance. Vatutin knew well what they were trying to do—clear both sides of the stream so that, in the morning, the main armored forces could ford the water obstacle and move out against the Russian lines.

At 10:30 that night, July 4, the world caved in upon the German lines. Vatutin had enough information to turn loose his big guns, and the massed artillery along the entire Sixth Guards Army front exploded into action. Thousands of shells rained down upon the attack force as it assembled, the great blasts sending the Germans rushing for cover and throwing into disorder the attempt to ready the German units for the assault that was due to take place.

Again and again the great guns hammered at German armor, infantry, motorized units, engineering battalions, tearing up convoys, ripping fuel dumps, turning the night sky into a single constantly flickering sheath of flame. German artillery, nearly overwhelmed by the sudden and unexpected fury of the Russian bombardment, finally got around to sending off counterfire, whereupon Vatutin played his second hand.

Several hundred big guns that had kept quiet until this point now roared into action, and the German artillery positions discovered themselves to be the target for a devastating new round of shells. Vatutin had tremendous artillery strength at his disposal, and he was making full use of that force. The guns hammered throughout the night and by dawn Vatutin brought in even more of the great artillery pieces. He ordered the massed artillery of Sixth Army and Seventh Guards Army to take under fire the German targets along their fronts.

What had begun as a limited advance by the Germans—and successful it was—had been transformed into a terrible shelling by thousands of Russian guns. The Germans suffered heavy casualties, but they were hurt even more by the disorganization resulting from the merciless, nonstop shelling.

Bad as was the barrage, the Germans knew how to function under heavy fire, and the darkness kept the Russians from gaining accurate information about the effectiveness of the bombardment. They could

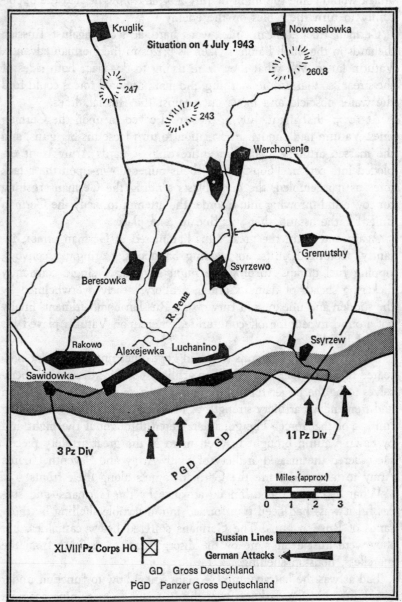

Kruglik

Nowosselowka

Situation on 4 July 1943

247

260.8

243

Werchopenje

Gremutshy

Ssyrzewo

Beresowka

R. Pena

Ssyrzew

Rakowo

Alexejewka   Luchanino

Sawidowka

11 Pz Div

3 Pz Div

P G D   G D

Miles (approx)

0   1   2   3

XLVIII Pz Corps HQ

Russian Lines

German Attacks

GD   Gross Deutschland

PGD   Panzer Gross Deutschland

take their punishment and endure their losses. They would lose time in setting up for the attack early in the morning for their role in Citadel, but still they would strike and add their great strength, especially with the panzer divisions, to the full blow against the Kursk salient.

It was at this point that nature turned against the Germans along the Voronezh front. The weather that had threatened during the hot and oppressive afternoon fulfilled its promise that night, and what was apparently a squall line with towering thunderheads burst open directly across the embattled ground. In the four small hamlets occupied by the Germans, where every effort was being made to gain secure footholds on both sides of the stream that ran along the towns, the earth turned into a thick quagmire. Especially between Ssyrzew and Sawidowka did the earth disappear into a bog.

The Germans watched with dismay as the stream rose swiftly along its banks and then began to spread out on each side, effectively widening what had been a gently flowing rivulet into a small, raging river. Roads and tracks leading to the German positions became seas of mud. Trucks turning off these vehicle-bogging roadways found the ground beneath the water even worse. Wheeled vehicles were helpless, and cursing German drivers had to wait for tracked vehicles to pull them free.

As the night progressed, the rains continued without letup, at times whipped by gale-force winds. Lightning flashes mixed with the bright flickering blasts of heavy guns, and the skies quaked under a continuous din of roaring artillery and the heavy cannonading of thunder.

It was a stroke of tremendous fortune which the Russians did not waste. Under cover of their own ceaseless artillery barrage and the drastically reduced visibility of low clouds and heavy rain, they rolled heavy guns and tanks into the wrecked buildings on the outskirts of the town. Red troops set up their weapons where the Germans must assemble, and as the gray, leaden dawn began to streak the horizon, the Russian gun commanders had before them a perfect target—the densely packed elements of two German divisions trying to ford a stream several feet higher than it had been hours before, and with the banks of the stream virtually impassable.

The moment for launching Citadel according to plan had come and gone, and all that Hoth had been able to accomplish with his "re-

shaping" of the front was to crack the first line of Russian defenses—and leave his forces wide open to the Soviet second line, which was quickly proving to be far more powerful than German intelligence had indicated. The events of the night had proved to be, stated Mellinthin, "of the greatest advantage to the Russian second line to the north of the stream and immensely increased its already considerable defensive strength."

Meanwhile, the official hour for launching the artillery barrage on the central front was nearing its point of commitment, and here, too, the Germans were to be caught seriously off balance.

16

THE SURPRISE SOVIET BARRAGE

On the evening of July 4, Zhukov was closeted with the commander of the central front, Rokossovsky, and his staff. We have seen earlier that the Russians had ordered every scrap of intelligence information from the front lines fed at once to each front headquarters, for on such small items could hang the precarious balance of gaining an immediate advantage in the forthcoming battle. Several prisoners and at least one defector made it clear through their reports that the Germans would attack before the next dawn. Other last-moment intelligence gathered directly from the front lines seemed to confirm beyond all question that the Germans would roll from their positions sometime in the morning of the fifth.

Zhukov had spent hours checking with all elements of the various fronts. He was on the telephone talking with Vasilievsky (southwest front) at his headquarters, receiving from that officer a compilation of intelligence reports gathered from skirmishes in the sector near Belgorod. From Vasilievsky, Zhukov also obtained the information that a prisoner from the 168th Infantry Division had been "prompted"

to reveal to his captors that the offensive would begin before the night ended.

Other reports were more sketchy, but leaned in this same direction. Then, just after 2:00 on the morning of July 5, the command post telephone rang with a call for Rokossovsky. It was General Pukhov, commander of the Thirteenth Army, with another piece of "hard" information. A sapper captured from the 6th Infantry Division stated that the German offensive would roll at 3:00 that same morning. Less than one hour away.

Rokossovsky turned to Zhukov. "What shall we do? Inform supreme headquarters or issue orders for the preliminary bombardment ourselves?"

Zhukov's reply came at once. To the master of mass warfare they had been provided with a stroke of good fortune. Information of this nature must never be wasted—nor must the time advantage that came with it.

"We can't waste time," Zhukov answered. "Give the order according to plan, and I will call Stalin and report the information."

As Rokossovsky went about ordering the bombardment, Zhukov reached Stalin at Stavka (supreme headquarters) and passed on the information obtained from the prisoners, as well as the decision to initiate the artillery barrage. Stalin was not surprised by the news, for he had just finished a conversation with Vasilievsky. He gave immediate approval to the orders to commence firing against the German lines and asked that Zhukov keep him informed.

The minutes passed slowly as the firing order went down the line. Colonel G. S. Nadysev, the front's artillery chief of staff, was in constant telephone conference with Stavka artillery officers and with General V. I. Kazakov, artillery commander of the front. Finally Nadysev and Kazakov were through. The men waited.

"At 0220 on July 5th," stated Rokossovsky, "a tornado of artillery fire broke the predawn silence over the positions on both sides over a wide sector of the front south of Orel. It turned out that our artillery had opened fire in the defensive zone of the 13th Army and, in places, the 48th Army, where we had been expecting the enemy blow, ten minutes before the beginning of the enemy barrage.

"For thirty minutes, about 600 artillery pieces and mortars fired on

the nazi troops which were ready for the offensive. The enemy suffered heavy losses, especially in artillery; his troop control system was disorganized."

There was no question that the fire of the Russian artillery, massed for a blow of precisely this nature, was shattering. In addition to the heavy artillery and the mortars, the Russians fired thousands of M-31 (Katyusha) rockets, turning night into day. In central front headquarters, the command post itself rumbled almost steadily with the concussion waves roaring outward from the guns, and Zhukov remarked that the "boom of heavy artillery and the explosions of M-31 rockets were clearly audible."

The guns were hammering steadily when a telephone call came through from Stalin. "Well," he asked Zhukov, "have you begun?" Told the bombardment was in progress, Stalin asked: "What's the enemy doing?"

Zhukov was able to reply that the reaction from the Germans was still feeble, and that the enemy "was attempting to reply from a few batteries."

"All right," Stalin said, "I'll call again."

The Germans were caught almost completely by surprise when the massed artillery of the Russians opened fire. The Nazi forces had been preparing to launch their own salvos starting at 2:30 A.M. and continue heavy fire for thirty minutes, then lift the barrage so that German troops and armor could start toward the Russian lines.

Initially, about one hundred German artillery batteries were brought under the fire of Rokossovsky's guns. For some time confusion reigned in the German lines, and at least half the batteries were unable to return the Russian fire.

At 4:30, two hours and ten minutes after the Russians let loose with their heavy guns, the first enemy batteries began to fire with a consistent pattern to their efforts. The fire effect was for some time negligible, but by 5:00 the effect had improved considerably, and 5:30 a thundering crescendo of steel marked the increasingly heavy German fire.

Yet, whatever the Germans could accomplish with this growing barrage, the end result was far less than had been anticipated. Nowhere in the German plans was there an accounting for a massive

initial bombardment on the part of the Russians. The Germans had counted upon a devastating punch into the Russian lines with their opening salvos. Instead, the Russian fire had caught them flat-footed.

At that, the sheer weight of Rokossovsky's hammering of the German lines is what gave the Soviet forces their unexpected advantage. Russian artillery commanders were literally in the dark about German troop concentrations in the areas selected for jumping off toward the Russian lines. Neither was there specific information about the location of the German batteries. Kazakov, the Russian artillery commander in the line, therefore went to area bombardment, counting upon the sheer mass of Russian firepower for effect, rather than precise aiming. He had no other choice, of course, and this, as Zhukov has pointed out, "enabled the enemy to avoid excessive losses."

Whatever information the Russians could obtain concerning the effect of the barrage would have to come from German prisoners captured early in the battle. Rokossovsky, noting the slowly gaining strength of the German heavy artillery after they initiated fire at 4:30, decided there could never be too much of a good thing and prepared to let loose an even heavier assault upon the German positions.

He had good motivation for his move. Russian bombardment had knocked out many of the German artillery batteries, but these now had had the time to reorganize and clean up the heavy damage they had received, and were soon back in action. Thirteenth Army reported taking very heavy artillery fire from the Germans, then reported they were under strong attack by an estimated three hundred German bombers. At this point Rokossovsky ordered Kazakov to initiate another heavy bombardment of the German positions, only this time with nearly double the weight of the explosives.

More than a thousand heavy guns, mortars, and rocket positions opened fire at once, and for the next thirty minutes the German and Russian forces were engaged in a devastating duel with perhaps more than two thousand heavy pieces firing continuously at one another. German air attacks increased in intensity with first light.

That the Germans had prepared for the struggle with an overwhelming assembly of heavy weapons was evident at 5:30 that morning. German armor, engineers, and infantry went over to the offensive

along the whole front of the Russian Thirteenth Army and along the right flank of the Seventieth Army.

The effectiveness of the Russian artillery barrage was to be questioned—especially its timing—and Zhukov later voiced the opinion that he, and the front-line commanders with him, had acted too soon. In this respect Zhukov is applying hindsight to the battle, but the point is to be made and considered in judging what took place along the central and Voronezh fronts.

When the Russian guns initiated the mass artillery barrage, most of the German troops were still asleep and still well protected within their deeply imbedded trenches, dugouts, bunkers, and foxholes, against which the effect of the Russian artillery fire was blunted. Many of the German armored forces were still moving to their forward positions and offered poor targets for the Russian artillery, again diluting the effect of the Russian fire.

Yet the storm of Soviet artillery fire certainly influenced the immediate—and the future—situation. The German troops may have been well protected, but the thundering crash of thousands of shells tearing up the earth all about them kept them under cover and prevented them from forming up to move out to their jumping-off positions for the offensive. Almost everywhere the Germans had assembled they found themselves cut off from their command posts, and Zhukov (and other Russian commanders) found satisfaction in the fact that the bombardment had its greatest effect in tearing up communications, as well as observation and control systems "almost everywhere" within the German assembly areas.

How badly would the Russian defense lines have been torn up had not the Russian artillery first opened fire? How much more effective would have been the dense German artillery had the big guns of the Wehrmacht been permitted uninterrupted and carefully aimed fire?

Zhukov and his commanders note that the recuperative power of the German forces was little less than extraordinary. Despite the initial surprise bombardment of six hundred guns, and a second violent duel between German artillery and a thousand Russian weapons of heavy caliber, by 5:30 on the morning of July 5—only two and a half hours off their original schedule—the German panzers and supporting

forces were on the move and punching into the Russian defensive system.

Again there is the ultimate question of *if*. The Germans made some immediate gains into the bristling defenses of the Red Army. What they *might* have accomplished had their forces been free of the disruptive fire of the Russian bombardment is a moot point. In any event, the German forces absorbed heavy casualties during the artillery barrage on the central and Voronezh fronts, they suffered severe disruption, their timetable was thrown off, the offensive when it started was poorly organized and resulted as much from the issuance of previous orders as it did from the commands to move out.

There is every chance that the Battle of Kursk might well have produced different results without the sudden artillery attack decided upon by Zhukov, Rokossovsky, and the others.

For there is another element of military strength that failed the Soviets. The front-line commanders had counted upon a heavy strike by Russian bombers—with strong support by fighters—against the German lines. They were destined to be disappointed. Zhukov admits (and he is one of the few Russians to do so) that Russian bombers in the opening phase of the Battle of Kursk performed with a dismal record. He states that "aerial support was insignificant and, to be frank, ineffective. Our strikes at the enemy's airfields at dawn were too late. . . ."

17

NAZI FIGHTER PLANES
AVERT EARLY DISASTER

Zhukov, in his evaluation of the role of Russian air power early in
the Kursk struggle, makes it clear that aerial support of his own forces
was insignificant "because the preliminary bombardment took place
at night."

Night attacks apparently were not considered to pose undue
hardships to the Luftwaffe, for by 3:30 on the morning of July 5
a front-line combat force of seventeen hundred fighters, bombers,
ground-attack and antitank aircraft, according to Cajus Bekker in *The
Luftwaffe War Diaries*, were "at that moment . . . to be over the
front and start attacking not only the enemy airfields, but the fortifications, entrenchments and artillery positions of the deeply staggered
Russian defense system."

With rare exception Russian historians choose to muddle through
the role played by the Red Air Force in the opening phases of the
Kursk battle. With good reason, it would seem, for it was the Luftwaffe that raged across the battlefield and fulfilled its promise. That
the Germans did not prevail was not the fault of the air force units,

which fought with great effectiveness—and were hampered through-out by insufficient numbers on their own part and by growing numeri-cal superiority on the part of the Russians.

As with many other aspects of the struggle in the Kursk salient, at-tempts to pin down specifics about the numbers of weapons bog down quickly in the multiplicity of sources and the inherent conflicts of statements contained therein. Estimates of the numbers of German aircraft extend from a low figure of seventeen hundred machines of all types—but these are first-line combat aircraft that were to be flying attack missions. Any such force is always increased in number by air-craft undergoing maintenance, by immediate reserves, and by re-placement machines held at the ready to be dispatched to the front. As a battle continues, the number of machines participating rises steadily, and so it becomes inevitable that when one specifies a num-ber of aircraft, one must also give other particulars.

But there seems no question that there were seventeen hundred machines ready to fly their missions against the Russians on the morn-ing of July 5. One thousand aircraft would support Hoth's Fourth Panzer Army in the southern part of the battle, and the remaining seven hundred were delegated to cover Model's Ninth Army.

The Germans expected heavy opposition from Russian fighters, yet they expressed surprisingly little concern about the ability of the So-viets to disrupt the attacks of the ground-attack machines. No matter what may be claimed by any historian as to the relative merits of Russian or German aircraft, there can be no argument that the Ger-man fighter pilots considered the Russians to be dangerous only when they were provided with the advantage of a huge superiority in num-bers. Yet the fighter cover was critical, for most of the flying would be very low, with the German planes going in as close as possible to sup-port their armor and infantry advancing into the Russian defense systems.

The German fighters were composed of their excellent Focke-Wulf FW-190 and Messerschmitt Me-109 single-engine machines. The ma-jority of the ground-attack aircraft would be the venerable Junkers Ju-87 Stuka, but this would be used as other than the dive bomber for which it had gained notoriety.

Special antitank teams, using heavy cannon, had been assem-

bled for the Kursk fighting, including in their number the famed tank-busting Stuka pilot Hans Rudel. A separate force of Henschel Hs 129 twin-engine antitank killers had been rushed to the front, and this machine would prove extraordinarily effective in the ground-skimming operations. The antitank planes were expected to be a complete surprise to the Russians, equipped as they were with high-velocity 30-mm. cannon, and with the pilots trained to make their target runs so that their shells would pump into the sides or rear of the Russian tanks; head-on firing was expected to be useless against the thick armor of the T-34 and KV-1 tanks.

There were also the standards of the German bombing fleet—fighters carrying heavy bomb loads, large numbers of the versatile Junkers Ju-88 twin-engine bombers, and lesser numbers of the antiquated Heinkel He-111 twin-engine bombers. Other types found their way into the first-line forces, for the German air force was scraping barrels in every direction to assemble its air power for Kursk.

The Germans hoped to utilize their qualitative superiority in several clearly defined roles. First, the fighters would protect the bombers against Russian fighters. They would also be expected to keep Russian attack planes from carrying out damaging strikes against German ground forces. Third, the fighters would be given almost free rein in sweeping the battlefield, both responding to ground calls for air support and searching for targets of opportunity.

The tank busters had their missions clearly defined—strike first at Russian tanks, and, as secondary targets, go after self-propelled guns and motorized vehicles. The bombers were also given well-defined and familiar roles; they were to respond to the needs of the ground forces and provide close, swift, heavy air support where needed by knocking out major Russian targets.

Most Soviet aircraft flew their missions in direct support of ground units, with far less emphasis upon wide-reaching aspects of air power. To the Russians the airplane was simply an extension of the long-range gun, and this was its sole purpose. Their fighters were assigned to the most basic role—attack the German fighters at every opportunity and keep the German tank busters and bombers from their targets.

There was one airplane on which the Russians were placing great reliance—the Ilyushin IL-2 Stormovik, a single-engine ground-attack

machine with an extraordinary, almost unbelievable ability to survive the punishment of enemy fire. The crew of the Stormovik sat behind thick armor plating; indeed, the most critical parts of the airplane were shielded by such thick armor that the Stormovik could absorb enough blows to down several other aircraft and continue flying. Even the German pilots, who held in contempt most Russian machines, had nothing but head-shaking admiration for the "flying bunker" thrown into battle by the Red Air Force.

The story—and it was true—went the rounds of the Luftwaffe of a Stormovik attacked by four German fighters. The intercept was a "piece of cake"—a single Russian bomber nailed by four fighters heavily armed with machine guns and cannon. The first fighter pulled up behind the "flying tank" and emptied its entire load of ammunition into the Russian, seemingly without effect. One by one, the remaining three fighters did the same, and still the Stormovik continued on its course.

A disbelieving German fighter pilot called by radio to another fighter, asking what could possibly be keeping the Russian plane in the air. The classic answer came back at once:

"Herr Oberst, you cannot bite a porcupine in the ass."

Two days after the offensive began the Stormoviks would have their greatest day of the war against the 9th Panzer Division, when massed squadrons of the Russian planes would destroy seventy German tanks in twenty minutes.

The German plan to provide massive air cover for the opening blows of Operation Citadel came within a few minutes' time of complete disaster. Again the final outcome of a major battle was to be influenced greatly by the tense moments of a fight carried out *off* the battlefield.

Preparing to launch its aircraft from five airfields in the Kharkov area, the German air force kept its pilots and crews at "cockpit readiness" from midnight on. There was no problem, of course, with cold engines or other "starting aches" that plagued the air force in winter. Even the weather was cooperating. Threats of thunderstorm activity in the Kharkov area had dissipated, and the meteorology office promised that a fine, clear dawn would meet the German planes in the air.

Everything had been brought to a razor's edge of readiness, and the crews were waiting only for the signal to man their aircraft and start engines. The Germans planned to send their bombers first into the air; they would rendezvous over the fields as they gathered in formation and await their fighter escort that would take off at the last moment.

The fighter escort was considered critical. The Germans still believed that the precise time of their opening the Citadel offensive was a well-kept secret from the Russians. German air activity in recent days had been heavy, as much to accustom the Russians to frequent strikes as a matter of course as it was to prepare for the offensive. But the Luftwaffe commanders were confident that the heavy blow against the Russian defense lines would carry with it enough surprise to let them get through without serious opposition. If the plans held up, then they could also catch a major portion of the Russian bombers and fighters on the ground preparing for takeoff. The Russians were notorious in avoiding night combat missions, and the Germans felt everything was falling neatly into place for a massive blow that would knock out much of the Red Air Force on their fields.

The crews were in their planes when the radio warning service flashed an alert to the command post of General Hans Seidemann at VIII Air Corps headquarters at Mikoyanovka. There was a sudden and heavy increase in Russian radio traffic. Exchanges had more than tripled between various Soviet air regiments, a sure sign that the Russians were about to undertake major air activity. The fighter units were notified to stand by for emergency takeoff, and a short time afterward new reports electrified Seidemann's headquarters.

The Freya radar stations located in the Kharkov area had picked up several hundred Russian aircraft already in the air and on a direct course for the crowded airfields near Kharkov. The German controllers demanded verification of the report, for if true, it could only mean that the Russians were fully aware of the time the Germans were scheduled to open their offensive, and they were about to inflict upon the Luftwaffe precisely what the Germans were planning—to destroy the enemy on the ground before he had the chance to become airborne.

The Kharkov fields were particularly vulnerable to such a strike.

Every available foot of space had been crammed with the fighters and bombers, and the airfields were powder kegs with heavy stores of ammunition, bombs, and fuel. Even if the German bombers were to start rolling toward the runways, too much time would be lost in getting them into the air, and Russian fighters would have a field day attacking them. The airplanes were packed so tightly together it would be impossible for the Russians to miss their targets.

At the fields the bombers were ordered to hold their positions. The scheduled time for takeoff came and went, and the crews received postponements of takeoff from one minute to the next.

Meanwhile, the fighters were rolling. The pilots at Mikoyanovka were waiting near their planes, and at the first alert signal they scrambled into cockpits, where mechanics standing by started engines at once. JG 52 went roaring into the air in a desperate reach for altitude and distance to intercept the approaching Russians before they could arrive at the Kharkov airfields.

There, JG 3 had exploded into action. The bombers were waiting along the approach to the runway, engines turning over, when they received orders to hold fast where they were. The fighters of JG 3 taxied through their ranks, turning and wheeling to avoid the bombers as they broke through to the runway, starting takeoffs without waiting for tower clearance. It was obvious to the pilots what was at stake. As Cajus Bekker wrote: "During these minutes *Operation Citadel* . . . would be doomed before it started. For without maximum and continuous air support the battle could not be won."

The German fighters raced into the air from different directions, some pilots ignoring the wind, taking off on taxiways—anything to get airborne and climbing. At Mikoyanovka thunder began to fill the sky, and the German headquarters staff looked up to see the massed Russian formations passing overhead, droning toward Kharkov.

Well before they reached their objective the Focke-Wulfs and Messerschmitts were in their midst, like wolves after lumbering cows. Two complete groups of German fighters tore into an estimated four hundred to five hundred Russian bombers, ground-attack planes, and fighters, and there developed one of the largest and most bitterly fought air battles of the Russian front.

General Seidemann, watching the swirling mass of planes, remem-

bered the great air conflict as "a rare spectacle. Everywhere planes were burning and crashing. In no time at all some 120 aircraft were downed. Our own losses were so small as to represent total victory, for the consequence was complete German air control in the VIII Air Corps sector."

The reader may question for himself the figure of 120 Russian planes shot down so quickly. That the German fighters were effective in their intercept is the real point. They harried the Russian bombers all the way to Kharkov, staying with the chase through their own flak, continuing to attack and doing everything they could to break up the Russian formations. From all indications they achieved what they had set out to do. Bombs scattered wildly across the countryside, and there can be no question that the Russian raiders wasted a bold attempt to break German bomber strength on the ground. For within minutes of the originally scheduled time for the German bombers to take off for their strikes against the Russian lines, they were rolling down the runways. The German fighters landed, refueled and rearmed, and were in the air in time to escort the bombers to their targets.

Much of the details of the air fighting through the long Battle of Kursk has been lost in the overwhelming immensity of the struggle. But it seems clear that the Russians continued with their set pattern of utilizing their aircraft as extensions of artillery and in providing direct support for their troops.

In what appeared to be an innovation in aerial tactics, however, the Russians brought together large numbers of new-model Stormoviks for mass attacks on German armor and mechanized units, when such assistance was called for by endangered Soviet ground forces.

The Nazis were sorely in need of more aircraft and particularly in need of the tank busters they had developed to a fine degree of efficiency. The old and reliable Stuka was still present in large numbers, and it was employed in the tried-and-true method of operating as a flying wedge directly before the advancing German armor. With their advanced airfields so close to the front lines, the Germans were able to utilize their crews and planes for as many as six strike missions per plane per day. By rotating different groups—one bombing the target, another on the way home, another taking off for a mission—they did their best to keep their planes always over the battlefield.

The Russians did much the same, although it appears as if the Red Air Force operated on a principle of keeping everything moving to the battlefield, no matter how weary the pilots or worn out the planes. The Russian use of air power was much the same as their use of artillery and infantry on the ground: throw everything that could fly at the enemy, and where air power was needed for an immediate remedy to a dangerous tactical situation, do everything possible to saturate the Germans on the ground, even if this meant ignoring German fighters and taking heavy losses.

For the Germans, Kursk was the first opportunity to use their tank-busting teams on a wide scale, and they made the most of the enormous number of targets provided by the great clash of armor. On the fourth day of the offensive, the southern reach of the pincers the Germans were trying to close on the Kursk salient had managed to grind its way about twenty-five miles north of its starting point. The advance was not without its particular dangers, for Fourth Panzer Army was now left with a dangerously exposed and extended eastern flank.

The land was made to order for Russian combat—sprawling woodlands providing excellent cover to Red Army units that, in this area under heavy German dominance, had still escaped the crunch of the panzers. By now the Germans had suffered so heavily in tank losses they were unable to protect their flank, all armor being committed to the hardest fighting. The army turned to the Luftwaffe for a constant air reconnaissance of the area, having to settle for immediate notification of any danger and then responding to the threat as the aerial studies revealed its nature.

Early in the morning of July 8 the worst German fears were realized. Where the flank was fully exposed, without protecting ground forces, German planes discovered a mass of Russian armor, supported heavily by infantry units, working its way from the dense forests. The Russians were first sighted by Captain Bruno Meyer, who was leading a special section of the Henschel Hs-129B-2 tank-busting aircraft.

Meyer's radio reports caused no small consternation in headquarters of Fourth Panzer Army, for as he continued to circle the woodlands, more and more tanks appeared until he could count at least

forty of the rolling fortresses, preceded by "dense blocks of infantry, like a martial picture from the Middle Ages."

This was the ultimate test of German hopes for their new system for attacking Russian armor from the air. Not with bombs, but with high-velocity 30-mm. cannon designed especially for the task. Meyer ordered the entire force of Henschels at Mikoyanovka—four squadrons each with sixteen planes—to take off at once for the attack.

Fifteen minutes later the Russian force came under fire from the first squadron. The German pilots rolled down from the sky in tight formation. There were no signs of Russian fighters, their only real fear. Having remained for so long under heavy forest cover, the Russians had not provided for an air escort, preferring to keep their planes in combat rather than simply flying patrol.

It was as perfect a situation as the Germans might ask for. The heavily armored Henschels, ignoring the ground fire directed at them from the infantry units and machine guns on the tanks, struck from abeam and astern, drilling their cannon shells into their targets. Each firing pass per aircraft meant four to five shells pumped at the Russian tanks, and as each plane completed its firing run, it pulled up sharply and roared about for another pass.

Within moments of the initial run the first tank was burning, and Meyer reported by radio, within five minutes of opening the air attack, that at least six tanks were aflame and that the Russian armored brigade was failing to hold order. Meyer radioed for fighters to attack the infantry while the Henschels continued their strikes against the tanks.

Before the next twenty minutes ended, Focke-Wulf FW-190 fighters had decimated the packed infantry, striking with fragmentation bombs and making repeated strafing runs, each aircraft firing its armament of four 20-mm. cannon and two heavy machine guns. No specific number is given for the Russian tanks knocked out, but Meyer reported back to his command post that the countryside was "littered with knocked-out and burning tanks." More to the point, he stated that the surviving tanks of the brigade, with infantry streaming wildly among them, had fled back to the cover of the dense forests. The sudden threat to the flank of Fourth Panzer Army was considered ended.

In the long run, however, the role of air support would prove to be

relegated to a secondary place in the overall picture of combat. Where the Russians were concerned, a battle of this nature meant absorbing heavy losses, and it mattered little if those losses were inflicted by German aircraft or by tanks and guns on the ground. Had there been more aircraft available on either or both sides, obviously air support would have been considered in the moves of the massive armies grinding against one another. But to Zhukov's way of thinking, the queen of battle was not to be found in the air, but on the ground, and it was the tank and not the airplane that would decide the ultimate outcome at Kursk.

18

THE CENTRAL FRONT

The massive confrontation of Kursk moved ponderously into action along two separate and distinct battlefields on the morning of July 5. To the north there was the central front under Rokossovsky; to the south the Voronezh front under Vatutin. Although each front cannot be separated from the Battle of Kursk, it is clear that the bitter fighting of each was a major offensive distinct from the other, and the two would be joined as a single entity only when and if the Germans managed to close the pincers they needed so desperately to pinch off Kursk.

Shortly after 5:30 in the morning of July 5 the Germans moved from their defensive positions toward the Russian lines, to begin Operation Citadel. Along the sector of the Thirteenth Army, the Germans advanced with the full strength of three tank divisions and five infantry divisions as the first line of attack. Spearheading the drive was a mass of German tanks with motorized infantry in close support. As the tanks and troops advanced slowly into a withering storm of

Russian defensive fire, the Germans fanned out along the assault line. They spread their forces (the 9th, 18th, and 20th tank divisions and the 6th, 78th, 86th, 216th, and 292d infantry divisions) to hit not only the Russian Thirteenth Army but also the adjoining flanks of the Forty-Eighth and Seventieth armies.

The Germans concentrated their forces along a front of twenty-eight miles, and as Zhukov and his command staff were to learn at a later time, the thunder and fury of the attack was intended essentially as a diversion to draw Russian attention away from what was to be the main thrust of the Wehrmacht—a powerful drive by Ninth Army against Vatutin's Voronezh front to the south. Little matter at the moment, of course, to Rokossovsky, for advancing against his sector was a magnificent and powerful adversary certainly possessed of the strength to break through his lines.

Within thirty minutes or so the Russians were fully aware of the armored wedges the Germans were trying to drive through the defense lines. At the head of the striking forces were two powerful groups, made up of the most experienced panzer and motorized infantry on the front. Each group counted approximately forty to fifty tanks with tight infantry support.

The sun rose on a scene of shattering devastation as the Russians met their attackers with a howling blast of fire. Heavy artillery was firing point-blank at the German spearheads, and the Russians were also laying down a savage curtain of fire from mortars, lesser artillery, the pakfronts of 76.2-mm. guns, and tremendous barrages of Katyusha rockets. Overhead, Russian fighters and antitank planes flew almost to treetop level after the German armored vehicles and the more exposed infantry. The dense curtain of fire almost at once set grass and cornfields ablaze, destroyed farm groups and small villages. The flame and smoke, billowing across the battlefield before a westerly breeze, was quickly mixed with the dense palls of black, greasy smoke from blazing tanks. It seemed that the earth itself was burning as shell bursts by the thousands erupted in every direction, adding to the din and the debris floating through the air.

Whatever the Germans had expected, they found more than they had bargained for in the Russian defenses. The pakfronts were bad enough, but the Russians had infested every group of antitank guns

with covering defenses. The Germans knew what to expect in the way of Russian minefields, and they discovered the earth sowed with thousands of the lethal charges within the ground. But as the engineers and sappers aided the tanks through the fields, the Germans were unaware that the easiest way through the minefields, where the number was somewhat less than in other areas, was precisely where the Russians wanted the German tanks to move.

The sappers cleared the way, and the tanks followed along channels that were being kept under constant aim by Russian gunners. When a tank moved into the field of fire of a pakfront, the Russians cut loose with a furious blast of fire from as many as ten guns blazing away together. Not even the thick armor of the Tiger could withstand the 76.2-mm. high-velocity antitank weapon of the Russian at point-blank range. And when a tank was caught in one of the channels, it might come under the fire of several pakfronts. Wherever possible, the Russians had zeroed in their heavy artillery, and a tank had no chance against such a heavy weight of fire and explosives.

Before the tanks had advanced a mile from their starting positions, a large number of the armored vehicles had fallen victim to powerful mine charges and were disabled. A tank with a tread blown away, or stopped because of damage, can almost always be made to fight again, especially if it is removed quickly from the type of devastating firepower the Russians were mounting. But the Germans now were to be haunted by the orders they had received before Citadel rolled forward from the German lines:

> . . . *in no circumstances* will tanks be stopped to render assistance to those which have been disabled. . . . Tank commanders are to press on to their objectives as long as they retain mobility. Where a tank is rendered immobile but the gun is in working order . . . the crew will continue to give fire support from a static position.

In the Kursk salient that order amounted virtually to a death sentence for the crews of damaged tanks. The Russian guns were mounted in such heavy concentration that any disabled tank not removed from the field of fire by another tank was an immediate target for heavy and destructive fire.

The tanks, of course, were expected to take out the gun positions opposing their advance. This proved impossible because of the number and location of the pakfronts, as well as the special measures taken by the Russians to protect their vital gun positions. Each pakfront, in addition to the small arms of its crews, had been so situated that it lay within the crossfire coverage of machine gun and mortar positions. Where tanks were stopped by the pakfront guns, the German infantry was ordered to move ahead and eliminate the heavy weapons. No one had reckoned on these nests of machine guns and mortars protecting the pakfronts. The Russians had issued strict orders to the men behind these machine guns and mortars that they were to fire *only* against Nazi infantrymen attacking the pakfronts to which they had been assigned as cover. The result was chaos for the attackers. The pakfronts were tearing up the tanks, and the supporting infantry was being cut to pieces by the Russians firing rapid-fire weapons from all sides, from positions extremely well dug in and protected against return fire.

As the battle raged, with mounting German losses that were shredding the assault, the Russians unleashed another nasty surprise, one that befitted well the character of the Russian soldier. Throughout the minefields the ground was ribboned with deep, zigzagging trenches, across which the tanks, after sappers had cleared the fields of mines, were allowed to move at a steady pace.

After the tanks had passed, special squads of handpicked Russians, all members of tank-destroying teams, arose from the deep slit trenches and went after the Nazi armor with fanatical zeal, causing no small consternation among the enemy, stunned to find Soviet soldiers *behind* them in the thick of battle.

Fully expecting to be confronted by the threat of thickly sowed minefields, the Germans were ready with countermeasures. Heavy tanks pushed ahead of them rollers that pressed down heavily against the ground to set off the pressure detonators in the mines. They also put into use one of the odder contraptions of the war—a small unmanned tank controlled remotely by radio or wire that hustled across the minefields until its explosive charge was set off by the controller. The diminutive iron beetles, strangely named Goliath, scurried ahead of the tanks, but their effect, finally, in the face of devastating Russian

firepower and the brilliantly established defenses, went for naught.

Steadily, inexorably, the Nazi assault began to come apart at the seams. The Russian technique of using very heavy mortar and machine gun fire against German infantry, while the pakfronts attended to the tanks—all of this effort being supported by waves of low-flying attack planes—paid off handsomely. German infantrymen found themselves cut off from their tanks, the tanks themselves were being shredded by the withering crossfire from the Russians, and the offensive bled itself white. Under a ripping, harassing fire, the Germans retreated to their starting point.

At 7:30 that morning, the Wehrmacht, having regrouped and taken stock of the Russian defenses that had proved so much heavier than anticipated, rolled again from prepared positions. This time the Germans threw themselves at the left flank of Thirteenth Army, preceding the new assault wave with an intensive artillery bombardment that was to last for an hour. The panzers and supporting units were on the move behind the artillery bombardment, gaining momentum, when the bombardment ended at 8:30. Now the main assault force ground steadily toward the Russian defense lines, this time with far greater strength than the opening bid several hours earlier.

In the lead were the powerful Tigers, and to lend enormous punch to the wedges that were to crack open the Russian line, was a special force of the huge Ferdinand self-propelled guns of some seventy tons weight, protected by 200-mm. armor plating. The Tigers and Ferdinands smashed headlong against the 15th and 81st rifle divisions of the Soviet Thirteenth Army, but they proved to be only the tip of the massive arrowhead set in motion by the Wehrmacht. Behind the heavy German armor came several hundred Mark IV medium tanks, in concert with armored personnel carriers packed with shock troops. It was a German force with all the steel and cutting edge of the original blitzkrieg of which the Russians had such grim memories.

Once the Russians had a proper appreciation of the scale of the German offensive, they brought in everything that could move to counter the enemy thrust. Sixteenth Air Army concentrated all its aircraft on this one sector of fighting, keeping several hundred fighters, ground-attack planes, and bombers at any one time over the battle-

field. General Horst Grossman (6th Infantry Division) remarked: "The Russians used aircraft in numbers such as we had never yet seen in the east."

Yet the Germans still had ultimate confidence that their powerful wedges would penetrate the Russian defense lines, especially the ninety Ferdinands of XLVIII Panzer Corps. Even at point-blank range, the Russian 76.2-mm. shells bounced harmlessly from their massive armor, and they seemed to roll with impunity over explosive mines that were stopping tanks dead in their tracks. The outcome of battles between the Ferdinands and the Russian defenses, meanwhile, was bolstering German hopes. The T-34 tanks proved helpless against the huge Ferdinands. At the close range of the savage fighting, the flat-trajectory, high-velocity guns of the Ferdinands split the Russian tanks wide open, one after the other. Even the Soviet pakfronts could not handle the German monster.

Acting in concert, the huge armored wedge of Ferdinands and Tigers became an ax that crashed through the Russian defense line. Nothing Russian guns could do availed, and the German infantry poured after the bludgeon that was proving so effective.

Then they were in the midst of the deep defense zone, and the interlocking system of pakfronts and covering machine gun and mortar nests began to take a fearful toll of the German troops. Little by little the infantry became separated from the armor, while the Russian gun commanders, accepting the inevitable, shifted their fire from the lumbering Ferdinands to the medium tanks and began to wreak havoc within their ranks.

The Ferdinands continued ahead, invincible, devastating, until they were in the midst of the Russian infantry concealed within slit trenches and underground bunkers. Russian infantry, hardened, fanatic, hateful, who saw the Ferdinands separated from the lighter tanks—*and now without any protection against men on the ground, moving in from the sides and rear.*

It was the Russian soldier in the thick of battle who sealed the doom of the mighty Ferdinands. The tank-destroying squads emerged from their trenches and ran wildly to the huge self-propelled guns. Russian infantrymen shouted their cries of attack and clambered aboard the Ferdinands as they thundered over the ground. There the Russians

secured footholds and brought the nozzles of flamethrowers to the ventilation slits of the German monsters. One long blast of flame and the Ferdinand was done, its crew choked to death through flame inhalation or burned alive. Those who managed to throw open their hatches in a frenzied attempt to escape were cut to ribbons by the massed guns pointed at them.

Guderian had warned about the danger of sending such weapons —the Porsche Tigers and the Ferdinands—into battle without secondary armament. He passed his judgment of the Ferdinands against the Thirteenth Army by saying:

> They were incapable of close-range fighting since they lacked sufficient ammunition [high-explosive as well as armor-piercing] for their guns and this defect was aggravated by the fact that they possessed no machine guns. Once they (the Ferdinands) had broken into the enemy's infantry zone they literally had to go quail-shooting with cannon. They did not manage to neutralize, let alone destroy, the enemy rifles and machine guns, so that our own infantry was unable to follow up behind them. By the time they reached the Russian artillery they were on their own. Despite showing extreme bravery and suffering unheard-of casualties, the infantry of Weidling's division did not manage to exploit the tanks' success. . . .

The Russians missed no opportunity to seal whatever breaches the Germans had managed to carve in the central front's defense zones. Engineer units during the first day of fighting swarmed into the thick of fighting and almost under the guns of the Germans fighting fiercely to advance, spread six thousand new mines in the sector of Thirteenth Army. The effectiveness of the minefields was so beyond expectations that the Russians were able to count more than a hundred German tanks and self-propelled guns either destroyed or heavily damaged during the first day's fighting. Another significant effect was wrought by the minefields, which had brought the tanks under fire of the pakfronts as well as inflicting their own deadly destruction upon German armor. As the day wore on, the tank commanders became decidedly chary of wandering away from the cleared lanes through the mines, and thus imposed upon themselves severe restrictions of maneuver, increasing even more their vulnerability to the pakfronts, heavier ar-

tillery, and the tank-destruction squads emerging from their slit trenches on the battlefield.

Late in the day, obviously willing to accept whatever losses were necessary to maintain pressure against the Russian lines, the Wehrmacht committed to battle the bulk of the armor under Model's command. Because the slow advance had been turning into a "go for broke" move, Model called for maximum air support to counter the Russian aircraft over the battlefield by pulling them away from the German armored forces, and also to help punch holes in the Russian defenses. It was the kind of aerial support effort for this day, July 5, and the day following, that brought even Zhukov to admit that "on both days German planes spread havoc."

German success was measured in slow, grinding movement paid for by terrible casualties in men and fearsome losses in weapons and equipment. The Wehrmacht made five separate major attacks against the Soviet defense system, and the gains the Nazis sought eluded them until the latter part of the day, when they threw in almost all the weight of their armor. At that, Model could only be less than satisfied. The Russian 15th and 18th divisions had yielded their first defense line, but simply moved back to the second and even more heavily armed zone, barely three to five miles from their first positions. Driving toward the Russian town of Gnilets, the Germans threw back two Russian divisions but found their gains limited to no more than three miles.

Another massive assault was made against three divisions, where the Thirteenth and Forty-Eighth armies linked together, in a furious Wehrmacht push to break through to Maloarkhangelsk. The Germans gained initial success, storming under a massive weight of aircraft and armor into the Russian defense zone. But the Russians immediately counterattacked and swarmed against the weary invaders. Before night fell the Germans had been hurled from their briefly held positions in the Russian defense zone and could count no ground won.

All that night the Nazis toiled desperately to get their house in order. Losses had been so severe it was imperative that any damaged tanks, self-propelled guns and other weapons be reclaimed from the battlefield for repair and return to service. Easier said than done. This was a new breed of Russian soldier the Germans were facing, and he

took to the darkness with a ferocity unrecorded in the war on the eastern front.

To regroup, the Germans had to operate within the areas they had occupied during the day, but darkness proved that such occupation was not without its special hazards. Many of the forward tank elements were now separated from the main body of the German forces. Small groups of Tiger tanks that had managed to maul their way far into the Russian defense zone were stranded without the infantry they needed so urgently to protect them against Russian sappers on the prowl for just such prey.

The only way the Germans could take advantage of their slight gains during daylight on July 5 was to move up infantry under cover of darkness, and the entire night was spent in just such activity, but not without heavy casualties. The contested ground had become a lethal no-man's-land, filled with Russian patrols on the hunt for Germans trying to reach their dangerously isolated tanks. Machine guns, grenades, and rifles sounded the night through, and in many of the slit trenches the two enemy forces came together in flare-lit glare and shadows, to battle violently to the death.

The German sappers had been told that the minefields must be cleared at any cost for the tank forces to move up through the defense zone wrested from the Russians. Here, too, the individual Russian soldier was proving his mettle, for the battlefield was strewn with Russian snipers who emerged from their warrens long enough to gun down mine-clearing crews, then disappear, reemerging elsewhere along the trenches known so well to them.

The dawn arrived with the first defensive zone solidly in German hands, but at a terrible price in casualties suffered during the long, battle-filled night. A price the Germans were surely to figure was too high for what awaited them in daylight.

The long and meticulous Russian preparations for the battle were now paying their special dividend. Rokossovsky and his staff had to assume they would be thrown back from the separate defense lines. Every gun in zone two had been provided with exact aiming points for zone one in the event the latter was invested by the enemy. In addition, the Russians found a way to make up for the guns they had lost in the areas occupied by the Germans. During the night they

brought up hundreds of tanks and parked many of these hulls down, protected by heaping mounds of soil so that only the turrets showed, to serve as impromptu artillery and antitank weapons.

The German attack, renewed on the morning of July 6, thus ran into a withering Russian fire just as heavy as it had been the day before. And they found the Russian soldiers just as fierce in battle as they had been on the first day of the offensive. Where the Germans overwhelmed Russian defenses, the Red soldiers often fought to the last man. Zhukov personally singled out as representative of the courage of the Russian trooper "a battery commanded by Captain G. I. Igishov [that] took the brunt of the attack and destroyed nineteen tanks during the day. All the men of the battery died heroically in the battle, but did not let the Fascists pass."

By the end of the second day of the offensive on the central front, the Germans had managed a total advance of only six miles. The six-mile advance had been achieved along a front of only twenty miles in width, and for this Model's forces had lost at least ten thousand men killed, with another fifteen thousand missing and wounded.

The major advance had taken its toll of German troops, but the Wehrmacht discovered that storming an area successfully did not terminate the pile-up of casualties. The countryside into which the Wehrmacht had advanced was almost made to order for the defenders, and as the German soldiers set out to clear the copses and woods, the towns and settlements, the rolling hills, they found themselves exposed to steady fire from diehards who seemed to spring up everywhere.

On the night of July 6 the German position, despite the progress already made, was far from enviable. Twenty-five thousand men who could not be replaced were missing from the ranks commanded by Model. At least two hundred tanks and self-propelled guns had been destroyed by the withering, heavy crossfire of the Russian defenses, and these, too, lacked replacement. The Wehrmacht had expended vast stocks of ammunition, and Ninth Army was so low on supplies that Model sent a personal message to Zeitzler at OKH (army high command) for the immediate dispatch of 100,000 rounds of ammunition for the tanks and other heavy weapons.

To the consternation of the German commanders, the Russians

continued to sow mines in every direction, but especially *behind* the armored wedges the Germans had rammed into the Russian defensive systems. This meant that the supporting forces, moving up behind the panzerkeil wedges, had to commit themselves to the tedious and time-consuming job of clearing a path through the mines just when they were most desperately needed at the first line of fighting.

Model could find little joy in the tip of the spearhead he had managed to pound into the Russian defenses. The greatest advance of the panzers was now stopped dead by a wide range of low hills to the north of Olkhovatka.

Model received reports from his reconnaissance aircraft that the Russians were now bringing heavy armored reinforcements into the battle from the east. Then he received confirmation that powerful Russian columns were moving westward, south of Maloarkhangelsk, toward Olkhovatka and Ponyri.

"Failing to achieve a decisive success in the center and on the left flank of 13th Army," states Rokossovsky, "the enemy switched his main effort to the village and railway station of Ponyri which, in the circumstances, was of considerable operational-tactical significance. Holding Ponyri, our troops could strike flank blows at the enemy advancing to Maloarkhangelsk and Olkhovatka and also keep in their hands the Orel-Kursk railway."

On July 7, at dawn, Model hurled his forces against Ponyri. It was in this vicinity during the next four days, along a staggered line running from Maloarkhangelsk to Nikolskoye, and especially in the area of hills between Ponyri and Molotychi, that the Germans were destined to batter themselves raw.

The attack, made with the fury of men who know they must win, at this place, or see their long-range battle plans shattered, turned the countryside into flaming carnage. Rokossovsky kept to his device of burying his tanks hull down to contest the advance of the Nazi heavy and medium tanks. Orders went out from him that any Russian tank in the open must avoid combat with heavier German armor and concentrate upon infantry and light armor as targets.

Within hours heavy smoke hung everywhere, shadowing the bright sun, as fields burned in all directions. Whatever had been the fury of the tank battles so far, they were eclipsed now as the two enemy forces

maneuvered and dug in, hammering constantly at one another. The massive exchanges of steel projectiles and fire yielded now to hand-to-hand confrontation between German and Russian. The Russian troops were entrenched on both sides of commanding heights. The land below had been cut and sliced into a maze of trenches, bunkers, and foxholes, bristling with weapons of every description.

To force their way through the terrible crossfire of the Russians, the Germans resorted to human-wave attacks, one row after the other hurtling forward into the deep roar of heavy Russian guns, the scream of rockets, and the constant background din of rifles. The best troops the Wehrmacht had in the area charged into the valley depressions first from the west, and then from the east, but no matter their direction of charge, they were met with an overwhelming defensive fire that never seemed to slacken.

The casualties suffered by the Germans were enough to have broken the back of any army, and it is a tribute—acknowledged by both sides—that these men fought with uncommon courage and dedication. One regiment in its first hour of battle lost every officer killed or wounded. Battalions were decimated until they were at only company strength; still they fought on desperately until their numbers were reduced to platoon strength.

In such a vast struggle the sacrifices and successes of most men are swallowed without recognition or even knowledge of their deeds by the terrible casualties suffered, and those who do survive and whose exploits become known are, of course, representative of the far greater number who fell where they fought.

The 2d Battery of the 540th Light Artillery Regiment of the Supreme Command Reserve of the Russian army provides a closer look at the sort of fighting and bravery that marked the savage grueling conflict. The 2d Battery took up a direct fire position north of Ponyri. One of the gun crews was commanded by Starshina K. Sedov; Sedov and his men were to distinguish themselves by extraordinary performance in a sea swelling with uncommon valor.

Sedov and his men, watching the advance of heavy Wehrmacht armor, held their fire until the Germans were barely more than six hundred feet from their position. They opened fire with a direct hit against the lead tank, piercing the armor and wreathing the vehicle

in flames. A second tank exploded and immediately afterward, as the Germans responded with steady, accurate fire of their own, several more tanks were hit.

For hours the battle raged between Sedov's gun battery and the tanks blocked by the stubborn Russian resistance. Crewmen manning the antitank guns were hit one after the other and fell where they were. Others moved in to take their places until there remained only the men clustered about their weapons. On Sedov's own gun, the paint was burned away from the barrel. Wounded soldiers had their hurts bound by friends and returned to the fight. The struggle became one of attrition, and it was Sedov and his men who held out the longest. Before the Germans pulled back slowly, this one gun position was officially credited with the destruction of eight tanks and approximately a hundred officers and men from the attacking force killed.

Human wave after human wave rumbled into the mouths of the Russian guns. At one point the Germans moved into a hollow near Ponyri more than 150 tanks and an unspecified but large number of armored personnel carriers for a flanking attack on the Russian lines. Spotted by fighters flying reconnaissance, the German force was quickly brought under heavy artillery bombardment and a devastating air strike by 120 Stormoviks and twin-engined bombers. The Germans retreated in disorder with heavy casualties.

By afternoon of July 7 Model was desperate and called for heavy air support. This time the German raiders went after Russian troops rather than the heavily entrenched tanks and artillery. Nazi soldiers rallied behind the heavy, sustained bombing strikes and rushed forward. Once again their ranks were slashed badly, but still they came on, and two battalions of troops supported by fifty tanks pounded their way into the northwestern outskirts of Ponyri. Just when Model had his first real grasp of success with a vital Russian center in his hands, the Russians mounted a furious counterattack, overrunning the German forces in the town and destroying both battalions.

Darkness fell slowly across a battlefield through which the sun had long been no more than a dim and shadowy disk seen through a smoke-ridden world. Model knew he dared not relax his pressure, and he rushed into the fighting an additional two infantry regiments and sixty tanks.

The fresh replacements ripped wide holes in the defenses of the 307th Division, which fell back slowly beneath the pressure of the German assault. During the night, when both sides ended their movement on the front, the Russians whipped together the disorganized 307th Division and with the first light of dawn hurled a counterattack against the enemy, dislodging the Germans from their bitterly won ground and assuring the continued safety of Ponyri.

Heavy tank battles that began on July 7 near Olkhovatka continued through the entire day and well into July 8. What was left of the German force in this area—some three hundred tanks with heavy support from submachine gunners—threw themselves against the 3d Tank-Destroyer Brigade northwest of Olkhovatka. The battery, already mentioned for its outstanding performance under fire by Zhukov, was commanded by Captain G. I. Igishov. The Germans finally pulled back after a bitter exchange, unaware that the only force still opposing them was made up of one gun and three desperately tired, wounded Russians.

July 8 produced another manifestation of desperation wherever the Germans were on the attack. The village of Teploye, along the western end of the combat line, became the scene of a furious assault launched by the last armored reserve available to Model. The tanks of this final reserve—4th Panzer Division—teamed with armor of the 2d and 20th panzers, along with a powerful striking force of motorized infantry, to carry out an attack that "must succeed" from sheer weight of firepower and arms against an already weakened and weary defense.

Rokossovsky had laid down a grueling reception for this offensive thrust. The village of Teploye and the heights behind the small community swarmed with a massive Russian defense composed of a division of artillery, two divisions of riflemen, two brigades of tanks, and a brigade of assault guns. Three times the Germans battered their way through the Soviets to the uppermost heights of the battlefield, and three times the Russians counterattacked to hurl them off the bloody ground. There was no fourth time for the Germans; their attack had been broken.

July 9 was the last day on which Model's forces made even the slightest headway against the savagely fighting Russians. By July 10

the losses in tanks were so severe, and losses among the German soldiers were mounting so rapidly, that the Wehrmacht assaults almost visibly began to break down in the field of battle. There were no advances registered that day anywhere along the central front.

The battle there was considered, in its defensive phase, to be ended. The Germans had blunted themselves against a Russian force the like of which they had never before encountered, and the machinery for a massive counterattack was already starting to grind its gears.

But the truly great battles, as the Germans had intended all along, were to the south, along the Voronezh front.

19

THE VORONEZH FRONT

The morning of July 5 saw Gross Deutschland confronted with a serious problem. The land between Ssyrzew and Sawidowka, where the powerful German division was to launch a full-scale offensive against the Voronezh front, had been turned into a sea of mud during the night by torrential rains. The river that separated the two villages had overflown its banks, transforming the rolling fields into a great swamp. Many lesser streams and brooks had become fast-moving water currents in the midst of the morass. Accordingly, dawn found the German division packed densely on its side of the swamp—staring at a great force of Russian artillery that had been moved up under cover of darkness, waiting for just this moment.

The hastily assembled artillery cut loose with a tremendous barrage against the ranks of Gross Deutschland, sending men and vehicles scurrying for whatever cover could be found. The rate and weight of fire increased as Russian tanks rolled to the top of hills on their side of the stream and pumped hundreds of shells from their high-velocity guns into their quarry.

Wehrmacht guns answered the barrage, and frantic calls to the Luftwaffe brought heavy air cover to the scene. Nazi fighter craft fought with particular tenacity. Their particular target was Soviet planes that were harrying the engineers of Gross Deutschland division. The latter group were exposed to constant shelling as they tried desperately to throw bridges across the rain-swollen streams. The Germans were also being constantly blocked by exploding mines, and the bridge engineers had to work through and around the mine-detector teams.

If German air cover had been strong in the battles of the central front approximately a hundred miles to the north, on the Voronezh front it was almost overwhelming. What the Germans lacked in artillery response to the pounding they were taking from Russian guns, they made up for in repeated waves of heavy bombing by the Luftwaffe.

The air cover would have been even more effective had not the Wehrmacht forces been spread so thin.

It had been the Russian decision to let the artillery fend for itself and use Russian ground-attack aircraft where they would do the most good—that is, in striking at the German tanks where they were to be found in the greatest numbers and where they had been, because of the rain and mud, rendered largely immobile, thus becoming excellent targets.

"Many tanks fell victim to the Red Air Force," Mellinthin said later. "During this battle Russian aircraft operated with remarkable dash in spite of German air superiority."

July 5, the second day of the assault by forces under Hoth, was compounded with heavy losses and frustrations for the German army. Mellinthin admits that in the areas occupied in the "softening up" operation on July 4 Russian snipers and tank-destroying teams "appeared from nowhere," and considerable forces from the Gross Deutschland division were diverted to deal with the fanatical Russians who posed a strong danger to the division's rear-area security. It took the engineers of the division a minimum of twelve hours to bridge the swollen streams and swamps, and by that time night had fallen, without any forces having traversed the new bridges. Alexe-

jewka and Luchanino, the immediate objectives of Gross Deutschland were for the moment, safe from the German drive.

Along the left flank of Gross Deutschland, the 3d Panzer Division
rammed into a stone-wall defense at Sawidowka that stopped the armored forces in their tracks. The 3d Panzer reported an incredible
density of mines in its area of operations that were knocking out tanks
and motorized vehicles almost everywhere. Valuable time was being
lost in clearing lanes through the fields of buried explosives. While
the Nazis were thus occupied, the Russians, enjoying the benefit of
high ground, were hammering the division with long-range artillery,
as well as slamming shells from Russian tanks into the packed German ranks.

Instead of gaining ground on July 5, 3d Panzer was forced to suffer
its mauling from Russian guns and stand fast against sudden fierce
counterattacks. Again, it was only the Luftwaffe that enjoyed any
appreciable success as Nazi planes struck fiercely at Russian gun positions and the marauding tanks. However, the Russians had moved
such a massive amount of matériel into the area that they were able
to absorb the full brunt of the assault.

After a long and bloody interval, the Soviets gradually realized
that the Wehrmacht forces arrayed against them along the Voronezh
front were far more powerful than Rokossovsky had faced on the central front. Hoth committed immediately to massive pressure against
the Russian lines, and he launched his opening blow with approximately 1,000 tanks and 350 self-propelled guns—300 of the rolling
monsters assigned to Gross Deutschland alone (which was, of course,
bulked together waiting for the streams and swamps to be bridged).

If Hoth saw part of his assault wave stopped for the moment in
certain areas, he had enough power to apply pressure at other points
to achieve some penetration against the formidable Russian defenses.
He had five panzer divisions to the north of Belgorod and three more
panzer divisions to the south of that city.

Finally, in line center, Hausser's S.S. divisions in savage fighting
achieved the only true German gains of the day. As darkness man-
tled the battlefields, the S.S. sliced into the first defensive zone of
the Russians and held fast for the night. South of Belgorod, the III

Panzer Corps clawed out a small but vital bridgehead over the Donets. All that the Germans could count, for the fighting on July 5 and 6, was three comparatively small breakthroughs. None extended more than seven miles into the heart of the Russian lines, whereas Hoth had been counting on pushing forward at least twenty miles or more.

During the night of July 5–6 the Russians brought in heavy reinforcements. The Sixth Guards Army received special tank-destroying teams, and the First Tank Army moved up behind the second defense line to add to the already massive defenses there. The rifle formations of Sixth Guards were judged to be dangerously low on support of heavy guns, and several hundred tanks were moved into positions and dug in up to their turrets.

On July 6 the Germans began to break out. Hatches closed, the heavy tanks and self-propelled guns moved away from their protected positions and started to advance across the sweeping cornfields of the battleground. A radio operator of a Tiger tank recorded the following:

> As we advanced the Russian artillery ploughed the earth around us . . . the whole front was a girdle of flashes. It seemed as if we were driving into a ring of flame. Four times our valiant *Rosinante* shuddered under a direct hit, and we thanked the fates for the strength of our good Krupp steel.

Fourth Panzer Army on July 6 was making steady progress toward its goal of Oboyan, directly on the road to Kursk. To cover the hard-fighting army, the Luftwaffe flew seventeen hundred missions in support of the advancing panzers. The effect in this area was pronounced and added to much of Fourth Panzer Army's success, but it cost other forces dearly in thin air coverage where it was needed desperately. Support air operations against Russian forces fighting XLVIII Panzer and II S.S. Panzer corps were drastically insufficient, for the German pilots found themselves fighting for their lives against inceasing swarms of wildly flown Soviet fighters.

Wehrmacht pressure, despite intense Russian defensive fighting, was mounting, and the Germans were moving slowly but inexorably toward their goals. At Oboyan, fifty miles south of Kursk, a Soviet

commander watching the German tanks rolling across country said later:

> I suppose that neither I nor any of our other officers had ever seen so many enemy tanks at once. Hoth had staked everything on a knight's move. Against every one of our companies of ten tanks were thirty or forty German tanks. Hoth well knew that if he could break through to Kursk, no losses would be too great and no sacrifice would be in vain. . . .

The situation improved slowly but steadily for the Wehrmacht, as the panzers battered down Russian resistance and broke open a hole through the leading ranks of 67th Rifle Guards Division, streaming out toward Oboyan and a crossing of the Psel. Hausser's S.S. panzers ripped through the 52d Guards Rifle Division, setting their aim for a steady tank march to Prokhorovka. Another powerful force was rumbling toward Rzhavets after fording the Donets, but Hoth's expectations for a rapid advance of this force began to fade when Soviet resistance on that front stiffened unexpectedly.

Nevertheless, Hoth was prepared to make the most of the advantages gained. He needed room for his panzers to move swiftly and decisively, so he turned his attention to the breakthrough that would gain him the open country in the area southeast of Oboyan. There he could use the slashing wedge of the panzerkeil, as he had wished to do all along, and hurl a powerful blow at the Russian left and rear. If successful, if carried out with great speed and determination, he could crack wide open the Russian defensive positions—and Kursk would no longer be an impossibly distant target. Hoth knew he had to move quickly, for Model's forces to the north were mired in fanatical Russian resistance on the central front, and he could expect no help to his offensive from that quarter.

Hoth could not have selected a better time and place for his enormous gamble. In a slashing tank battle south of Oboyan, the panzers had been bloodied severely, but they had also taken a grisly toll of Russian armor. It was after this struggle that Vatutin ordered a huge force of his tanks be dug in and protected as hardpoint artillery to make up for losses already taken at the hands of the advancing Ger-

mans. But as Hoth viewed the situation, his Fourth Panzer Army, despite its own serious losses, still mounted the tremendous punch of six hundred Tigers, Panthers, Mark IV's, and self-propelled guns. The Russians, on the other hand, were low on armor that could be sent in large numbers into the battlefield, and mobility was swinging to the side of Hoth.

The Russians were acutely aware that they must commit their armored reserves to the battle, even if this maneuver meant speeding up Zhukov's timetable of holding back his biggest punch until the last possible moment. If they did not do so, Hoth had every chance of breaking through to Prokhorovka, turning his armed forces sharply and cutting beyond Oboyan toward Kursk.

If he could be stopped here and now, then his advance would be a march into a terrible valley of death, from which German hopes for continuing the offensive would never emerge. Vatutin, therefore, sent his troops a stern order: "The Germans must not break through to Oboyan under any circumstances."

He backed up his own command with a powerful reinforcement of two regiments of assault guns where the fighting was going poorly for the Russians, but the move was made in a case of too little arriving too late, and the panzers decimated the stunned, newly arrived Russians.

The danger to Oboyan, and to Kursk itself, was considered so grave that Vatutin's headquarters was "honored" with the presence of Nikita Khrushchev, carrying with him all the political weight of Moscow.

"The next two or three days will be terrible," stated Khrushchev. "Either we hold or the Germans take Kursk. They are putting everything on one card. It's a matter of life or death for them. We must take care to see that they break their necks."

He did not need to add: *or else.*

On the morning of July 7 the panzers began to make good the promise Hoth saw in the growing battles. Advance forces stormed into the village of Dubrova, sending the Russian defenders reeling back to Syrtzevo on the Pena River, which was considered by both combatants to be the last bastion of defense before the Germans could rip straight into Oboyan. As the Russians withdrew steadily to Gremutshy and Ssyrzew, they came within range of heavy German artillery and were

cut to pieces, fleeing in a disorderly stream. Heartened by the sudden success, the panzers drove at full speed to the northwest, hoping to carve a deep and lethal chunk out of the Russian defense lines, giving them the freedom of maneuver that would allow them to strike in any direction where resistance seemed the weakest. It was not to be.

The fleeing Russian forces, meeting reinforcements racing to the near debacle, stopped in their tracks and wheeled about to dig in, resuming the fight with a ferocity that caught the advancing Germans wholly unaware. The tremendous fire rippling out from the newly dug-in Russians first stopped the panzers in their tracks, then forced them to fight for survival as thousands of shouting Russians rose from their battlements to counterattack behind lines of T-34 and KV-1 tanks.

To the right of the suddenly entangled panzers a regiment of Gross Deutschland promised a sudden blaze of success, when they reported they had stormed the town of Werchopenje, which meant a truly significant piercing of the Russian lines. At once the German command rushed a special battle group into the breach to take swift advantage of the startling success.

When the special group caught up with the regiment, the Germans discovered they were the victims of poor map-reading and were still far from Werchopenje. For this fighting task force, July 7 ended with the two enemies battling fiercely for individual hills, then subsiding into mutual exhaustion for the rest of the night.

The long battlefront was no longer a single cohesive fighting line, but had broken up into separate combat areas, measured by seesawing defeats and victories on both sides. During the night of July 7, 3d Panzer was engaged in taking advantage of its successes during the day, gouging out pockets of Russian resistance from their positions along the Pena. XLVIII Panzer found darkness a blessing in that Russian artillery and tank fire fell off unexpectedly, and the advance forces began crossing the Pena with a strange lack of resistance from the defenders.

There were still other marks of success for the armored wedges being thrust so deeply into the Russian lines. Well to the right of XLVIII Panzer, three S.S. divisions had hacked long, deep gains into the Russian defense zones. But the S.S. never had the chance to profit

substantially from these gains. They were never able to bring together the three deep penetrations, so that all day on July 8 and well into the ninth, the three S.S. forces moving northward found Russian resistance to the *sides* of their penetration taking a grim, mounting toll of German armor and men. The tip of the wedge of each S.S. force was still as strong as ever, but the flanks were being shot to bloody pieces.

Starting at dawn on July 8, individual skirmishes continued to rage back and forth. The special battle group of Gross Deutschland that had hoped the day before to expand the "German occupation of Werchopenje" was hammering its way through stiffening Russian resistance. The panzers chopped their way forward from one hill to the next, the Russians yielding ground slowly, exacting a grisly toll of their enemy, seemingly willing to give up some ground in order to bleed the panzers of their number and their momentum. The Germans fought with an amazing spirit and drive, taking advantage of every break in the fighting, exploiting every weakness, meeting head on the worst of Soviet firepower when there was no other way to advance.

One powerful assault team of the special battle group raced past Werchopenje, bypassing the embattled town to the east, so that the village might be brought under concerted fire from several sides. The Russians held not only Werchopenje but more important, a steep hill (shown on German combat maps as Height 243.0) directly north of the town.

Russian tankers mounted the hill and trained their guns on the advancing Germans below. Nothing the panzers did, from the ground with their own heavy tanks and guns nor fierce air attacks, succeeded in dislodging the Russian tank crews who smashed every panzer assault on the vital height. As the German drive faltered and began to break down under steady losses, Russian tanks seemed to appear from all sides and drove headlong at the German armored wedges, preventing the panzerkeil formations from linking together for mutual strength and protection.

Early on the morning of July 8, forty Russian T-34s charged a group of Tigers of XLVIII Panzer, but with little success. Actually, they suffered heavy losses, and the surviving T-34s were compelled to flee to the safety of the defensive lines on the other side of the Pena.

In the afternoon seven more futile attacks were mounted by the T-34s against the Tigers—and this time with twenty-one of the Russian tanks destroyed. Still the Russians kept up counterattacking, the T-34s making swift, hit-and-run sorties while artillery units continued their barrage and the Red Air Force gained in strength and effectiveness with every passing day.

On the front where the Germans had gained speed and ground, their drive began to come apart at the seams.

"Neither Height 243.0 nor the western outskirts of Werchopenje were taken on that day," wrote Mellinthin, "and it could no longer be doubted that the back of the German attack had been broken and its momentum was gone."

The Germans would replace individual failure on the battlefield with renewed victory. Each side gained and lost the initiative on numerous occasions, but time was beginning to weigh heavily on the side of the Russians.

No matter how many men they lost, there seemed always to be fresh reserves. No matter how many tanks were destroyed in battle, the next morning brought waves of tanks from a seemingly inexhaustible supply. No matter how fiercely the Luftwaffe fought in the air, the day following brought waves of new Russian fighters and ground-attack planes. No matter how many supplies were destroyed, how much artillery was wiped out or captured—there was always more.

By July 9, after five days of fierce fighting for the Germans on the Voronezh front, they had made substantial gains in some areas, yet their forces were being shredded. There were virtually no replacements for German armor, even if great forces had not yet been committed to the battle. What the German panzer leaders recognized, totally aside from the consideration of numbers, was that *qualitatively* the battle was swinging to the enemy.

The Ferdinand self-propelled guns on Model's front to the north had proven to be lumbering monsters incapable of defense against infantrymen, and now, in the south, the Panther medium tanks for which the panzers had held out such tremendous hope had also proved to be minor disasters in their own right. The tank design was superb; no question of that. But it still needed a long period of shaking out to get rid of the bugs in its system. Both the Ferdinands and the Panthers

were sent into battle without sufficient ammunition for the task at hand. They were also set ablaze by hits that would not faze a Tiger, and the oil and gasoline fuel systems were so poorly protected that a small fire could immediately blossom into an inferno.

And what of the Porsche Tigers? They suffered much the same fate as did the Ferdinands, and they came under the same scathing indictment of Guderian as had the lumbering self-propelled guns. Without secondary armament (unlike the Henschel Tigers) the Porsche Tigers fell to the same doom as the Ferdinands. The moment they were removed from heavy infantry support, the Russian tank-destroying teams swarmed against the Tigers, rendering them hulks almost at will.

The German troops had been in the field and on the move for five days. They had gone into battle with their rations on their backs—set for five days—and there had been no replenishment of their supplies. They were exhausted and in desperate need of rest. Ammunition was running low for troops, machine gunners, tanks, artillery, mortars. And Russian artillery fire, if anything, was getting stronger, as were the Russian air attacks, making it extremely difficult for the German combat field services to replenish tank fuel, ammunition, and other supplies and to repair the tanks where they were most needed—directly in the field of battle.

There wasn't really that much to add up for the panzers on the morning of July 9. Hoth's forces, fighting since July 4, had managed to pound their way (XLVIII Panzer Corps) to within sixteen miles of Oboyan, but the leading tip of the armored wedges was still fifty-five miles from Kursk and, even more important, still at least ninety miles from the Ninth Army under Model. At this point no one held out any real hopes for Model's battered and bleeding forces to regain any meaningful strength against the armies commanded by Rokossovsky.

Painful lessons had been administered to the pride of the Wehrmacht. The Russian soldier was proving to be something vastly different from the subhuman portrait painted so vividly by the propagandists of the Reich. He had emerged from his ground to defeat the great Ferdinand self-propelled guns that could not be stopped by the

best of Russian firepower. The dreaded Tiger tanks, especially those without machine guns, also fell swiftly to the fiery blows of the tank-destroying teams swarming across the battlefield. The Luftwaffe, which held itself on some high pedestal, found itself unable to stop the Russian in the air and proved impotent in its attempts to prevent Russian aircraft from raking German forces on the ground.

The Panther had been regarded by military experts as the finest tank of its type in the world when it was rushed into Operation Citadel, but the Russians found they burned splendidly. The Russians discovered among many other critical lessons, another simple but extraordinarily important one.

The 88-mm. gun of the Tiger was a weapon superior to the 76.2-mm. gun of either the T-34 or the KV-1. Especially vulnerable to the can-opener characteristics of the Tiger, however, was the T-34, which lacked the massive armor of the KV heavy tank. The lesson observed so sharply by the Russians was that the 88-mm. gun of the Tiger was superior *only when Russian and German tanks were standing well off from one another*. When it came to getting in close and fighting it out in the orchards, riding up and down the gullies, swarming through and around the copses, then it was a battle of armor at point-blank range.

And at this in-tight range, the T-34 proved it could smash open a Tiger just as easily as the Tiger could hole a T-34.

This turned the weight of battle inexorably to the side of the Russians, who had many more T-34 tanks than the Germans did Tigers (the panzers still relied heavily on their older Mark IV tanks).

As the sun rose higher on July 9, the only real German progress was to be found with Gross Deutschland division, which drove a powerful battle force through a Russian village that straddled the main defense line of the defenders. That afternoon, and well into the night, the Germans did everything possible to exploit the breakthrough, sending a strong reinforcing battle group, including forty tanks, after the lead force.

The Germans poured their reinforcements through the gap in the Russian line and then struck out with renewed fury to the west, working their way behind the Russians so that they might chew away the foundations of defenses that had stopped the bulk of armored

wedges. That night (July 9) the Russians surprised their enemy when they slipped away from Rakowo, where they had blocked a further advance of panzers.

Impelled by the necessity to capitalize swiftly on the penetration already achieved, Hoth ordered his commanders to send assault guns and shock troops into the breach, clean it out of Russian diehards, and bring up a tank force that had the experience, supplies, and firepower to rip deeply into the strategic area between Kruglik and Novoselovka. If they could break through they would be shattering the very core of the Soviet defensive alignment.

For the next two days the truly critical fighting of the Voronezh front took place between these Russian towns as 3d Panzer and Gross Deutschland fought savagely around the clock. In the hilly slopes of the Pena the German infantrymen pounded and battered their way from one small village to another, inflicting heavy casualties against the Russian defenders, but taking severe losses themselves. Nazi rifle teams rushed from house to house, dropping to their knees, then rising to plunge on in the face of defending fire from windows, doors, and barns. From room to room, up artillery-shattered stairways, the fight carried on. Russians and Germans met in bitter, hand-to-hand clashes, their struggles often reduced to clubbing at each other with reversed weapons when ammunition ran out.

Progress was made, but it was terribly costly and maddeningly slow, for by the evening of July 11, when a mangled Russian force slipped into woodlands near Berezovka for survival, the Germans could measure their furious fighting and brutal casualties as having earned them a salient about fifteen miles across and only nine miles deep. This was the total extent of the gouge they had managed to make in the Russian lines.

Yet for Hoth it must do. He had no choice but to exploit what this salient could give him, and the advantage was immediate to those involved. The tank forces finally had the room, to reassemble and bring themselves back into shape, while doing two things: remaining in the front lines and keeping out of reach of the persistently deadly Russian artillery. It also permitted Hoth to gamble. The men of Gross Deutschland were weary to the point of utter exhaustion. Without some rest and refitting they would be useless for continued combat.

The German troops dug in, and Hoth ordered 3d Panzer to take over the lines being released by Gross Deutschland.

It would be a brief respite, perhaps measured only in hours, for Gross Deutschland was to reassemble on a road leading to the north. The men would bivouac alongside the road and sleep, and then they would be kept ready for a move far to the north. There, Model's offensive against Rokossovsky was a bloody mess, and unless pressure could be applied on the central front—which was Gross Deutschland's assignment—there could be no hope of victory for Operation Citadel.

The replacement of Gross Deutschland by 3d Panzer Division went without incident; that is, until the last groups pulled away from their positions. The night sky lit up with brilliant stabbing flashes, and there was no German unable to recognize the beginning of a mighty Soviet artillery barrage.

The 3d Panzer was still not settled in its positions when the shells began to rain down in its midst. The troops did their best to dig in deeply and securely, but inevitably there were more casualties, which the Wehrmacht could ill afford. The barrage cut off suddenly, but there was no rest for the weary infantrymen. Advance scouts reported the sounds and movement that promised a Russian counterattack. It came that same night, with sufficient power and speed to hurl 3d Panzer from the positions in which it was barely settled.

The dawn would bring with it the greatest tank battle of all time.

20

"THE TIGERS ARE BURNING"

The tension in Moscow was almost a physical presence when the Russians received their first word that the battle of the Kursk salient was joined with the German army. Those who knew the details of the war were acutely aware of the great conflict building for so many months, and there seemed to be an intrinsic appreciation in the Soviet capital of the stakes involved. The details, of course, were unknown to the populace or even the foreign correspondents in Moscow, but lack of details could hardly shroud the positioning of the vast armies and the strange lull preceding Operation Citadel.

There was no doubt that if the fight building near Kursk did not go well, Russia would be in straits as dire as those after the Nazi blitz-krieg unleashed across its borders in the summer of 1941. Foreign diplomats, newsmen, Russian officials, experience and intuition—they all pointed to the same thing, that the nation had reached an ulti-mately critical juncture in the war. The tension, as might be expected, built until it was almost unbearable.

The first official news that the dam had broken came in a fervently nationalistic report rushed into print in *Red Star*:

Our fathers and our forebears made every sacrifice to save their Russia, their homeland. Our people will never forget Minin and Pozharsky, Suvorov and Kutuzov, and the Russian Partisans of 1812. We are proud to think that the blood of our glorious ancestors is flowing in our veins, and we shall be worthy of them. . . .

The news trickled in from the front, and Moscow hung by its radios, waiting for any shred of news. What they learned was that the Germans had risked the bulk of their forces on the successful outcome of this one struggle. It became obvious almost at once that Russian defensive preparations for the enemy offensive went far beyond anything ever known to date in the war. Moscow and Stalingrad had represented high marks of beating off a powerful and deadly enemy, but even those heroic accomplishments must pale against what Zhukov had assembled to hold off, and then to destroy, the enemy hammering at the gates of Kursk. Finally the first official communiqué was issued:

Since this morning our troops have been fighting stubborn battles against the large advancing forces of enemy infantry and tanks in the Orel, Kursk, and Belgorod sectors. The enemy forces are supported by large numbers of aircraft. All the attacks were repelled with heavy losses to the enemy, and only in some places did small German units succeed in penetrating slightly into our defense lines. Preliminary reports show that our troops . . . have crippled or destroyed 586 enemy tanks . . . 203 enemy planes have been shot down. The fighting is continuing.

The reaction to the communiqué was electric. No one doubted that the greatest battle of the war was raging to the south of Moscow, and on everyone's tongue was the magic number. Five hundred and eighty-six German tanks destroyed! That one number revealed more than everything else put together, and the populace went to sleep that night fairly itching to receive further word on the morrow.

On the second day of the battle, July 6, the Soviet government ad-

mitted to a withdrawal on a small scale, but did not attempt to disguise the fact that severe German pressure had necessitated the move. No matter to the millions watching with bated breath, for again it would be the numbers that told everything, and the numbers, though some-what less than the day before, were still staggering. The Russian ar-mies, announced the government, had destroyed 433 tanks and shot down 111 planes.

The third day, July 7, the tally was announced as 520 tanks and another 111 aircraft.

The first indication of the hardness of Russian steel came on July 8, the fourth day of battle, when Moscow stated that its forces had counterattacked in several areas of the front. The German losses for the day's action were put at 304 tanks and 161 aircraft.

By this time there could be no doubt, even if the figures were exag-gerated, that the Wehrmacht was taking a bloody and possibly fatal battering at the hands of the dug-in Russians. The losses in tanks especially were staggering, and they could only reflect German losses in men, vehicles, weapons, and other war matériel. Either the Ger-mans had an inexhaustible supply of its war goods, or they must break before too much longer.

Tension in Moscow had yielded to excitement and the promise of each continuing day. And then, on July 9, there came from the bat-tlefield the first detailed report of the massive fighting in the Kursk salient.

It was the title of the report that swept Moscow and all Russia by storm. An appropriate title: *The Tigers Are Burning*.

It was but the prelude to *the* battle.

Unknown to one another, both the Germans *and* the Russians were preparing for an all-out assault on July 12, approximately one week into the fighting on the Voronezh front.

Hoth, as we have seen, needed desperately to break out into the open country to the southeast of Oboyan, near Prokhorovka, where he would have the room in which to maneuver large forces of his ar-mor for a shattering blow against the enemy and open the way for his panzers to streak toward Kursk.

The Russians felt the time was essential for a counterblow against

Hoth and had made provisions for such a stroke with the armor under Vatutin's command. Vatutin had planned to use the armor commanded by General Mikhail E. Katukov (First Tank Army), but this force was now strongly dug in as a defensive fortification against continuing German attacks. Zhukov released to Vatutin's control, then, almost the entire bulk of the uncommitted Russian mobile reserve—the Fifth Armored Army (also known as Fifth Guards Tank Army), led by Rotmistrov, an experienced and brilliant tank general. In addition, Zhukov moved to Vatutin's control General A. S. Zhadov's Fifth Guards Army from the steppe front.

All told, Zhukov was about to launch a series of counteroffensives all along the Kursk front. Four armies would strike on the morning of July 12. There would be a hammer blow against the Orel bulge with Sokolovsky in command of that force; forty-eight hours later, Popov would launch another sledgehammer on the adjoining front.

But the deciding fight would be between the tank forces under Rotmistrov and the armor of II S.S. Panzer Corps. Under Hoth's command the Germans (who scraped all armor together from the combined forces of the panzers struggling to reach Oboyan) would clash head on with Rotmistrov.

The two main antagonists of the battle of July 12, Rotmistrov and Hoth, were no strangers to one another, for they had clashed violently once before at Stalingrad in 1942, when the Germans made a desperate attempt to break through to their forces trapped by the Russians. Rotmistrov had emerged the superior of Hoth from that encounter, and he went into the new struggle with confidence. He knew that while Hoth masterminded the battle shaping up on the twelfth, as Vatutin was the top commander on the front of the Russian forces, it was Hausser, commanding the II S.S. Panzer Corps, whom he would meet in direct struggle.

The battle would be fought, if Rotmistrov planned correctly, in the countryside adjacent to Prokhorovka. If Hausser acted as Rotmistrov calculated he must, then the German commander would bring his panzers in a powerful rolling armada of steel along a comparatively narrow strip of land that lay between the Psel River and a railway embankment. It was a bitter countryside for such a monstrous clash,

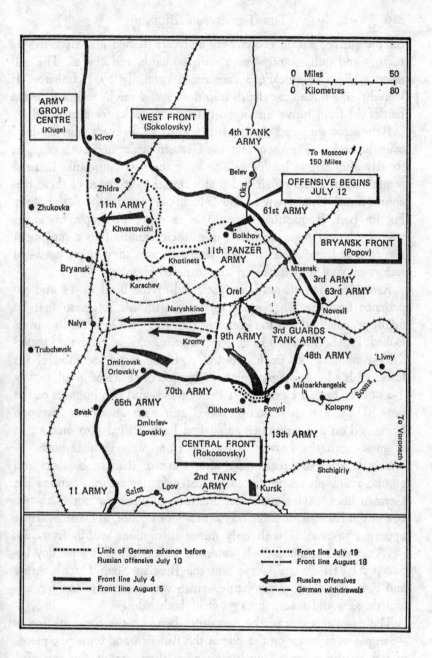

ARMY GROUP CENTRE (Kluge)

WEST FRONT (Sokolovsky)

Kirov

Zhidra

Zhukovka

11th ARMY

Khvastovichi

Bryansk

Khotinets

Karachev

Naryshkino

Nalya

Trubchevsk

Kromy

Dmitrovsk Orlovskiy

Sevsk

65th ARMY

Dmitriev-Lgovskiy

70th ARMY

CENTRAL FRONT (Rokossovsky)

2nd TANK ARMY

11 ARMY

Seim

Lgov

4th TANK ARMY

Belev

Oka

To Moscow 150 Miles

OFFENSIVE BEGINS JULY 12

61st ARMY

Bolkhov

11th PANZER ARMY

BRYANSK FRONT (Popov)

Mtsensk

3rd ARMY

63rd ARMY

Orel

Novosil

9th ARMY

3rd GUARDS TANK ARMY

48th ARMY

Livny

Olkhovatka

Ponyri

Maloarkhangelsk

Kolopny

Sosna

13th ARMY

Shchigriy

Kursk

To Voronezh

Miles 0 — 50

Kilometres 0 — 80

Limit of German advance before Russian offensive July 10

Front line July 4

Front line August 5

Front line July 19

Front line August 18

Russian offensives

German withdrawals

for the surface sloped everywhere and was slashed and ribboned by ravines and gullies and strewn with orchards and copses. The soil dried easily and quickly, a fact noted carefully by Rotmistrov. It would throw huge dust clouds into the air and might well isolate the battlefield from heavy air support, once the tanks were engaged.

Rotmistrov intended to take full advantage of every edge he held over the enemy. He knew that the German armor had been engaged for day after day in battles sure to leave the surviving tanks in need of maintenance and repair and that a certain percentage of these machines must break down in the field because of mechanical failure. For his part, Rotmistrov's armor was in excellent shape, his crews were fresh and eager for the battle, their ammunition complement was full, and they were supplied with whatever they might need—all factors of vital importance in any armored clash.

Rotmistrov had always been possessed of the need to see and experience firsthand what was happening with his forces so that he might personally direct the events of the struggle. On a hill that overlooked Prokhorovka—and the area that would become the battlefield—Rotmistrov set up his control post. He could see most of his forces with a long sweeping glance—850 pieces of armor in all, mostly T-34 tanks, but also some KV-1 heavy tanks, and two brigades of the new SU-85, a massive self-propelled gun with an 85-mm. weapon (mounted on a T-34 chassis) that had been rushed into production as an authoritative answer to the Tiger and new Panther tanks.

Shortly after daybreak, wave after wave of Russian bombers and ground-attack planes, protected by heavy fighter escort, pounded the German lines, paying particular attention to enemy armor. The success of the Russian air strike was somewhat in doubt, as German armor appeared to proceed with only minor disruptions within its ranks.

(A separate armored clash would be under way that same day between XLVIII Panzer Corps and the Russian Sixth Guards Army and First Tank Army; this battle, which was destined to last for several days, would take a heavy toll of both sides.)

The exact moment of the encounter between the two tank forces —850 pieces of armor on the side of the Russians and some 700 pieces in use by the Germans, including more than 100 of the powerful

Tiger heavy tanks—took place in a manner wholly unexpected by either combatant and helped decide the final outcome.

As Rotmistrov's force began to roll, lookouts reported the German armored column, almost as large as the Soviet, thundering toward the Russian lines. The Soviets could hardly believe their eyes. They had planned to surprise the enemy with their massive tank attack, and here came a force approximately equal to their own, pounding over the earth beneath a gigantic dust cloud.

The tanks were buttoned up on both sides, and men rode into battle in stifling heat and choking dust, their clumsy vehicles lurching and slamming about in the rough countryside. Planes of both sides swept earthward to attack enemy armor, but air support was quickly thrown off the battle by the dust clouds and boiling smoke that made pilot recognition of friend or foe almost impossible. As a result, the air armada turned to claw at one another in a series of dogfights and skirmishes that went on for most of the day.

Then came the critical moment. The panzers rolled inexorably along their predetermined course, and the Russians, enjoying the advantage of having their tanks located on higher ground, wasted no time in exploiting the favorable situation. Rotmistrov ordered his armor to attack at full speed, and the T-34s charged recklessly down from the slopes.

Deliberately avoiding any kind of head-on clash, the T-34s managed to slip beneath the deadly 88-mm. guns of the German tanks before the enemy could wheel to meet them. With the Nazis boasting superiority in having thicker armor and bigger guns that fired higher velocity shells, their strategy lay in touching off a tank-to-tank slugging match. The Russians wiped out these advantages in a wild charge, taking the German tank armada in the flank and racing in a diagonal line at point-blank range straight through the lines of the panzers.

Never before had there been a charge of armor on such a vast scale, nor to this date has it ever been duplicated. It was the single most extraordinary running assault of tanks, and the bold, tactical stroke of the Soviet tank fleet inexorably dictated the manner in which the battle must be fought.

The entire world seemed to tremble from the continuous din erupting from the battlefield. It was a hellish crescendo of firing guns,

exploding shells and bombs, exploding and blazing tanks, crashing airplanes, screaming engines—all mixed together in a mass thunder that went on unabated for eight hours.

Where the Tigers and the Panthers could traverse their turrets and put to good use their long-barreled high-velocity guns, they carried out a savage execution of their quarry. At close quarters the 88-mm. gun was a devastating weapon, and it usually required only one round to tear up even the sloping armored protection of the T-34. But there was little opportunity for the German tanks to stand off and cut their enemy to pieces. The T-34s were faster, they were being handled with remarkable spirit and skill, and they seemed to be everywhere. Once again the Germans were being taught that the lesser gun of the T-34, at ranges of a hundred yards and less, lost nothing in its ability to rip open even the thick armor covering the Tiger or the Panther.

In an astonishingly short interval, more than fifteen hundred tanks and self-propelled guns were engaged in a wild, confused mass of blazing guns and thick clouds of dust and smoke. The Russian "cavalry charge" had broken the back of the carefully laid German plans to handle their opponents in a set pattern. The T-34 attack was executed so swiftly that there was no opportunity for the panzers to wheel about and meet the assault. Before the Germans could even react, the leading elements of the Russian tanks had charged through the entire first echelon of the panzers.

A German tank commander wrote of that incredible moment:

We had been warned to expect resistance from the pakfronts and some tanks in static positions, also the possibility of a few independent brigades of the slower KV type. In fact, we found ourselves taking on a seemingly inexhaustible mass of enemy armor—never have I received such an overwhelming impression of Russian strength and numbers as on that day. The clouds of dust made it difficult to get help from the Luftwaffe, and soon many of the T-34s had broken past our screen and were streaming like rats all over the old battlefield.

The Germans never had the opportunity to stand fast in carefully arrayed ranks and fight. Armored units milled about in a vast confusion of roaring guns and livid streaks of flame, the sudden bursts of white

fire marking the death knell of a tank or self-propelled gun. Again and again the Germans tried to break off combat so as to reform their ranks, but the "rats" streaming all over the battlefield made that maneuver impossible.

The field of battle seemed too small for the huge number of fighting machines, and within the first hour the sloping hills were spotted with blazing, smoking hulks, many of them torn open, their turrets blown away to land fifty or a hundred feet from the vehicles. Those crews who survived a burning or exploding tank found any moves across open ground to be suicide; they would have to run a gauntlet of high-velocity shells, strafing planes (which could hardly tell enemy from friend), and the blazing machine guns of the tanks themselves.

Finally the battle resolved into groups of tanks maneuvering to concentrate their firepower against similar enemy groups, the forces all the while taking advantage of the cover of gullies and trees.

Rotmistrov must have been both overwhelmed and frustrated by what he saw from his vantage point on his hilltop. In the thickening dust destroyed tanks burned like torches—*hundreds* of them—and the dust was itself mixed with the ever-increasing plumes of black and greasy smoke from the shattered vehicles. There was no way from such a distance to determine who was attacking and who was being struck.

One fascinating example of individual fighting involved the 2d Battalion of the 181st Brigade, XVIII Tank Corps, which made its attack against the enemy along the left bank of the Psel. Immediately the battalion clashed with a powerful group of Tigers. The German tanks lurched to a halt, their guns swinging around to take the Russian tanks at the greatest range possible. Had they been permitted to do so, the Russians would have been cut to pieces. The heavy KV tanks used by 2d Battalion could handle the Tiger at close range, but at any considerable distance German steel could resist the 76.2-mm. shells of the Russians.

Captain P. A. Skripkin, the battalion commander, signaled for his armor to follow him in a headlong dash at the Tigers, and he rolled his own KV at full speed directly into the center of the massed German tanks. Skripkin took the Germans by surprise, and before the Tigers could fire, the KV had slammed a shell at close range into one

German heavy tank, holing the armor and setting off a violent explosion within that killed the crew.

Skripkin turned the KV sharply, racing at another Tiger, pumping three rounds into his second target to set it ablaze. By now the Germans had brought about their guns, and several Tigers combined their fire against this astonishing Russian. One 88-mm. shell ripped through the side of the KV tank; another shell exploded partway through and seriously wounded Skripkin.

The driver-mechanic, Alexander Nikolayev, and the radio operator dragged Skripkin from the burning KV and hauled him into a deep shell hole. The Russians were prepared to sit out the battle hiding in this manner, but they had been seen by the crew of a Tiger that now rolled toward them to finish off the survivors. Nikolayev dashed from the crater back into the blazing KV tank, restarted the engine, and lurched forward under full throttle.

What the Germans thought of a Russian heavy tank, flames billowing from its body, as it rushed toward them is anyone's guess. The lead Tiger came to a stop, slamming a shell at the KV. It missed, and the Tiger jerked into motion to move aside from the blazing steel projectile approaching it. Too late! Nikolayev's flaming tank rammed the Tiger at full speed, and both tanks were enveloped in a titanic explosion.

It was the type of fighting the Germans were to find everywhere on the battlefield. Nikolayev's reckless and heroic act was the sort of action that was multiplied in incident after incident, and it tipped the scales of victory away from the panzers.

The night that fell across the battlefield was never without light, a fearsome puncturing of darkness by swirling fire and blazing sparks from the shattered hulks of tanks and planes that had been destroyed during the day. It was a battle that strategists might call without decision. The Wehrmacht had lost at least 350 and perhaps 400 tanks; by any accounting at least half their number had been destroyed, and the surviving armor was in sad mechanical shape and desperately short of supplies and maintenance. There had been another savage loss—more than ten thousand men in skilled tank crews and supporting infantry, as well as dozens of aircraft and their crews.

There are judgments of that tank battle that insist the Russians did not win, but merely achieved a stalemate. This appears to be a myopic evaluation of what transpired, for the Germans had gone into battle with the type of tank force they believed could never be defeated. One hundred Tigers and a lesser number of Panthers represented what the purist would consider the finest armor of the entire war, but it had been unable to break its Russian opponents. The Soviets were severely outnumbered in heavy tanks, yet Rotmistrov's men in their few KV-1s, and the fast-moving T-34s, had certainly met the enemy on equal ground and dished out destruction as violently and effectively as they had received.

There are sharply opposed accounts of the night following the massive tank struggle. Some insist the Russians remained on the field of battle to claim their damaged tanks and save their surviving crews. Others say that Rotmistrov had failed to destroy the panzers that were his objective and he withdrew from the field of combat in order to regroup. Strong arguments may be made for either case, but in the long run it availed the Germans not at all. The panzers had lost at least half their number on this day, and Hoth could count barely 350 tanks at his disposal, whereas Rotmistrov still had at least 500.

If Hausser, indeed, was left the hideous, torn earth of the battle-field as a prize, it was useless to him, and soon there would be no pan-zers at all in the area. The battle of July 12, no matter what individual struggles with losses to the Russians might come in the future, had smashed the ability of the Germans to dictate when and where the field of combat would be.

Hausser was removed from his command by an enraged Hitler, and the panzers soon retired to lick their wounds and face the problem of massive Russian attacks all along the many fronts of the Kursk salient. The ability to attack and advance was wrested from the Germans, who were never again to regain the upper hand.

July 12, on that narrow strip of land between a river and a railway embankment, sounded the death knell for the panzers. On that same day Russian armies were striking massive blows along adjacent fronts. Three days later, the Red Army had pounded out advances of fifteen to thirty miles.

Twelve days after the greatest single tank battle ever fought, on

SYMBOLS.

▬▬▬ Front line by the beginning of July 1943

╌╌╌╌ Position of the Soviet troops by August 28 in the area of the Kursk salient

•••• Position of the Soviet troops by the end of September

▰▰▰▰ Front line by the end of 1943

July 24, the Russians recaptured every foot of ground taken by the Wehrmacht since Operation Citadel opened on July 5. In the Orel-Kursk and Belgorod areas the Germans had hurled seventeen tank, two motorized, and eighteen infantry divisions at the Russians, and for their pains they had lost an estimated 70,000 men killed, and 2,900 tanks, 195 mobile guns, 844 field guns, 1,392 planes, and more than 5,000 motor vehicles destroyed.

Yet the battles that had been fought to date were only the initial phase of the great decimation of German military forces. The Soviets would consider the Battle of Kursk not to be ended until fifty days had followed the opening shots on July 5. Those fifty days would go into the history books of the war as the huge summer offensive of 1943 by the Red Army.

The most critical phase of those fifty days—when the Wehrmacht and its panzers, in their attempts to take Kursk and reopen the road to Moscow, posed a huge threat to the Russians—ended on July 24. From that point on the Russians would be forging new gains and wrecking the ability of the Germans to initiate any more meaningful offensives. It would be a grievous error, however, to pass off the remaining period of the summer offensive as one during which the Russians stampeded their enemy. Badly hurt as they were, the Nazis remained a powerful force in terms of weaponry, manpower, and determination.

That Operation Citadel had chewed up the fighting heart of German armor, was a fact no German leader could, or would, deny, no matter in what form that admission might be couched.

There was another side of the coin that requires telling, however, and the battle for Kharkov in August 1943 is especially illuminating. The massive gains gouged out by Russian armies, the victories that were flashed to all the world, obscure the details of fighting in which the Wehrmacht, at times, bested its enemy, and exacted the bloodiest toll from the Russians who sustained their offensive on the basis of the Zhukov creed that no casualties are ever too great if the objective is accomplished.

Even the most critical German commanders regard the huge Russian counteroffensive in the area of Belgorod as exceptionally well managed by Soviet generals. They are less generous in their judgment

of orders issued from Moscow and make it clear that such orders were motivated by political rather than military considerations.

On the first day of the massive Soviet thrust—in what the Germans consider to be the Belgorod counteroffensive beginning on August 5—massed Red tanks crowded the area around Bogodukhov, northwest of Kharkov, and Graivoron. Then, reported a German panzer leader in briefings after the war with American officers in Neustadt, the Russian tanks "flowed like lava into the broad plain east of the Borskla, where they were halted by German counteroperations from the Poltava-Akhtirka area."

It is especially interesting to note the German mood in its interpretation of the situation involving Kharkov. A statement provided during the Neustadt interrogation of panzer leaders tells us that

> Kharkov constituted a deep German salient to the east, which prevented the enemy from making use of this important traffic and supply center. All previous Russian attempts to take it had failed. Neither tank assaults nor infantry mass attacks had succeeded in bringing about the fall of this large city. Boastful reports made by the Russian radio, and erroneous ones by German pilots, announcing the entry of Russian troops into Kharkov at a time when the German front stood unwavering, did not alter the facts. When the Russian command perceived its mistake, Marshal Stalin ordered the immediate capture of Kharkov.

It was an order from Moscow that would cost the Russians dearly, although in the opening phase of the huge offensive Stavka was convinced the rehabilitated Russian Fifth Tank Army would have little difficulty in ridding Kharkov of its enemy occupation forces. Stavka failed to recognize the full strength of the Germans in the area and did not anticipate the speed with which the Wehrmacht army would react to the threat of the Soviet drive.

Five divisions of the German XI Infantry Corps effectively sealed off Kharkov in a long arc the moment the Germans saw signs of the armored pressure being brought against them. To the defenders, the Soviet plan was almost dictated, without room for variation, by the strength of the Wehrmacht and the local terrain. The Germans

were thus able to gamble that the Russians, even with their willingness to absorb terrible losses, would not carry out a frontal assault on the projecting Kharkov bastion, but would throw their strength against the narrowest part of the defending arc west of the city. If they succeeded in breaking through at this point, they would be able to envelop the defenses and seal off the city.

Presuming the Russian plan of battle must follow this logic, the Nazis set up thick antitank defenses. Along the northern edge of the bottleneck the German troops shoved and rolled their deadly 88-mm. flak guns into position, aimed where the tanks must come, and then backed up this initial defense line with more batteries of 88s on the high ground overlooking the anticipated battlefield.

Notwithstanding these weapons, the Germans were not at all sanguine about their ability to hold Kharkov, for they were aware the Russians would attack with extremely heavy armored forces. On the day before the anticipated Russian assault, the defensive alignment was augmented by the arrival of the 2d S.S. Panzer Division (Das Reich) in the city. These strong armored forces were rushed to the most endangered sector.

Ninety-six Panthers, thirty-two Tigers, and twenty-five heavy self-propelled guns rolled into position the night of August 4–5—barely in time to meet the Red tanks rumbling forward in a mass armored blow.

Russian maneuvers up to this point had been largely confined to assembling their armor in the villages and flood plains of the valley before advancing in battle formation from their assembly point. The Kharkov defenders countered by launching heavy air attacks.

It was an air strike the like of which had never before been witnessed on the Russian front. So heavy had been German losses in supplies that the Stuka dive bombers lacked the bombs normally assigned for strikes against armor. All that was available was a supply of four-thousand-pound bombs that had been intended for use against Russian battleships. There was no choice but to use the two-ton monsters, and the Stukas took off with their massive loads and headed for the Russian assembly area. Fortunately for the Wehrmacht a strong and effective fighter escort went along on the raid, otherwise the German bomber force would have been shattered.

Russian fighters rose in a cloud to defend the assembly area but were overwhelmed by aggressive Nazi pilots in Messerschmitts and Focke-Wulfs. Rather than having to run the gauntlet of Russian fighters, while they were severely overloaded, the Stukas came on in wedge formation, eased into their dives, and screamed earthward against the enemy armor.

For miles in every direction the earth shook and heaved as the massive bombs exploded with earthquake force in the target area. Each time a four-thousand-pounder struck, the shock wave boomed outward like an enormous crack of thunder. Left relatively free from attacks by Russian fighters, the Stuka pilots with "majestic calm," plunged earthward, executing their bomb drops with careful precision. Within minutes of the first wave of air strikes—and more were on the way—the villages occupied by the Russian tanks blazed from one end to the other. Mixed with the upward-shooting flames of homes and farms could be seen the more intense, whiter flame of blazing fuel and ammunition as Russian tanks exploded and burned.

By day's end, after several intense air strikes, Stalin's order to attack went unfulfilled. The setting sun cast a garish glow upon a scene that resembled hell. All across the valley arose dark, curling mushrooms of smoke from wrecked tanks. It was, for the Germans, an excellent combat performance by the Luftwaffe, and a great stroke of fortune. Without risking a single tank or soldier they had bloodied the enemy and bought the time to further reorganize the defense system.

The next morning, August 6, showed how well the Russians had learned their lesson from the Stukas. There was no mass grouping of tanks as dawn broke, but scattered groups of armor appeared, crossing the valley in many different areas and then disappearing into the sprawling cornfields that lay between the two enemy hordes. It would be only a temporary cover for the Red tanks, for the cornfields ended at the east-west main highway that lay several hundred yards before the main German line of resistance.

As the morning wore on, the Russian crews kept working their way steadily to the hollows and depressions at the southern edge of the cornfields. The Germans watched as best they could, but the enemy tanks were hidden from sight. Then, as the Germans expected, the

signal was flashed to the Russians to move out at full speed. The mass scramble of T-34s became a widespread bludgeon, Russian drivers gunning their engines, the clanking and whine of treads fading before the machine gun fire of the T-34s and the crunching thud of their big guns.

The Panthers were ready and waiting, and the air seemed to split with the screaming crack of the flat-trajectory 88s in the German tanks. The panzer crews had arranged their Panthers to catch the oncoming T-34s in a withering flanking fire, and within moments the fields were spotted with blazing T-34s, turrets blown away, sides holed, fuel and oil tanks blazing from the deadly close fire of the Panthers. The first wave of T-34s stumbled into the howling 88s, and the attack failed. It did not falter; it failed through sheer destruction of the Russian tanks.

But there were more Red tanks; there were always more, it seemed, and the Fifth Guards Army, its leaders lashed by Stavka to take Kharkov at all costs, broke from their concealment a second, and third, and then a fourth wave of T-34s. Many more were hit, and the number of burning and wrecked tanks increased. But the T-34s through sheer weight of numbers and dogged persistence punched out of the protecting hollows into the teeth of the Panthers and gouged their way into the most forward defensive positions of the Germans.

What had happened to German armor one month earlier when they stormed the pakfronts of Russian defense lines was reborn before the gates of Kharkov, only this time the Soviets found themselves on the receiving end. The T-34s cracked the first German line, gathered speed to storm the next bastion, and rolled directly into a deadly nest of antitank and 88-mm. flak guns and, totally unexpected, a powerful force of Hornets (88-mm. tank destroyers) and Wasps (self-propelled 105-mm. light field howitzers).

The ripping crossfire, with well over a hundred of the deadly 88s blazing away at one time, supported by still more firepower, tore to shreds the Russian attempt to maintain tank formation and split the advancing armor into widely separated groups. Now the 88s and especially the Hornets, jockeying for the most favorable position, took the T-34s in their flank and began a systematic butchering of the enemy.

Still the Russians came on, disregarding appalling losses, ignoring the odds turning steadily in favor of the Germans. Still the T-34s ground over the earth, firing steadily, taking their enemy head on, in the flanks. More tanks were brought up from the rear, and in the face of that savaging defensive fire, the Russians managed to concentrate new groups of tanks to force a penetration through sheer weight of numbers and guns. The T-34s were massing against the second defense line when suddenly they were struck violently from another quarter, as German reserves of powerful Tiger tanks and self-propelled assault guns arrived.

When the fighting ended, and the Russians retreated from the field of battle, they left behind them 184 destroyed T-34s.

One Russian force did not yield its position. A battalion of motorized infantry had pounded into a heavy wooded area west of Lyubotin, set up defense positions, and resisted very heavy assaults by the Germans. Cut off and isolated now from their main force, the Russians were promised relief in a radio message, and they dug in deeper to fight it out through the night.

August 7 opened with a variation in the Russian assault tactics. There was no mass frontal attack this time. The Germans, their lines secure, their casualties replaced, watched an incredible armored attack of several hundred tanks rolling simultaneously in a single huge wedge that shook dust into the air from the vibrating earth. The wedge appeared unstoppable, but as it moved toward the German lines, the defending crews made the most of their rare opportunity. Tank commanders sighted their guns, effective at much greater range than the T-34 weapons, and the command to fire flashed through the lines. At a range of two thousand yards, the 88-mm. guns of the waiting Tigers and Hornets began to slam rounds into the T-34s that could not yet return, with any effectiveness, the withering rain of shells. As the great armored wedge moved across open terrain along the railroad, the Tigers and Hornets kept picking off their targets and an increasing number of T-34s fell away from their formations, badly holed and burning.

By late afternoon, stopped several times by this deadly long-range fire, the Russians were finally ready for their main blow, and once again the T-34s burst from the protecting hollows of the cornfields

and dashed into the teeth of the German defenses. What the Russians had faced the day before was far worse now as the massed firepower of every available Tiger, Hornet, Panther, self-propelled gun, and the antitank and flak guns opened up with rapid fire. The ground covered by the Russian armor seemed to come alive as thousands of high-velocity shells burst with loud cracking roars, the chaos increasing with the thickening smoke and piercing blasts of exploding tanks.

One hundred and fifty-four Russian tanks were either burning, exploded, or shattered by the time the assault ended, but the Russians had left themselves in an almost indefensible position. Large rifle units, seriously weakened by the loss of protecting armor, lay naked to the deadly fire of the German 88s, and a bloody slaughter took place as the explosive shells decimated the fleeing infantry.

Another fierce battle raged in the nearby woods where the encircled Red battalion had refused all offers of surrender and fought like madmen against overwhelming odds. Late in the day the Germans intercepted a radio message from the battalion that informed Soviet headquarters that they had lost the struggle. There was intermittent firing for a while to counter the withering point-blank storm from the big German guns, and then silence. The Russians, to the last man, including radio operators, had died fighting.

To the complete surprise of the Germans, July 8 passed without another attack. The entire day, beneath scorching summer heat mixing with the smoldering iron corpses on the battlefield was spent by the Russians dragging damaged tanks from the field to restock their shattered armored ranks.

The day was almost ended—it was shortly before midnight—when the alarm sounded through the German defenses. Sleepy panzer crews and dug-in German infantry could hardly believe their ears. From the darkness, carrying easily through the almost complete silence of the night, came the sounds of massed engines and turning treads.

Just before the invisible enemy reached the foot of the elevated terrain leading up to the German defense line, the night vanished in a mass rippling of eye-searing flame. Under this light, from hundreds of T-34s firing as rapidly as the loaders could slam shells into

their weapons, they could see an unprecedented mass attack of everything that could be made to move by the Russians.

During the first few moments of firing, as the German guns answered the attack, both sides lost several tanks to sudden violent explosions, and the spattering illumination from flaming fuel garishly lit up the battlefield. The "tank torches" kept increasing in number, for now the fight was taking place at close quarters, and more armor was ripped apart and set aflame.

Nothing the Germans had ever encountered before could match this moment. The antitank gunners almost wept in frustration, for in the shifting glow of burning tanks they could not distinguish between friend and foe, and their deadly effect was thus minimized. Not so with the commanders of the Tigers and Panthers. Buttoned up, they shouted orders to their men to charge into the midst of the Russian tanks, firing steadily. Both sides began to take increasing losses at this gun-barrel range, and the German tank commanders, aware they were fighting within their own defense system, began to ram whatever Russian armor survived the 88s before them.

The Germans held their front lines long enough for reserve armor to be brought into the wild contest, and as more Tigers and Panthers rushed into the fight, the night sky waxed steadily brighter—not only from the burning tanks but from an almost ceaseless flash of heavy guns and the growing number of flares sent hissing like flying snakes into the sky. Then isolated farm buildings began to burn, and there was still more light, and the Germans discovered that at a distance of one to two hundred yards they could identify the Russian tanks by their silhouettes.

What had been a great hammering thunder from all sides increased to an even greater pitch as rapid-fire orders went out to the German tank crews, and an all-encompassing din rattled the earth from one horizon to the other. The sudden bright flashes began to appear well beyond the high plateau on which the great night battle of armor was fought. Russian tanks that had penetrated in darkness and confusion to a point far behind the German lines were running wild, tearing up and destroying anything that appeared before their guns.

By next morning the armored clash was ended. Once again the Red armored column had suffered heavy losses. More than eighty

T-34s were left on the battlefield as burned-out hulks. Only one pocket of savage fighting remained. Behind the German lines, in dense woods, a motorized Russian force with a few tanks and antitank guns was holed up, and beating off vastly superior enemy forces. Nothing could be done to dislodge the determined Russians—nothing, that is, until flame-throwing tanks moved up and burned the entire woods pocket to the ground, exposing the Russians to overwhelming fire-power. Only a few dazed, stunned prisoners were taken.

In three days of mass armored fighting the Russians had suffered a battering that cost them 420 tanks and losses in men and matériel so great that, according to German intelligence, the Russian Fifth Tank Army "ceased to be a combat factor for the foreseeable future. Kharkov remained in German hands until the high command ordered the troops stationed there to retire."

Yet only the final results matter, and in the fifty days that followed the opening of Operation Citadel on July 5, 1943, more than a hundred German divisions were mangled in the raging conflict they would all remember forever as the Battle of Kursk.

Isolated setbacks, even unexpected terrible losses, could not change the ominous meaning in the report received in Moscow on July 9, which spoke so eloquently for the fighting in the Kursk salient, and all the way to Berlin: "The Tigers Are Burning."

BIBLIOGRAPHY

BOOKS

Bekker, Cajus. *The Luftwaffe War Diaries.* Garden City, N.Y.: Doubleday & Co., 1968.

Carell, Paul. *Hitler Moves East, 1941–1943.* Boston: Little, Brown and Co., 1965.

Clark, Alan. *Barbarossa: The Russian-German Conflict, 1941–45.* New York: William Morrow and Co., 1965.

Constable, Trevor J. and Toliver, Raymond F. *Horrido!* New York: Macmillan Co., 1968.

Galland, Adolf. *The First and the Last.* New York: Henry Holt & Co., 1954.

Goerlitz, Walter. *History of the German General Staff.* New York: F. A. Praeger, 1952.

Guderian, Heinz. *Panzer Leader.* New York: E. P. Dutton & Co., n.d.

Jukes, Geoffrey. *Kursk: The Clash of Armor.* New York: Ballantine Books, 1969.

Keegan, John. *Barbarossa: Invasion of Russia, 1941.* New York: Ballantine Books, 1971.

Kerr, Walter. *The Russian Army.* New York: Alfred A. Knopf, 1944.

Killen, John. *A History of the Luftwaffe*. Garden City, N.Y.: Doubleday & Co., 1967.

Liddell Hart, Basil Henry. *The German Generals Talk*. New York: William Morrow and Co., 1948.

———. *The Red Army*. New York: Harcourt, Brace, 1956.

Macksey, Major K. J. *Panzer Division: The Mailed Fist*. New York: Ballantine Books, 1968.

Mellinthin, Major General F. W. von. *Panzer Battles*. Norman, Okla.: University of Oklahoma Press, 1956.

Neumann, Peter. *The Black March*. New York: William Sloane Associates, 1965.

Orgill, Douglas. *T-34: Russian Armor*. New York: Ballantine Books, 1971.

Pabst, Helmut. *The Outermost Frontier*. London: William Kimber, n.d.

Schroter, Heinz. *Stalingrad*. New York: E. P. Dutton & Co., 1958.

Werth, Alexander. *Russia at War*. New York: E. P. Dutton & Co., 1964.

Zhukov, Georgi K. *Marshal Zhukov's Greatest Battles*. Edited by Harrison Salisbury. New York: Harper & Row, 1969.

Zieser, Benno. *The Road to Stalingrad*. New York: Ballantine Books, 1956.

SPECIAL PUBLICATIONS

Combat in Russian Forests and Swamps. U.S. Army Study No. 20-231.

Effects of Climate on Combat in European Russia. U.S. Army Study No. 20-291.

German Defense Tactics against Russian Breakthroughs. U.S. Army Study No. 20-233.

Operations of Encircled Forces: German Experiences in Russia. U.S. Army Study No. 20-234.

Operations on the Russian Front: November 1942–December 1943. U.S. Military Academy, 1944.

Order of Battle of the German Army. U.S. Army, Military Intelligence Service.

Russian Combat Methods in World War II. U.S. Army Study No. 20-230.

Rear Area Security in Russia. U.S. Army Study No. 20-240.

Soviet Military Review. 1968, 1969, 1970, 1971. Moscow: Krasnaya Zvezda.

Strategy and Tactics of the Soviet-German War. (By officers of the Red Army and Soviet war correspondents.) Moscow: Soviet War News.

Terrain Factors in the Russian Campaign. U.S. Army Study No. 20-290.

INDEX